Iain M. Banks

# MODERN MASTERS OF SCIENCE FICTION

Edited by Gary K. Wolfe

Science fiction often anticipates the consequences of scientific discoveries. The immense strides made by science since World War II have been matched step by step by writers who gave equal attention to scientific principles, human imagination, and the craft of fiction. The respect for science fiction won by Jules Verne and H. G. Wells was further increased by Isaac Asimov, Arthur C. Clarke, Robert Heinlein, Ursula K. Le Guin, Joanna Russ, and Ray Bradbury.

Modern Masters of Science Fiction is devoted to books that survey the work of individual authors who continue to inspire and advance science fiction.

*A list of books in the series appears at the end of this book.*

# Iain M. Banks

Paul Kincaid

**UNIVERSITY OF ILLINOIS PRESS**
Urbana, Chicago, and Springfield

Library of Congress Cataloging-in-Publication Data
Names: Kincaid, Paul, author.
Title: Iain M. Banks / Paul Kincaid.
Description: Urbana : University of Illinois Press, [2017] | Series: Modern masters of
    science fiction | Includes bibliographical references and index.
Identifiers: LCCN 2016054031 (print) | LCCN 2016054150 (ebook) | ISBN 9780252041013
    (hardback : acid-free paper) | ISBN 9780252082504 (paperback : acid-free paper) |
    ISBN 9780252099564 (e-book)
Subjects: LCSH: Banks, Iain, 1954–2013 —Criticism and interpretation. | Science fiction,
    English—History and criticism. | BISAC: LITERARY CRITICISM / Science Fiction &
    Fantasy. | BIOGRAPHY & AUTOBIOGRAPHY / Literary.
Classification: LCC PR6052.A485 Z69 2017 (print) | LCC PR6052.A485 (ebook) |
    DDC 823/.914—dc23
    LC record available at https://lccn.loc.gov/2016054031

Printed and bound in Great Britain by Marston Book Services Ltd, Oxfordshire

# contents

# ACKNOWLEDGMENTS

Any number of people deserve to be thanked on a project like this. Singling out a few is always invidious because you risk forgetting the many. However, there are some people who have directly contributed to the work you hold in your hand, and I am delighted to acknowledge their help.

To start with, this would not be the book it is without David Haddock, source of all esoteric knowledge when it comes to Iain Banks. He was encouraging from the start and has provided an unexpected wealth of interviews, essays, letters, books, and other material that would have been all too easy to miss. Without his help, this would have been a much poorer book.

Tony Keen provided unpublished material he has written about Iain Banks, which was invaluable in helping to focus my own ideas. He also read and commented on some of the chapters as they were written, which has helped rescue me from some of the worst sins of my first draft.

Thanks also to Ken MacLeod, who took time out from writing his next novel in order to patiently answer my impertinent, if not downright nosy, questions.

Jude Roberts was generous in allowing me to use her interview with Iain Banks in this book.

And, as ever, I must thank my wife, Maureen Kincaid Speller, copyeditor and proofreader extraordinaire, whose keen eye was essential.

Finally, to everyone whose encouragement or support helped, whether you knew it or not, thank you.

Iain M. Banks

## CHAPTER 1

## CROSSING THE BRIDGE

On April 3, 2013, Iain Banks posted a "Personal Statement" on the Iain M. Banks website: "I am officially Very Poorly." He was typically matter-of-fact about his condition: "As a late stage gall bladder cancer patient, I'm expected to live for 'several months' and it's extremely unlikely I'll live beyond a year."

"I've asked my partner Adele [Hartley] if she will do me the honour of becoming my widow," he continued. They married on March 29, 2013. While the pair had a short honeymoon in Venice and Paris, a host of messages started to appear on social media and on the "Banksophilia" website set up for the purpose. Returning from holiday, Banks wrote a May 20 "update" on the site: "I've been reading the posts on the site. So far I've reached page 60, which is getting on for a third of the way through." Many of these messages related anecdotes about meeting Banks, but the vast majority were from people who knew him only through his books. The novels had forged a personal connection between the author and his readers. Time and again, people spoke of his books restoring their faith in science fiction or in literature more broadly; they said his books started them reading again, that his work shaped their own ideas. As one example among many, one reader wrote: "Your concept of a post-scarcity society has become my manifesto, and something like the Culture a way to get there."[1]

As that comment suggests, the Culture, which featured in nine novels, a novella, and a couple of short stories, had become for science fiction readers an iconic image, a utopia that was dynamic and liberal. Banks posited a post-scarcity society in which there is no need to work, because all drudgery is performed by AIs; in which there is no money, because anyone can have whatever they desire; in which there are no hierarchies; and in which anyone can become whatever they wish—so, for instance, people regularly change sex. Little wonder that, from its first appearance in *Consider Phlebas* (1987), the Culture acquired a consistent following.

But Banks was not initially known as a science fiction writer. His first novel, *The Wasp Factory* (1984), which featured murder, madness, and what some regarded as very sick humor, was probably the most controversial literary debut of the 1980s, a book that sharply and violently divided critics. In part because of that controversy, the novel became a bestseller, and his next two novels, *Walking On Glass* (1985) and particularly *The Bridge* (1986), which could be his masterpiece, confirmed the appearance of a major talent. Each book was very different from its predecessor, but they shared a narrative vigor, an often black humor, and he managed huge vistas with deft skill.

After *The Bridge*, Banks's career took an unexpected turn with the publication of *Consider Phlebas* under a different form of his name: Iain M. Banks. That Banks should write a science fiction novel was not particularly surprising—there were enough hints in the first three novels to make this a natural progression—but he chose to write in what was, at the time, considered to be a worn out and generally despised subgenre, the space opera. In doing so, he almost singlehandedly revitalized the form. From that point on he maintained two distinct writerly personas. As Iain Banks he wrote "mainstream fiction" that varied from the story of a contemporary pop star (*Espedair Street*, 1987) to a richly comic novel of a dysfunctional family (*The Crow Road*, 1991, with its famous opening sentence: "It was the day my grandmother exploded" [*Crow*, 3]) to a violent crime novel (*Complicity*, 1993) to a fable about the effects of war (*A Song of Stone*, 1997). These were interspersed with the "science fiction" of Iain M. Banks, which tended to be novels of the Culture, often displaying daring structural experimentation (*Use of Weapons*, 1990; *Excession*, 1996), though he did occasionally venture outside the Culture, most notably with *Feersum Endjinn* (1994).

This apparent bifurcation in Banks's career, between the work of Iain Banks and Iain M. Banks, is in fact no less flexible and open to interpretation than the distinction Graham Greene drew between his novels and his entertainments. Nevertheless, it has led to the popular view that, since the novels of Iain M. Banks are overtly science fiction, then the novels of Iain Banks, including those published at the very start of his career, must be mainstream. The distinction, however, is nowhere near so clear-cut. Even before we come to the liminal case of *Transition* (2009, see chapter 4), there is considerable overlap between the two branches of Banks's career, ranging from the future setting of *Canal Dreams* (1989) to hints of the supernatural in *The Crow Road* to the issues of identity and the nature of the self that are as explicit in *Feersum Endjinn* as they are in *Espedair Street*. As Christie L. March says, "This shading between his science fiction and his mainstream narratives allows him to edge past such parameters, playing with narrative form and linguistic convention in ways that slyly makes SF readers out of mainstream audiences."[2]

We could as easily say that Banks makes mainstream readers out of sf audiences, for I don't think that either form is dominant in his work. What is clear, however, is that the resonances between the two sets of novels are so significant that it is impossible to give serious consideration to the work of Iain M. Banks without regard to the works of Iain Banks, and vice versa.

All of his novels, mainstream or science fiction, appeared on the bestseller lists. He remained a massively popular writer to the end of his life; even late in his career, when some of his work seemed otiose (*The Algebraist*, 2004) or to recapitulate earlier, better novels (*Stonemouth*, 2012), the books sold consistently well. Iain Banks was not just another popular novelist but a writer whose work inspired a devoted following, incredible excitement, and intellectual engagement. He was called, by *The Times*, "the most imaginative

British novelist of his generation."[3] And throughout his career he presented a consistent set of ideas, marked by political and religious skepticism and ready humor, that spoke directly to a varied but enthusiastic readership.

Iain Menzies Banks was born in Dunfermline, Fife, on February 16, 1954. A sister, Martha Ann, had died at six weeks old from spina bifida before Iain was born, so he was the only child of a mother who was a professional ice skater and a father who worked for the Admiralty. To be close to the Rosyth naval yards, they lived in North Queensferry, just across the Firth of Forth from Edinburgh and in the shadow of the Forth Rail Bridge—"my bedroom window looked out onto it," he recalled.[4] The bridge would provide a narrative shape for an early draft of *Use of Weapons* as well as for *The Bridge*, and perhaps inspired the monumental structures in so many of his books. The place certainly impinged itself upon his imagination; as soon as his writing gave him the financial independence to return to Scotland, he set up home in North Queensferry and remained there for the rest of his life.

Banks seems to have enjoyed his childhood. In *Raw Spirit* (2003), supposedly a travel book about visiting all of Scotland's whisky distilleries but also the closest he came to writing an autobiography, he recounts the story of an American student who approached him at a 1989 launch party for *Canal Dreams* held in Edinburgh. When the student said he'd just read *The Wasp Factory* and "you must have had a really disturbed childhood," Banks pointed him to "that little old grey-haired lady" and moments later "I heard my mother's voice floating over the assembled heads; 'Och, no, Iain was always a very happy wee boy'" (*Raw*, 44). One can understand the student's question: from *Use of Weapons* and *The Crow Road* to *Matter* (2008) and *The Quarry* (2013), betrayal, mistrust, and physical danger often come from within the family. Nevertheless, such a consistently recurring theme appears to have had no basis in his own life. But then, he seems to have lived in his imagination from a young age.

When Banks was nine years old his father's job took him to the Clyde, and the family moved to Gourock. He began writing around the age of eleven. By the time he was fourteen he had written, in longhand, a thriller called *Top of Poseidon*, though when he counted up he found the finished story was far too short for a novel. Instead he reused the plot for a novel called *The Hungarian Lift-Jet*, a spy novel in the style of Alastair MacLean that featured lots of military technology and mayhem. This was followed by a massive satirical novel called *The Tashkent Rambler* that borrowed its influences variously from Joseph Heller's *Catch-22* (1961) and John Brunner's *Stand on Zanzibar* (1968). This novel featured characters with names like Dahommey Breshnev and Toss Macabre. "The stories became pun-driven, pun-led; I made the stories up as I went along and at every junction of the tale, whenever there was a choice about what was going to happen next, I invariably went for the route that seemed to promise the highest number of puns" (*Raw*, 108).

It was presumably this novel, in exercise books filled with lots of Terry Gilliam–style collages made out of pictures cut from (mostly) Sunday color supplements, and with ridiculous pun-filled parody adventure stories, that was the first thing by Banks that Ken MacLeod read when they met at Greenock High School. Banks had transferred to the school in 1971 to complete his Highers, as final secondary school exams are known in Scotland, and MacLeod, who would himself go on to become an award-winning science fiction writer, edited the school magazine. As Banks tells the story, he was lying on a grass slope overlooking the school playing fields when MacLeod approached him: "'I hear you write stories,' he said in a sing-song voice. . . . 'Would you like to write one for the school magazine?'" (*Raw*, 214). Banks did write the story, but it was rejected because it contained mild swearing. He then adds: "Ken's version of how we met is entirely different and possesses the additional merit of being true" (*Raw*, 214).

MacLeod suggests that they met when MacLeod was reading Banks's copy of the satirical magazine *Private Eye* over his shoulder. Another version is that they got to know each other in a creative writing group formed by a teacher, Joan Woods, and held in her home, where they quickly discovered a mutual love of science fiction. They would read the magazine *New Worlds*, primarily for the criticism by John Clute and M. John Harrison. In the first issue of *New Worlds Quarterly*, published in 1971, Harrison had an essay titled "A Literature of Comfort" that had a particular effect on the two would-be writers. In the essay, Harrison refers to science fiction as "a literature of shoddy, programmed pap,"[5] arguing that it had betrayed its roots in favor of safe thrills. Space opera was very much the paradigm of the "clammy witlessness,"[6] as Clute called it, that the two critics were railing against in contemporary science fiction. Most art forms have a natural life: flourishing for a while, providing a venue for innovation and excitement, then, in time, either transmogrifying into something new or settling into a period of exhaustion in which the familiar and the repetitious increasingly outweigh the inventive and the engaging. Space opera had flourished during the 1930s; by the 1940s the more interesting parts of the subgenre were already transforming into what became known as hard sf; by the 1950s what remained of space opera was a tired rehash of what had gone before. Space opera was a conservative expression of the great man theory of history, in which one heroic figure, almost invariably a man, could set right all wrongs, defeating nasty, differently colored aliens, and change the world. Militaristic, its spaceships invariably modeled on naval vessels with hierarchical chains of command, space opera was clumsily written, naïve, and formulaic. Even its immediate successor, hard sf, had grown dull and unadventurous, but by the 1960s and 1970s space opera was simply parodic. That it was still being published and republished, and was in fact what the term science fiction brought to mind for most people, must have been acutely embarrassing for the iconoclasts of the New Wave, for whom Harrison and Clute served as ideologues. The New Wave envisaged science fiction as a vehicle for literature that was structurally experimental, psychologically challenging, and that opened up new ways of looking at the world and our place within it. Space opera, and indeed most of the science fiction still being written, did none of that, and hence, in the eyes of both Harrison and Clute, was failing to live up to the possibilities it contained.

Banks and MacLeod were both voracious readers of science fiction who loved space opera because it presented a bright and open-ended future, but they recognized what Harrison was attacking. At this point they began to develop the idea of writing a big space opera that would still meet the strictures expressed by Harrison and Clute. These ideas didn't feed through immediately into Banks's fiction, however. *The Tashkent Rambler* eventually reached half a million words, and he felt confident enough in his abilities now that it was the first novel he submitted to publishers. It was rejected seventeen times.

In 1972 Banks enrolled at the University of Stirling. Having already determined that he was going to be a writer, he chose his subjects carefully, as he explained in an interview broadcast on Scottish TV in 1997: "I want to be a writer, so English Literature, obviously [. . .] books have got to have a meaning, so Philosophy; and books have got to have convincing characters, so obviously Psychology." The interviewer asked: "Did it work?" to which Banks replied, "I don't think so, no."[7] As we shall see, however, psychology in particular was to prove influential in his early novels. It was here, too, in the Creative Writing Group at Stirling University, that Banks wrote the poem "Feu de Joie" that would later form the basis for *Song of Stone*.

It was at university, while still collecting rejections for *The Tashkent Rambler*, that Banks turned his attention seriously to writing science fiction. He began and abandoned one science fiction novel (Ken MacLeod, who was reading the work as it was written, complained that all the dialogue sounded like students[8]), then started work on the novel that would eventually become *Use of Weapons*. This was a conscious attempt to reclaim the moral high ground of space opera for the left, the first of his works to give expression to the vision of science fiction that Banks and MacLeod had absorbed from Clute and Harrison. Banks began with the idea of the ultimate mercenary who was on the side of good, and developed a universe to accommodate such a character. He decided to build the best possible society he could imagine: Suppose all your technological dreams came true—what would you do with them? In an unpublished interview with Dr. David Smith of Brunel University, he said: "Money is a sign of poverty. A cheque book is really a ration book."[9] In line with this ideal, his perfect society had to be a communistic one in which there was plenty for everyone, but a society that had come about not through revolution but through information. The notion that information can lead to the betterment of all people was a position he maintained all his life, and is at the heart of the Culture as he began to develop it in this novel. Ken MacLeod has summed up the idea of the Culture as "pan-sentient utilitarian hedonism":[10] the greater good for everyone no matter what their nature leads inevitably to the greater pleasure for everyone.

The problem with *Use of Weapons* was structural. It was a young man's book, written with great joie de vivre and daring, but it was overly ambitious. The initial plan was to give the book a vast formal structure inspired by the shape of the Forth Rail Bridge, with the chapters arranged by theme rather than chronology. Unfortunately, this structure gave the novel two climaxes, both of which came in the middle of the book. Although Banks submitted the novel to several publishers, it would be some time before the structural problems would be finally and triumphantly solved.

Immediately after leaving university, Banks wrote another, more straight-forward science fiction novel, *Against a Dark Background* (1993), which may have sprung from the work he'd abandoned earlier since it was based on ideas worked out in his first year as an undergraduate. At this time, he was working in a variety of jobs that allowed him time to write. This included a spell as a "Non-Destructive Testing Technician (Trainee)" (*Raw*, 178) with British Steel, working at Portmahomack near Nigg, on the coast north of Inverness, where his work involved checking the structural reliability of the steel that would be used on North Sea oil platforms. The landscape around Nigg on the Cromarty Firth would prove to be a major inspiration for the setting of *The Wasp Factory*.

In 1977 Banks went down to London to take part in a demonstration, staying on for a while with Ken MacLeod, who was doing his MPhil at Brunel University in Uxbridge and living in what he called a shared house and what Banks referred to as a squat in Hayes. It was on this trip that Banks used the library at Brunel to conduct the research into contemporary affairs that he needed in order to write *The State of the Art* (1989). He was trying his hand at writing short stories at the time, with no more success than with his novels, although some of them would resurface later, but *The State of the Art*, his second visit to the Culture, soon grew from the original short story into a novella.

At this time Banks made his first visit to the United States, a trip that included being hired to drive someone's car from Washington D.C. to Los Angeles, which may have helped to cement his love for high-powered cars and fast driving, and which certainly gave him the idea for part of *The Player of Games* (1988). In Texas he came upon a place where the median strip on the highway had burned without the land on either side of the road being affected. This gave him the idea of a circular island where fire burns up the vegetation that in turn needs the fire to germinate. Upon his return Banks wrote *The Player of Games*; the burning median strip became the planet Echronedal, where the climax of the novel is played out. He was still fruitlessly submitting everything he wrote to publishers, but *The Player of Games* attracted some interest, which may have encouraged him to continue.

Banks moved permanently to London in December 1979. He took a job as a costing clerk with solicitors Denton, Hall & Burgin in February 1980, and later that year Ken MacLeod also joined the company. Banks met Annie Blackburn, a secretary at the company, in April 1981, and in December they started living together in Dalston.

Between May and July 1981 Banks wrote the first draft of *The Wasp Factory*, with a second draft between February and April 1982. By this time, he had written upwards of a million words of fiction and had been collecting rejection notices since 1974. Now, as he told it, he deliberately wrote a mainstream novel in order to get published. In an interview with Andy Sawyer he said, "*The Wasp Factory* was my attempt at writing an ordinary conventional novel."[11] A couple of years later, he added: "I had thought that, having written so much sf before, I'd try something that wasn't science fiction so I'd have a better chance of getting published."[12]

Banks expanded on this idea in his preface to the 2013 paperback edition of *The Wasp Factory*:

> Maybe I wasn't just a science fiction writer after all. Maybe I should try writing an ordinary, boring, mainstream novel [. . .] *The Wasp Factory* represented me admitting partial defeat, heaving a slightly theatrical sigh, stepping reluctantly away from the gaudy wall-size canvases of science / space fiction [. . .] lower[ing] myself to using a more restricted palette and produce what felt like a miniature in comparison (preface, x).

The story had obviously grown with the retelling, but it was, at best, disingenuous. As he revealed to Andy Sawyer, "*The Player of Games* came quite close to getting published,"[13] which hardly suggests that continuing to write science fiction was likely to prove unfruitful. Moreover, the next novel Banks wrote after *The Wasp Factory* was *Consider Phlebas*, which he put aside without submitting for publication only because *The Wasp Factory* had been accepted. Writing so overtly a science fiction novel as *Consider Phlebas* was a curious decision for a writer who had supposedly decided to pursue publication by writing mainstream fiction.

Nor did *The Wasp Factory* have an easy route to publication; it was rejected by Jonathan Cape, Andre Deutsch, Victor Gollancz (whose reader's report apparently described it as "quite well written, but far too strange ever to get published,"[14] and this from a publisher well used to strange fiction), The Bodley Head, Hamish Hamilton, and Michael Joseph. Clearly, nobody saw the book as an ordinary, conventional novel, as Banks himself comes close to admitting when he says his "normality-challenged teenage eccentric" allowed him to "treat it as something resembling science fiction" (preface, x). Indeed, the reason that Iain Banks finally made it into print with *The Wasp Factory* may well have nothing to do with whether it was science fiction or mainstream, but simply the fact that it was "the first book . . . that I did a second draft on."[15]

Eventually the novel was submitted to Macmillan, where (according to Banks) Hilary, future wife of editor James Hale, found it in the slush pile and took it to her husband-to-be (*Raw*, 250), though Mary Pachnos, rights director at Macmillan at the time, recalls that it was Lord Hardinge of Penshurst, who ran the crime list, who passed the manuscript on to Hale.[16] The usual formulation here is to say that Hale decided to take a chance on the book, but before it was published, on February 16, 1984, Banks's thirtieth birthday, Macmillan had already spent £10,000 on publicity—"way over the top for a first novel"—and the paperback rights had sold for £30,000, "more than many writers see in a lifetime,"[17] suggesting that the publishers clearly had some confidence in the book right from the start.

*The Wasp Factory*, at first glance, conforms to the idea of a small scale conventional novel. It is narrated by a teenage boy, Frank, growing up on a small island along the Scottish coast. The name of the narrator is significant: as Kirsty MacDonald suggests, Frank's "sincerity of belief is foregrounded by his very name";[18] at the same time it hints at his connection to Frankenstein's creature, for he is clearly a "made man"; moreover, as an excessively unreliable narrator he is far from frank. Frank lives with his eccentric father and is awaiting the arrival of his elder brother, who has just escaped from a secure mental hospital. From the first sentence, however, it is clear that this is far from being a realist novel: "I had been making the rounds of the Sacrifice Poles the day we heard my brother had escaped" (*Wasp*, 7). These Sacrifice Poles immediately call to mind the pig's-head totem in William Golding's *Lord of the Flies* (1954), another story of boys gone wild on an island. Perhaps more pertinent, the Poles tell us that this is not a rational world, but a world of symbol and ritual: "All our lives are symbols. Everything we do is part of a pattern we have at least some say in" (*Wasp*, 117). The story is of a life constantly shaped and guided by beliefs and rituals that are themselves the necessary constructs of a life disconnected from friends, from family, from reality, and even, we learn, from gender. As Maureen Kincaid Speller puts it:

> Almost every action of his day has some significant function; indeed, I think it's of the greatest significance that the actual Factory in part comprises a huge clock-face, a modern symbol of order (aren't we all slaves to the clock, though Frank, quite literally, seems to have all the time in the world) and from a bank, another potent symbol of order. It's as though he needs the ritual to keep his world, and his understanding of his world, under control.[19]

The problem for Frank is that the more he shapes his life around these rituals and symbols, the more out of control it becomes. He is, to an extent, a nonperson: "I have no birth certificate, no National Insurance number, nothing to say I'm alive or have ever existed" (*Wasp*, 13–14). He is detached from the world physically as well as legally, living on an island that is connected to the mainland by a footbridge, though the fact that there is a gate part way along the bridge makes us see this more as a barrier than a link. Frank's questionable legal status means that he must pretend he is only an occasional visitor to his own home, and so he goes into the nearby town only rarely, usually to get hopelessly drunk. Moreover, within this disconnected existence, he lives in a miasma of untruth: "If I was lucky, my father might tell me something and, if I was luckier still, it might even be the truth" (*Wasp*, 8). Frank can believe nothing, and since he is our only conduit into this extraordinary world, we can believe nothing we are told either. "On the one hand, the story is so bizarre, one simply can't believe that it might be true; on the other, the story is so bizarre, how could it not be true?"[20]

The story that Frank tells revolves around gender, though it is only late in the novel that we discover how problematic this is. Freudian psychoanalysis tends to regard women as defined by their lack of a penis, an idea that Banks would certainly have come across during his psychology studies. He literalizes that notion in the person of Frank, and by extension the whole Cauldhame family, though this, I will suggest, is not to encourage a Freudian analysis of the novel so much as to undermine it. In 2010 Banks told Jude Roberts that he was not convinced by Freud's ideas and "I've never deliberately included any Freudian imagery in my stories."[21] Frank was emasculated as a young child, his penis and testicles bitten off by the family's pet dog, Old Saul, at the precise moment that his younger brother Paul was born (an unmistakable reference to the Bible story in which Saul is transformed into Paul). In compensation, or so it would seem, he is aggressively, excessively masculine, making bombs and flamethrowers, which he uses against anything from wasps to rabbits. He murders three other children, including brother Paul, in increasingly bizarre ways that are somehow never laid at his door, while also reporting the even more extraordinary deaths of other relatives. To an extent this has a satiric edge; as Banks told Kim Newman, "The whole thing was to try and make Frank a type of symbol for the military establishment."[22] It is also part of the comedy of the novel—"I do make violence funny sometimes. That's a tricky operation. You should laugh at it first and then feel the horror, not laugh at it and forget it"[23]—an issue that would become increasingly problematic in later novels. But these issues are really beside the point: what we have in Frank is almost a cartoon figure, an exaggeration of all things male, so that when we arrive at the final revelation of his gender, the divided nature of his character is made clear.

All through the novel we see people being divided by the differences between the social or cultural demands being placed upon them and their own experience. Frank's older brother, Eric, is a key example: working in a hospital, a socially responsible and morally satisfying role, he comes upon a baby with a fractured skull that has been so badly cared for that maggots have got through the fracture into the brain. It is a discovery that drives him insane. Frank, in turn, has to negotiate his way between the excessive order of a father who expects him to know the exact measurements of every piece of furniture in the house, and a daily life so untrammeled that he can commit three murders without ever arousing suspicion.

Scottish literature has characteristically centered on "characters with damaged or distorted identities,"[24] from James Hogg's *The Private Memoirs and Confessions of a Justified Sinner* (1824) and Robert Louis Stevenson's *Strange Case of Dr. Jekyll and Mr. Hyde* (1886) up to Alasdair Gray's *Lanark* (1982). Even works that are not overtly fantastic often share this characteristic, as for instance in *Trainspotting* by Irvine Welsh (1993) and *Morvern Caller* by Alan Warner (1995). Such doubled or divided characters also feature in the work of the Scottish psychologist R. D. Laing, especially *The Divided Self* (1960). Though Laing's work was being called into question by the 1980s, he was very widely read throughout the 1960s and 1970s and was a major influence on Scottish writers of the period.[25] Ken MacLeod, for instance, recalls reading the book in high school and discussing it in Joan Woods's creative writing group. But even if Banks didn't come across it then, he is likely to have encountered Laing's work when studying psychology at university, or at least found his ideas disseminated throughout contemporary fiction. Laing's study of schizophrenia identified what he called "ontological insecurity," in which someone "may feel his self as partially divorced from his body . . . [and] . . . the world of his experience comes to be one he can no longer share with other people."[26] This notion of division is a consistent feature of Banks's work. Cairns Craig, for instance, takes the narrative passages in the second person in *Complicity* as indicating "the divided nature of the self which addresses itself as though it was another."[27]

In Banks's work, Laing's notion of a divided self is tied in with an idea from *The Presentation of Self in Everyday Life* by Erving Goffman (1959), which Banks referred to in his interview with Michael Cobley: "It's about the way we use more or less assumed identities, take [*sic*] from films, TV, books, people around us, to construct defences to keep the world back."[28] It is the damaged and doubled characters, the constructed defenses, the worlds that have become a private rather than a shared experience, that make it impossible to read *The Wasp Factory* and its two successors other than as what I have called the Scottish fantastic.[29]

As *The Wasp Factory* accelerates toward its end, and we learn that the dog attack didn't happen as Frank was told, another lie, and that though he was raised as a boy, he is in fact a girl, so we notice the number of doubles that these divided selves have generated. For example, Frank, himself double as both boy and girl, also doubles with Eric, who was often dressed in female clothes. Andrew M. Butler identifies Paul and Saul, and Angus the father with Agnes, who is Frank's absent mother.[30] Kev McVeigh points out that "the doubling serves to internalise the novel, and Frank's physical distancing from normal society emphasises this,"[31] which is a way of noting how Laing's ontological insecurity holds sway in the novel. This is a parallel reality; the world on the island reflects the inside of Frank's mind (in much the same way that the island in William Golding's *Pincher Martin* (1956) actualizes the inside of Martin's head), a mind divided from itself through the distortions of gender identity and through the social and physical limitations imposed by this detached and enclosed place. This is why science-fictional readings of the novel tend to question everything we are told. McVeigh is perhaps an extreme example, proposing that Eric is in fact a projection of Frank's own psychosis and doesn't actually exist, and that Angus's genitalia are as fake as the wax models of Frank's supposed genitals, which would mean that Angus and Agnes are the same person. I am not entirely convinced by this argument, but reading Cauldhame (Cold Home) as a landscape of the mind, another reality reflecting Frank's divided status, is a more rewarding way of approaching the book.

The alternative, which is to accept the truth of what we are told, is to read *The Wasp Factory* as an uneasy hybrid of Gothic horror and psychological realism, and that is exactly how the book was reviewed. The book had a sensational reception; it was more widely reviewed than most debut novels can ever hope for, yet it divided the critics. Many, it is true, praised the book, almost to excess. The *Financial Times* said it was "a Gothic horror story of quite exceptional quality. It is macabre, bizarre and impossible to put down. There is a control and assurance in the book, an originality rare in established writers twice the author's age."[32] The *Daily Telegraph* added that "Iain Banks has written one of the most brilliant first novels I have come across for some time." *Punch* concluded that "*The Wasp Factory* is a first novel not only of tremendous promise, but also of achievement, a minor masterpiece perhaps."

But this praise was offset by an equal number of reviewers who were, if anything, even more excessive in their condemnation. "It is a sick, sick world when the confidence and investment of an astute firm or publishers is justified by a work of unparalleled depravity," the *Irish Times* thundered. The *Sunday Express* described it as "a silly, gloatingly sadistic and grisly yarn of a family of Scots lunatics, one of whom tortures small creatures . . . a bit better written than most horror hokum but really just the lurid literary equivalent of a video nasty." And, in a review that Banks liked to quote in interviews, *The Times* proclaimed: "As a piece of writing, *The Wasp Factory* soars to the level of mediocrity. Maybe the crassly explicit language, the obscenity of the plot, were thought to strike an agreeably avant-garde note. Perhaps it is all a joke meant to fool literary London into respect for rubbish."

There was no middle ground; the book was either brilliant or loathsome. But this very divided reaction indicated that something very different had appeared on the literary scene, something for which the critics were quite unprepared. I suspect it was the fact that this love-it-or-loathe-it response suggested something startlingly original that prompted Toby Roxburgh of the paperback house Futura to quote both the good and the bad reviews on the paperback edition. Banks certainly received a lot of attention as a result.

When he received the advance check from Macmillan, Banks treated himself to an electric typewriter, a new camera, and a few records, and he took Ken MacLeod and another old friend who read his manuscripts to dinner. In September 1983 he and Annie Blackburn moved to a house in Faversham to be closer to her parents in Canterbury. And though he told Max Hastings in December that he had no thought of leaving his job as a solicitor's clerk,[33] he handed in his notice just ten days before *The Wasp Factory* was published. From that point on he earned his living as a full-time writer.

Meanwhile, Banks was at work on his second novel, which was variously called *The Exile's Progress* and *Chinese Scrabble* before he settled on *Walking on Glass*. James Hale had advised him to write a book a year, and, with an occasional interruption, that was the regime he now maintained. *Walking on Glass* was delivered in April 1984 and came out roughly a year after the first novel. Perhaps because its genre roots are more overt, or possibly simply because *The Wasp Factory* had prepared the way, the book did not generate anything like the same controversy, despite the fact that the incest theme was clearly designed to shock. Nevertheless, this second novel is more interesting for its structure than its plot, a first indication of the part that unconventional structure would play in many of his subsequent novels, most notably *The Bridge* and *Use of Weapons*.

*Walking on Glass* is made up of three separate stories, told in alternating chapters, that seem to come together at the end, though this convergence is more implicit than explicit. The first story, the one that seems privileged because it is unequivocally realist, tells the story of one afternoon during which Graham Park walks from the Art College where he is a student to the home of the woman he hopes will become his lover. Even so, there are indications that symbols are as important in the construction of this world as they are in *The Wasp Factory*. Graham looks at his watch and sees that it is 3:33: "Three three three. A good omen. Today was a day things would come together, a day events would coalesce" (*Glass*, 11). Events would indeed coalesce, though not in ways Graham could possibly imagine. But more significant is his reading of the omens, because most of this section of the novel will be told in retrospect, recalling earlier moments in the development of his relationship with Sara, and in the end we will discover just how much he has misread every symbol.

It is also worth noting that Graham's friend, Richard Slater, who joins him for a part of the walk, relates an idea for a science fiction story. This brings in science fiction right at the start of the novel, and means it features in every section, but it also has the effect of equating the fantastic with story so emphasizing the fictionality of the sf elements in the rest of the novel, making them seem not quite so important.

The second story tells of Steven Grout on the same day as Graham's walk, though the two never meet. Steven is the sort of divided self that Laing wrote about, a man whose fantasizing and paranoia, an overt form of ontological insecurity, have led him to construct a private reality that no one else can share. He believes himself to be an exile from some great war between good and evil in another realm of reality, and that alien enemies are constantly trying to attack him with futuristic weapons such as the Microwave Gun, a device that sounds suspiciously similar to the Lazy Gun which we will encounter in *Against a Dark Background*. To defend himself against these attacks, Steven must take eccentric evasive action, wearing a hard hat at all times and stepping only on the cracks in the pavement. His paranoia makes it impossible for him to relate to fellow workers, so he doesn't hold on to jobs for long. The start of his day sees him losing his job filling potholes in the road, and during the course of his day we see him failing to sign on at the Labour Exchange, evading his landlady to whom he owes rent, getting drunk and being robbed, all the while being more aware of a shadowy other world than he is of this one.

If Steven believes himself to be exiled from some great war, then Quiss and Ajayi, the central characters in the third story, actually are such exiles. They are from opposite sides in the conflict, but each has committed some grievous error and has consequently been transported to an isolated, snowbound castle. Before they can be restored to their former positions, they must play ridiculous games: Chinese Scrabble, dominoes with unmarked pieces, and so forth. The successful completion of each game gives them the opportunity to answer a riddle—What happens when an unstoppable force meets an immoveable object?—and only by solving this riddle will they be redeemed and restored to their original positions. If the tutelary deity of *The Wasp Factory* is Stevenson's *Jekyll and Hyde*, then *Walking on Glass* would seem to pay homage to Lewis Carroll's *Alice in Wonderland* (1865), with perhaps also a nod to Mervyn Peake's *Gormenghast* trilogy (1946–59). The lives of Quiss and Ajayi are on hold (unlike the other two stories in this novel, in this section the action takes place over thousands of days); the labyrinth of the castle, the puzzles they must solve, and, above all, the games echo *The Player of Games*. In fact, games would come to play an important part in the iconography of Banks's novels. As he explained to Michael Cobley: "The reason games are attractive in that way is because they're ready-made symbols, the whole idea of the game is an automatic symbol of life, because all games are in a way small attributes of life, small sections that people try to codify."[34] In other words, games make explicit the world of symbols that so much of Banks's fiction inhabits. By codifying games, the characters seemingly impose control even though their lives are out of control, a feature that is explicitly part of later realist novels such as *Complicity* and *The Steep Approach to Garbadale* (2007). Graham may be too innocent to fully understand the complexities and duplicities of the world he inhabits, but Steven, Quiss, and Ajayi do understand these complexities and duplicities, or think they do, and as a result the world they inhabit is one of ontological insecurity.

Unlike Steven, whose response to this insecurity is entirely defensive, both Ajayi and Quiss attempt to explore and make sense of their world in their own ways. Quiss is extrovert and hence heads out to explore the castle, only to get lost because "they'd changed some of the corridors and stairways en route from the games room to the lower levels" (*Glass*, 79). And when he does find his way, he comes upon a kitchen far too large for the rundown and largely depopulated castle he inhabits, a vast and inexplicable room that might in some way presage the immense structure within which *Feersum Endjinn* is set. Beyond this, he finds a room where, if he puts his head into a bubble in the ceiling, he finds himself inside the mind of a being on another world (we recognize that this is a woman working the land in what is probably East Asia). This experience, analogous to the experience of reading, is so seductive that a little later he comes upon a place of seemingly infinite extent where countless people who were previously prisoners of the castle like him all now stand with their heads immersed in the bubbles, forgetting everything else. Ajayi, meanwhile, explores the castle in her own way, by learning to read the books that form the crumbling walls of the castle (the castle thus echoes Steven's room, with its piles of books forming walls and tunnels; while the novel repeatedly generates images of black and white, text on a page: this is a book about being in a book[35]). Both, therefore, come, through the castle, to immerse themselves in the mind of someone else. It is a measure of the ambition of the novel (if not, exactly, its achievement) that the last book Ajayi starts to read is *Walking on Glass*.

In the end it turns out to be Steven who binds all three stories together. His hard hat having been stolen, he is indeed felled by a bolt from the heavens—or, to be precise, a beer barrel flung from a truck caught up in the accident caused when Richard Slater's motorbike, its engine spiked when Steven put sugar in it earlier in the story, skids in a pothole left by Steven; the accident will in turn undo the duplicities of Richard and Sara in which Graham played the innocent dupe. While in the hospital to which he is confined as a result of his accident, Steven notices two elderly patients endlessly playing games, even though another patient keeps stealing some of the pieces. In the grounds, moreover, he finds a matchbox—"McGuffin's ZEN BRAND" (*Glass*, 217), "McGuffin" being Alfred Hitchcock's term for an object with no purpose other than to start the plot—which features the riddle Quiss and Ajayi, Q and A, have been trying to solve. We see that Quiss and Ajayi embody what Steven encounters in the hospital, and thus all that we have read is somehow collapsed into Steven's delusions.

*Walking on Glass* is an odd book that doesn't cohere as well as it should. It is a book in which structural experiment seems to outweigh plot, a work filled with jokey wordplay and half-developed references to some of Banks's so-far-unpublished novels. Yet it supported the idea that *The Wasp Factory* had generated, that a daring yet engaging new talent had appeared, a notion that would be confirmed with Banks's next novel.

Immediately after *Walking on Glass*, Banks wrote a long novel of around 180,000 words called *O*, "which I wasn't sure about and [James Hale] told me it wasn't good enough and he wasn't prepared to publish it" (*Raw*, 251). Hale did suggest that other publishers would be happy to pay a lot of money for any new Banks novel, such was the impact he had already made on the publishing scene, but by now Banks regarded Hale as his mentor and preferred to follow his advice. Instead, Banks cannibalized *O*, salvaging those bits he could incorporate into *The Bridge* and throwing the rest away. This was possible because *The Bridge* is actually a loose mélange of stories, dreams, and vignettes, held together by the structure rather than any overall narrative thread.

*The Bridge* was one of Banks's most political novels and a significant text within the Scottish literary renaissance that was then in full swing. In 1979 a referendum to establish a Scottish Assembly won a clear majority of the votes cast, but since this did not quite equal the cut-off figure of 40 percent of the entire Scottish electorate, the Westminster government declared that the referendum was lost on what was widely seen as a technicality—"The Fabulous Make-Your-Mind-Up Referendum was, effectively, pochled—rigged, in English" (*Bridge*, 213). Meanwhile, the incoming Conservative government was considered inimical to Scottish interests. For instance, in one episode of the satirical television show of the period, *Spitting Image*, the puppet Margaret Thatcher calls Scotland "the test bed," where her most destructive and divisive policies were first tried. Increasingly, the people of Scotland were feeling that they had lost any control over their own destiny. As Richard Todd put it: "Scotland in the 1980s got what England voted for."[36] In a country that was already politically to the left of the rest of Britain, and in which nationalism was gaining ground, there was a sense of resentment and entrapment. "[I]n reaction to a wider political environment that seemed to be running against Scotland's best interests, Scots expended a lot of cultural energy in rediscovering a sense of themselves—and with it, a sense of their difference from a British culture that no longer seemed to include them."[37] Out of this political turmoil emerged a primarily literary renaissance that incorporated many elements that were a traditional part of Scottish fiction, such as "characters deformed to fit the power structures that surround them"[38] yet struggling to construct their own identity, however warped. The sense of national helplessness tended to be expressed in a schizophrenic doubling along the lines of Laing's divided self, and accompanied by a strong political commitment and often surreal elements. Significant Scottish writers who emerged at this time and worked within this pattern include Irvine Welsh, Alan Warner, James Kelman, Janice Galloway, A. L. Kennedy, and of course Iain Banks; but the paradigmatic text, the novel that was recognized as starting the Scottish literary renaissance and that became the touchstone text of the Scottish fantastic, was Alasdair Gray's *Lanark* (1981). The influence of *Lanark* is almost immeasurable. Directly or indirectly it has had an effect on generations of Scottish writers, Banks's *The Bridge* being only the most overt, though later works such as *Marabou Stork Nightmares* (1995) by Irvine Welsh also borrowed structurally and thematically from both Gray and Banks. As Banks put it: "I was absolutely knocked out by *Lanark*. I think it's the best in Scottish literature this century. It opened my eyes. I had forgotten what you could do—you can be self-referential, you can muck about with different voices, characters, time streams, whatever. *Lanark* had a huge effect on *The Bridge*. I'm quite happy to acknowledge that debt."[39]

Gray's divided self is Duncan Thaw/Lanark, and the novel is partly a realist story of Thaw's life in postwar Scotland and partly a surreal account of Lanark's experiences in the postmortem world of Unthank. The ontological uncertainty of the novel is brought out by its structure, in which we first encounter Book Three, then a Prologue, then, in order, Books One, Two and Four; an arrangement that means we cannot privilege the real over the fantastic, or the surreal over the mundane.

The divided self of *The Bridge* is an unnamed narrator and John Orr. The hesitation implied by Orr's name is surely intentional, and though the two are never specifically linked, we are allowed to make that inference. It is partly a realist story of the narrator's life in Scotland from the 1960s to the 1980s and partly a surreal account of Orr's experiences in the strange community that exists on the seemingly endless titular bridge. Following Gray, the realist passages convey a dawning political consciousness, while the surreal passages take us inside a mind shattered by the compromises of everyday existence and obsessed with a sense of guilt. Banks has said: "It's not really in me to be a political writer with a capital 'P.' I'd sort of like to be, but I'm either too lazy or too pragmatic to force myself into a straightjacket that doesn't fit."[40] Nevertheless, the political tenor of *The Bridge*, and of many of his other books, both mainstream and science fiction, is inescapable.

The most obvious debt to Gray is that the ontological uncertainty of the novel is underlined by its structure, which is inspired by childhood memories of the Forth Rail Bridge:

I was doodling on the top of this sheet of paper; three flattened hexagons with two little linking sections between them, which is the shape of the bridge, and I'd been wondering just how to set the book out; chapters or what, and suddenly I realised the bridge itself had a perfect shape; three sections, the little linking bridges-within-bridges, the four feet on the stone caissons . . . everything; it was all there; a literal framework.[41]

After a brief, vividly impressionistic passage that recounts the aftermath of a car crash on the Forth Road Bridge from the point of view of the trapped and injured driver—"Trapped, Crushed. Weight coming from all directions, entangled in the wreckage (you have to become one with the machine). Please no fire, no fire. Shit. This hurts." (*Bridge*, 1)—we shift not to the alter ego Orr, but to a strange dream scenario. A carriage on a mysterious errand meets an identical carriage on a narrow road across remote moorland. Each makes identical manoeuvers, effectively blocking the other from going on. Later, there is another dream in which two pirate ships engage in a mutually destructive battle until, in extremis, the surviving crew of one ship boards the other vessel, only to find that the crew of that ship has boarded their vessel. The symbolism of these two dreams echoes the doubling that runs through all three of these novels, which Moira Martingale interprets thus: "Banks's conscious use of the ambivalent device of the Gothic 'double'—divided characters who are part of the same unity each undergoing a rite of passage—effaces the distinction between imagination and reality and the result, as Freud says in his essay on The Uncanny, is that what we think cannot exist, does."[42] Given Banks's own psychology degree and avowed antipathy toward Freud's work, however, Martingale's Freudian interpretation of *The Bridge* (actually a mélange of Freudian and Jungian) seems too simplistic. (Banks's disdain for Freud might be indicated in his novella, *The State of the Art*, when he has the loutish Li, who thinks only of sex, tout himself as the only person "interested in Freudian analysis" [*State*, 121[43]]). Indeed, the most Freudian examples of doubling occur in these two dreams, which turn out not to be dreams at all, but rather deliberate creations by Orr designed to appease the curiosity of his psychiatrist, Joyce. The dreams that Orr does experience, involving the recurring figure of the barbarian, if they are dreams rather than yet another layer of reality, are far more complex than the Freudian doubling that Martingale discusses. Better, I think, to read this, along with *The Wasp Factory*, in the context of Laing's divided self.

Each of the chapters that form the platform of the bridge has this same bifurcated structure, a dream to start with, or at least something to take us to a different place and perspective, followed by the continuing story of Orr's experiences on the bridge or, in the later chapters, in a series of increasingly threatening, war-torn scenarios. Interspersed among these chapters, the caissons that uphold the entire structure, is the story of a successful engineer and would-be poet, in particular his occasionally troubled relationship with Andrea.

The engineer, the narrator of the realist sections, the comatose figure that Orr watches on his television, remains unnamed throughout the novel. This loss of identity, a failure to know himself, is another connection to the idea of the divided self and is one of the themes that would recur throughout Banks's work. Banks does, however, provide two fairly blatant clues to his name. When the narrator is dating a girl called Nicola, there is an oblique reference to Nicholas and Alexandra, and he is also asked if he is related to the singer in the Eurythmics. Later, in *Complicity*, the central character, Cameron, meets Alexander Lennox and his wife Andi in a bar. "The idea was that *Complicity*, for all its final bleakness, does have a happy ending. It's just that it isn't its own happy ending, and it's not at the end" (*Raw*, 292).

It is worth noting how often the pattern of the bridge is repeated throughout the novel. Even in the sex scene, when Orr is making love to Abberlaine (Andrea's avatar), the Xs that decorate her lingerie become "a language, an architecture. Cantilevers and tubes, suspension ties," her body takes on the shape, "arms in a V behind her, extended and straining," so that in the end, Orr says, "I feel like I have just fucked the bridge" (*Bridge*, 154). Architecture and language are equated. One of the things that becomes apparent in *The Bridge*, though there were traces of it in *Walking on Glass*, is the importance of language, or rather the incomprehensibility of language and the way it blocks understanding. Sometimes this is dealt with humorously, as in the coarse Scots dialect of the barbarian's "langwitch" (*Bridge*, 142) which seems to presage the debased language of *Feersum Endjinn*; more often it is a serious issue, as when Orr first sees the figure in the hospital bed on his TV and comments, "I can't even tell what language is being used" (*Bridge*, 30). Language thus becomes a symbol of the struggle to understand, to make sense, which is at the heart of all three of these early novels.

*The Bridge* is, in short, the most successful expression of themes that run through these three novels and will continue into Banks's later work. Among these, of course, is the lyrical expression of a longing for Scotland that is implicit in the landscape of *The Wasp Factory* and the descriptions of Edinburgh and its environs in *The Bridge*, and explicit in a variety of small ways, such as the Scots dialect used by the barbarian. Within two years of the publication of *The Bridge*, Banks had moved back to Scotland, first to Edinburgh and eventually to North Queensferry, close to his childhood home and once more in the shadow of the Forth Bridge.

In the main, however, the themes repay reading the novels as fantastic rather than as straightforward realism. (Not everyone would agree with this reading; Simone Caroti accepts Banks's own judgement that they are mainstream novels because "Frank/Frances, Steven, Quiss, Ajay [*sic*], and Alex/John are people within (problematically) mimetic worlds,"[44] although it is difficult to see the ritualized landscape of Cauldhame, the castle of books, and the hierarchical society of the Bridge as in any way mimetic. I am not just referring to the way that they pick up on devices and ideas from the earlier (and at this stage unpublished) science fiction novels, such as the echoes of *The Player of Games* in *Walking on Glass*, or the barbarian's magic dirk in *The Bridge* that is clearly a variant on the knife missile we later find in so many Culture novels. The novels display a sense of the other, of parallel worlds that are the creation of the divided self and so are inaccessible to anyone else: the island of *The Wasp Factory*, the castle of *Walking on Glass*, the bridge of *The Bridge*, all are enclosed, isolated, places easier to enter than to leave. But for all that these spring from and reflect the minds of the characters, that does not make them any less real. Frank lives on an island that he has conjured to suit his own shattered personality, yet that does not mean we can in any way dismiss what he sees and does there, or count it any less "real." But reading the fantastic in the novel allows us to pick up the clues so that rather than reading the island through Frank, we are reading Frank through the island. Quiss and Ajayi may be reflections of the two old game players that Steven sees in the hospital, but that does not make understanding their bitter isolation, the strange alchemy of their prison, any less important in interpreting what the novel is doing. And the bridge is not just an escape from the confinement of Alexander Lennox's coma; it is a strange and complex world that is more important in its own right than it is as a commentary on Lennox's life. Just as, in Alasdair Gray's *Lanark*, we must take Unthank as more than a distorted Glasgow, so we must take the bridge as more than a distorted Edinburgh.

## CHAPTER 2

## BACKING INTO THE CULTURE

By 1986 Iain Banks had established a reputation as one of the best young writers in Britain. He was controversial, challenging, unafraid to try new structures, new approaches. His books were guaranteed to receive substantial reviews and high sales. Yet despite the interest in and engagement with genre that was obvious in his work, he had so far received little notice in the science fiction community. But already that was changing.

At this point we come to my own small part in the story of Iain Banks. In 1985 I was on the committee of a science fiction convention called Mexicon II. The idea of Mexicon was to provide a venue for serious discussion of science fiction as literature. At the first Mexicon in 1984 our guests had been Alasdair Gray and Russell Hoban, and we were now looking for guests who would offer the same combination of the literary and the innovative. At one meeting our chair, Greg Pickersgill, was praising *The Wasp Factory*, which was now out in paperback. On his urging I read the book, and also *Walking on Glass*, which had just been published, and agreed that Banks was clearly engaged with science fiction and thus exactly what we were looking for. So I wrote to invite him to be one of our guests, an invitation he accepted with alacrity.

I'm not sure any of us knew what to expect, but the result was mutual delight. His personality—extrovert, humorous, enthusiastic—won over everyone who met him. And he was equally pleased. "These are my people!" he proclaimed to Ken MacLeod immediately on his return,[1] and it gave him the impetus to talk his editor into looking again at the sf novels, especially the most recent, *Consider Phlebas*. By the time he was interviewed for *Interzone* in the summer of 1986, he could announce, "I've got an sf book tentatively scheduled to come out in November."[2] Publication would be pushed back until February 1987, but this was fast work. Banks was a young man in a hurry in those years; at the same time that he was revising *Consider Phlebas* he was also writing his next novel, *Espedair Street,* that would also appear in 1987.

Meanwhile, the first reviews of Banks's work were starting to appear in science fiction publications. In the April 1986 issue of *Locus*, the American edition of *Walking on Glass* was dismissed by Faren Miller as "artifice for its own sake."[3] More positive was the October 1986 mailing from the British Science Fiction Association, which contained my review of *Walking on Glass* in *Paperback Inferno* (I found the Quiss and Ajayi sections "a wild and inventive mélange of Peake, Kafka and Borges" but on the whole the "formal structure and the imbalance between the sections both tend to get in the way of the story"[4]). In the same mailing, there were two reviews of *The Bridge* in *Vector*; one by me ("an extravagantly inventive novel, delighting in wordplay and oblique literary allusion"[5]), and one by Mike Dickinson (Banks "has confirmed himself as the best British writer of his generation"[6]).

At this remove, it is difficult to ascertain how reluctant Macmillan were to publish *Consider Phlebas*. They weren't known for publishing science fiction at the time, and here was one of their brightest stars wanting to produce the stuff. Banks's reputation as an innovative writer to watch had been secured among precisely that portion of the literary establishment most likely to decry science fiction, so there was an obvious danger that he might damage his career. At the same time, he was a bestselling writer who by now must have had quite a bit of clout with the publisher. He was asked to use a pseudonym, and for a while he toyed with the idea of calling himself John B. Macallan after two of his favorite brands of whisky, but in the end he decided to satisfy his family. The manuscript of *The Wasp Factory* had carried the name Iain M. Banks, but the initial was dropped when the book was published in case it reminded people of the bad romantic novelist Rosie M. Banks in P. G. Wodehouse novels. Banks apparently received complaints from his family for dropping Menzies, so now he reinstated the initial M. When *Consider Phlebas* appeared; Macmillan must have been pleasantly surprised to find that they had another bestseller on their hands, and one that reached a new audience.

In many respects, this was a curious choice for Banks's first overt science fiction novel: it was the fourth work he had written about the Culture, so this complex society was, by now, familiar and well developed in his imagination. Yet for readers it would all be new. Over the next three years, *Use of Weapons*, *The State of the Art*, and *The Player of Games* would all be published, in reverse order of their composition. It was as if Banks was backing into his creation; yet this reverse order proved to be an excellent introduction to the Culture.

At the time, the fact that Banks had written science fiction was not particularly surprising. His previous books had clearly signaled an interest in the fantastic, and it was known that he had an sf novel in the works. What surprised people was that it was a space opera. As John Clute put it: "Iain's tales of psychosis paradigms dance out of range of genre fixatives, and Iain M has begun his career with a space opera."[7] Colin Greenland wondered "whether Iain Banks [. . .] is quite the right author for generic space opera, or any kind of fiction whose virtues are straightforward and conventional."[8] People enjoyed the story; Faren Miller described it as "a splendid, rip-roaring adventure by an author who's clearly at home in the genre and well equipped to make the most of it,"[9] and David Langford agreed: "manic, high-energy adventure of the sort they don't write any more," though he concluded, "[l]ittle subtlety, lots of fun."[10] The startlement, not to say disdain, with which Clute pronounces "space opera" or Langford opines "little subtlety" is tangible. Yet, *Consider Phlebas* and its successor volumes would help to revitalize the tired subgenre of space opera and would be credited as one of the key works that kick-started the so-called British Boom.[11]

In retrospect, and seeing *Consider Phlebas* in the context of the next three Culture books, what is surprising is not so much that Banks wrote space opera as the simple, almost crude structure of this novel. The three subsequent works—even the novella, *The State of the Art*—offer challenges and rewards in the way the story is presented, culminating in *Use of Weapons*; but *Consider Phlebas* is an episodic picaresque, a largely disconnected sequence of escapades that place our antihero in peril, reveal some new wonder of the universe, and explain some further detail about the Culture, usually all at once. Banks himself describes it as "a shipwrecked sailor who falls in with a gang of pirates and goes in search of buried treasure" (Eastcon 6).

We first meet our antihero, Bora Horza Gobuchul the Changer, a being able to take on the appearance of any other race, chained in a cell that doubles as a sewer, where he is on the point of drowning in effluvia. He is rescued at the last minute, but the ship in which he escapes is attacked, and he finds himself floating alone in space. He is picked up by pirates, joins their crew, takes part in a couple of spectacularly unsuccessful raids, is captured by a tribe of cannibals, escapes in the nick of time, kills and replaces the pirate captain, and finally descends into the massive network of tunnels beneath a planet of the dead in pursuit of his mission to capture a Culture AI, known as a Mind. In this last, over-extended sequence, virtually every character in the novel is killed. The story is bloody, fast-paced, often ghoulishly funny, and filled with objects on such a huge scale that the entire project might have been designed from the start to try the abilities of Hollywood special-effects wizards.

The inhabitants of the Culture are human; their enemies, the Idirans, are not. But before we start to imagine that this is some vision of our distant future, that we ourselves might attain the utopian state ascribed to the Culture, a series of appendices firmly places the Culture-Idiran war in our past. Clashes begin about 1267 C.E. and escalate slowly into a war that lasts until 1367 C.E., though, as Christopher Palmer says, it "take[s] place in the far future, as far as scientific and even social development is concerned. That is, to date [it] in relation to our time is pointless."[12] It is, in other words, the equivalent of "Once upon a time," or, as *Star Wars* has it, "A long time ago in a galaxy far, far away . . ."; as we will see later, this is space opera recast as fairy tale romance. The dates do not coincide with the Crusades (the sixth and last (major) Crusade had ended half a century before), but the identification of the Idirans as zealots conducting a religious war, and the passage from the Koran that opens the book—"Idolatry is worse than carnage" (*Phlebas*, v)—both suggest that such a connection is intentional (though Robert Duggan points out that the passage Banks quotes is now recognized as a mistranslation of the Koran[13]). However, the Culture-Idiran War does serve as a dating point for the rest of the sequence; every one of the Culture novels, with the obvious exception of *Inversions* (1998), is careful to state how long after the war it takes place. Or, in the case of *The State of the Art* and *Use of Weapons*, we know that the General Contact Unit *Arbitrary* visits Earth in 1977, and that Diziet Sma writes her memoir of these events 115 years later, having been interrupted in her composition by the events that constitute *Use of Weapons*.[14] Thus, by their internal chronology, the sequence after *Consider Phlebas* is: *Excession* comes some five hundred years after the war, *The State of the Art* is around six hundred years after the end of the war, *Matter* is at 660 years, *The Player of Games* and *Use of Weapons* take place at roughly the same time around 716 years after the war, *Look to Windward* (2000) revolves around the eight-hundredth anniversary, *The Hydrogen Sonata* (2012) marks one thousand years, and finally, *Surface Detail* (2010) is set fifteen hundred years after the war. If we assume this dating relates to the end of the war, the series ranges from the late thirteenth century C.E. to sometime towards the end of the twenty-eighth century.

The fact that the brief history of the war given in the appendix doesn't even mention the events recounted in the novel means, first, that we cannot place this story chronologically within the war. My sense is that it takes place early in the conflict, but we have no way of knowing. Second, it suggests that these events are of little consequence in the overall course of the war, "a revelation of futility," as Christopher Palmer puts it.[15] Though the events are of major importance to the players, they are not actually changing the course of history. We encounter the same thing elsewhere in these books—in *Use of Weapons*, for example, where a brief additional passage (which seems to be beginning the story all over again) recounts the recruitment of another mercenary, another weapon to be used by the Culture. This is a conscious reaction against the standard model of space opera, which dates back to Banks's reading of Clute and Harrison (see chapter 1). Banks's more radical vision was anti-hierarchical: the Culture has no naval ranks, for instance, so that no one person, male or female, could have much effect in the greater scheme of things. It was his way of "trying to act against what you normally expect to find in the genre."[16]

One of the things designed to make this different from other space operas is the nature of the Culture as utopia. Right from the start we are told that the Culture is a "communist Utopia," which Horza equates with "soft and pampered and indulged," (*Phlebas* 35) and that the Culture's beliefs and attitudes are spreading throughout the Galaxy as "the consensus of opinion was starting to resemble what the Culture had to say on the subject [. . .] because everybody believed the Culture's own propaganda, that it was fair, unbiased, disinterested, concerned only with absolute truth" (*Phlebas* 145). But mostly we have to take the idea of a post-scarcity utopia on trust, because other than a few brief scenes we see the Culture only as Horza sees it, and he opposes the Culture. He is a mercenary for their enemies, the Idirans, in "a conflict between civilisations based on the incompatibility of their core values . . . initiated by a group of fearsome and uncompromising religious zealots that has set out to destroy the nice liberal people of the Culture."[17] Or at least, so it is presented, so Horza believes. Thus, the flashes of the Culture that we get are filtered through Horza's antipathy composed, in more or less equal part, of disdain for its utopian politics, unease at its atheism, hatred of the role of machines, and reluctant admiration for its technology.

Therefore, our first glimpse of the Culture is of a society whose values and achievements are everything we might aspire to. The fact that the Culture was read as the embodiment of liberal ideals helped to make the books immensely successful in the United Kingdom. They were less successful in the United States, perhaps because of Banks's checkered publishing history there (even when often-belated U.S. editions were available from Houghton Mifflin, St. Martin's Press, or Bantam, it is noticeable that American critics still tended to cite the U.K. editions, and American magazines still tended to use British covers as illustrations), perhaps because of politics. In one of the earliest essays about Banks in an American science fiction magazine, for instance, Lawrence Person is enthusiastic about the way Banks plays with space opera, but he has problems with the politics of the book. He interprets the Culture as "third stage" communism and "I rank the plausibility of third stage communism right up there with the Tooth Fairy," which may be why he has "very little idea of how The Culture actually works."[18] To be fair, until "A Few Notes on the Culture" appeared in 1994, the civilization was only ever seen obliquely, so no readers are likely to have had a very clear idea of how it worked.

In fact, the Culture was far less straightforwardly utopian than was generally believed. The doubts and hesitations would become more overt in the later novels, but some of the contradictions in the Culture are highlighted in *Consider Phlebas*—for instance, when Fal 'Ngeestra reflects that the Culture is "killing the immortal, changing to preserve, warring for peace . . . and so embracing utterly what we claimed to have renounced completely, for our own good reasons" (*Phlebas* 332). The sense that the Culture should not be taken at face value becomes, over the course of the next three Iain M. Banks works, perhaps the most interesting thing about the Culture.

From this point on, Banks would alternate books by Iain M. Banks with books by Iain Banks, usually, though not always, writing one a year. But his next Iain Banks novel came only a few months after *Consider Phlebas*. *Espedair Street* should be considered as the first genuinely mainstream novel Banks wrote. Although ostensibly a rock-and-roll novel, filled with the enjoyment of music that is found throughout his work and using song lyrics Banks had written years before (his own music and lyrics would be used in the later BBC Radio Four adaptation of the novel), it seems to me to be far more about coming to terms with his own suddenly increased wealth and fame. Curiously, among the excesses Banks ascribes to his rock stars, the band's leader, Crazy Davey Balfour, "would occasionally swarm up the outside of the hotel rather than use the elevators" (*Espedair* 125). Around the time that the book came out, Banks himself was accused of exactly the same thing.

Following Mexicon II, Banks had become a regular and popular attendee at science fiction conventions throughout the country, his personal conviviality probably contributing to the popularity of his books. In August 1987 the World Science Fiction Convention was staged in Brighton, and Banks was, of course, there. At one room party in a suite he found himself hemmed in on a balcony. In order to get back into the room, he found it simpler to scramble across to the next balcony. The story escalated, until people reported seeing him scaling the outside of the hotel. Since police had coincidentally been called to another room in the hotel where there had been a reported theft, a further elaboration of the story had him being arrested and spending the night in the local gaol. It was, unsurprisingly, a story that Banks rather relished.

The next Culture novel, which came out in 1988, was the one Banks had come close to selling before *The Wasp Factory*. *The Player of Games* is a much subtler and better-crafted novel than *Consider Phlebas*, a view with which sf reviewers at the time tended to concur. Maureen Kincaid Speller (then writing as Maureen Porter), for instance, considered it "a more mature work [. . .] a thoughtful, sombre sort of story, less reliant on action,"[19] while Faren Miller similarly thought Banks's "fiction reveals a sophistication which can laugh at itself even as it instructs."[20] And it engages far more with the ambiguity of the Culture.

In 1702 the Abbé Raguet complained that boredom seemed inevitable in a utopia. Whether or not Banks had ever even heard of the good Abbé, he certainly took the message to heart. Having already introduced the Culture through the lens of its enemy, here, and again in *The State of the Art*, Banks displayed the Culture through the eyes of someone bored with its ease and plenty.

The novel opens with Gurgeh, our hero and the only protagonist in these first four Culture works who is not primarily presented as an anti-hero, playing a shoot-'em-up game as an unsuccessful cure for boredom. It's all false, he complains, and this sense of falseness crops up throughout the novel, such as when he cheats in the game against Olz Hap, or when he leaves the Orbital: "He couldn't help feeling like an actor, or a component in the ship's circuitry: like part of, and therefore as false as, the pretend-view of Real Space hung in front of him" (*Player* 100). Again, when Hamin and Olos try to bribe him to throw the game, Gurgeh replies, innocently, "You mean, lie? Participate in the construction of your false reality?" (*Player* 224). Of course, in the end, Gurgeh was acting a part, he was being used, it was all false.

Gurgeh's boredom allows Banks to show the hedonism of the Culture, epitomized by the style of a game opponent: "It looked impressive, but it was mostly show; fashionable, intricate, but hollow and delicate too; finally vulnerable" (*Player* 9). As the drone, Chamlis, tells him: "You enjoy your life in the Culture, but it can't provide you with sufficient threats" (*Player* 21). All the material and social needs of its inhabitants are met effortlessly within the Culture, but time and again Banks suggests that this is not sufficient for a full and meaningful life. Thus, in *Consider Phlebas*, we first meet Fal 'Ngeestra nursing an injury after climbing without "a floater harness, or with a rescue drone nearby" (*Phlebas* 86), while in *Look to Windward* we are introduced to a host of dangerous sports that are widely pursued. Without risk, it is implied, life within utopia is flat. Indeed, when it comes to the last three novels in the sequence, *Matter*, *Surface Detail*, and *The Hydrogen Sonata*, in which the Culture consistently shies away from the elevation to a new level of being known as subliming, a step long since taken by other Galactic civilizations, we might interpret the trilogy as arguing that utopian hedonism has undermined the will for such a collective step into the unknown. It is, therefore, the need for "sufficient threats" to give shape to his life that allows Gurgeh to be variously tempted and blackmailed into undertaking a mission for Special Circumstances, the nearest the Culture has to a military or espionage wing.

He travels to the distant empire of Azad where a complex game, which has given its name to the empire, is used to determine social position, political status, and even level of employment: "the set-up assumes that the game and life are the same thing, and such is the pervasive nature of the *idea* of the game within the society that just by believing that, they make it so" (*Player* 77). This is the clearest expression of an idea that runs throughout Banks's fiction, occurring, for instance, in *Walking on Glass*, *Complicity*, and *The Steep Approach to Garbadale*, among others. As Will Slocombe puts it, games "do not just reflect reality but inherently color our perceptions of it. [. . .] Moreover, the way in which we play the game reveals more than just our understanding of its rules: it reveals who we are."[21] The bulk of the novel, therefore, conforms to the basic conceit of Azad, in which the way Gurgeh plays reflects not only his worth but the worth of the society he represents.

To begin with, Gurgeh wins quite easily. Eventually he comes to realize that this is because his style of play had reflected the character of the Culture—"a net, a grid of forces and relationships, without any obvious hierarchy or entrenched leadership" (*Player* 269)—and his early opponents had tried to adjust to this novel style and thus failed. But he plays these games with a certain insouciance, because he has no stake in the outcome. As a visitor from outside the empire, his victories count for nothing within the Azadian hierarchy. He initially regards Azad with a mixture of bemusement and distaste; as a citizen of the exceptionally liberal Culture, he finds it difficult to understand the empire's rigid sexual differentiation, the strict demarcation of hierarchical roles. Gradually, however, during the course of the novel, the Special Circumstances drone Flere-Imsaho introduces Gurgeh to Azad depravities. The social conscience that is thus awakened, the political rage against abuse of power—"the journalist who can't write what he knows is the truth, the doctor who can't treat somebody in pain because they're the wrong sex" (*Player* 210)—could have come straight from one of Banks's more politically engaged mainstream novels, such as *Complicity*. However much Banks might have denied being a political writer with a capital P, even his more extravagant space operas, such as *The Player of Games*, are suffused with the same sense of social justice, the same anger that human nature is "the phrase they used whenever they had to justify something inhuman and unnatural" (*Player* 226). The more Gurgeh learns of the depravity and injustice of Azad society, therefore, the greater his personal stake in the game, and the more he becomes engaged in the battle. By the end of the novel the game board truly has become a surrogate battlefield for a war between the ideals of the Culture and those of the Azad empire. But in his concluding game against the emperor, Nicosar, Gurgeh comes up against an opponent who doesn't try to adjust to his style of play. Rather, Nicosar's game embodies the values of the empire: "The Emperor sent pieces to their destruction with a sort of joyous callousness where Gurgeh would have hung back" (*Player* 270). In these circumstances, as Cairns Craig puts it, "To defend himself and the Culture of which he is part, Gurgeh has to become his own opposite, has to acquire the warrior virtues from which his civilization should protect him."[22] Victor Sage is more succinct: "To uphold the values of civilisation, he has to become a barbarian."[23] So the contradictions suggested by Fal 'Ngeestra in *Consider Phlebas* have here become explicit.

This ambiguous sense that the preservation of civilization necessitates uncivilized behavior is something that recurs throughout Banks's work. It is present in *Complicity* and *The Song of Stone* as much as it is in the Culture novels, and it is central to his next novel as Iain Banks, *Canal Dreams*. Indeed, it is explicit when Dandridge, the leader of the fake rebels in that novel, proclaims: "You have to do bad things in a bad world, if you want to stay able to be good" (*Canal* 166). For once that notion is directly questioned in *Canal Dreams*: Dandridge has been corrupted by the bad things he does, whether or not they were initially for a good cause.

Though, by this time, Banks had returned to the source of his inspiration (he was living in a flat on the South Bridge in Edinburgh), *Canal Dreams* is the Iain Banks novel that took him furthest from Scotland, both in setting and in spirit. The story concerns a group of travelers on ships trapped in the Panama Canal by some vague, ill-defined war. The result is a disappointment: he has called it "probably the weakest of the books [. . .] it's the one I'm least proud of, and the book I found the most difficult to write."[24]

In a way, *Canal Dreams* fits into the pattern of the Scottish fantastic to which so much of Banks's supposedly mainstream fiction belonged. It is set in the (then) near future, around the turn of the century, and, as in *The Bridge*, the dreams of the central character, Hisako, play a major part in the narrative. Nevertheless, it can probably be best understood as harking back to Banks's earliest attempts at fiction, and in particular to the influence of Alistair MacLean. Certainly there is something of MacLean in the ending of the novel, in which a middle-aged Japanese cellist, acting entirely on her own, is suddenly able to take on and defeat an entire unit of highly trained and CIA-backed "rebels," in the process displaying an aptitude for handling large ships, scuba gear, and a variety of weapons that even hints about her background cannot fully explain.

What may be most significant about *Canal Dreams*, however, apart from being the first time Banks had used a female protagonist (with, of course, the ambiguous exception of *The Wasp Factory*), is that it used rape as a trigger for action. Having identified the CIA agent who is leading the so-called rebels who have taken over the ships, Hisako is raped; then all the other passengers and crew imprisoned on the ships are murdered, though it seems to be the willful destruction of her Stradivarius cello that actually drives her to action. The rape happens offstage, and Banks is careful not to sensationalize it or to dwell on it, but it does mark the beginning of the novel's climactic action sequence. Moreover, this is the first use of rape as a plot device in Banks's fiction, something that would recur in novels from *Complicity* to *Surface Detail*, and that would draw increasing criticism as Banks's career progressed.

Roughly coincident with the 1989 publication of *Canal Dreams* in Britain, Mark Ziesing brought out *The State of the Art* in the United States as a standalone novella from his small press. It was, to say the least, an eccentric edition, which included unjustified text, a near-unreadable font, and page numbering that began afresh at the start of each new chapter.

This was the only work by Banks that received its first publication in the United States. It would not appear in Britain for another two years, when it would provide the bulk of Banks's only collection of short fiction, also called *The State of the Art* (1991). It was also the only one of Banks's works to date that had not received the editorial attention of James Hale, a lack that Banks was to regret.[25] At this time James Hale left Macmillan to go freelance. Banks had come to rely so much on Hale's advice and editorial work that he, too, left Macmillan. From this point on he would use Hale as his freelance editor, and, for the first time, he took on an agent, Mic Cheetham, who would now guide his work to other publishers. The dedication of *Use of Weapons*, the first book to appear after this change in his business arrangements, is "For Mic." It is worth noting that Cheetham was particularly well known among the science fiction community and was one of the most popular agents for sf writers, which suggests that Banks was now seeing his science fiction as the main focus of his writing.

*The State of the Art* seems to bring together the two strands of Banks's writing, since it tells of a Culture mission to Earth in 1977. On the surface, it does appear to be primarily a satire on contemporary Earth politics. For instance, when asked if Earth is ready for contact, Sma says: "You seriously think we could mess the place up more than they're doing at the moment? [. . .] They could hardly make a better job of vandalizing their own planet if we gave them lessons" (*State* 91). Such a reading of *The State of the Art* is certainly what makes Lawrence Person uncomfortable with the novella, arguing that "the Culture is not a believable enough civilization for me to give their condemnation any credibility."[26] But in fact the focus of the novella is far more upon the Culture, using the troubled state of current affairs as a way of reflecting upon the utopian inertia of the Culture.

Thus, the ship, *Arbitrary*, talks of "infecting the whole galaxy with sterility" (*State* 91). When Linter decides to stay on Earth it is because, he says, "I feel alive for a change" (*State* 108), while Sma argues against staying by emphasizing the immobility of the Culture:

Can't you see how much this place has to alter . . . in just the next century? We're so used to things staying much the same, to society and technology—at least immediately available technology—hardly changing over our lifetimes that [. . .] I don't know any of us could cope for long down here. (*State* 111)

Linter replies: "We expect everything to be set up just as we like it, but these people don't; they're used to having good and bad mixed in together. And that gives them an interest in living" (*State* 113–14). He repeats this view later when he says: "They're real because they live the way they have to. We aren't because we live the way we want to" (*State* 131). Later still, he points out that the Culture "is too certain, too organized and stifled. We've choked the life out of life; nothing's left to chance" (*State* 165). It is as if every argument against the Culture that Banks has put in the mouths of Horza, its enemy, or Gurgeh, who is bored by it, has been rehearsed and expanded and repeated in this novella. However it may seem, this is not a story about a wonderful, technological heaven, a dreamland without poverty or discrimination; despite what Banks himself said, on occasion, about wanting to live in the Culture, this is really rather a pointed tale about how we would not, should not wish to live in such a dream. It is notable that Banks puts the strongest speech in favor of the Culture in the mouth of Li at his most pompous and idiotic: "The Culture could afford to let me be whatever it was within my personal potential to become; so, for good or ill, I am fulfilled" (*State* 148). But Li's manifold discontents, including a desire to claim the nonexistent position of captain of the ship, and an embarrassing banquet—to which he wears "a *2001*-style space-suit with a zig-zag silver flash added across the chest [. . .] a red cape which flowed out behind . . . [and] . . . he gripped a *Star Wars* light sword" (*State* 145)—that concludes with sweetmeats cloned from various earthly villains, suggest that he is actually far from being fulfilled.

*The State of the Art* was one of a number of short stories that Banks wrote in the late 1970s, trying what was then seen as a traditional route into science fiction publication. At the time these stories met with no success, but once his books began to appear, the short stories started to turn up in odd places. One appeared in *Interzone*, a couple were in the anthologies *Arrows of Eros* (1989) and *Tales from the Forbidden Planet* (1987), another was published as a chapbook by the Birmingham SF Group when Banks was guest of honor at their convention, Novacon 17, in November 1987. There weren't many; Banks was not a natural short story writer. Every short story he ever wrote, whether experimental fiction like "Scratch," mainstream fiction like "Piece," fantasy like "Road of Skulls," or straight science fiction like "Descendant," was gathered together in the collection *The State of the Art*, and published under the name Iain M. Banks. The belated U.S. edition, published by Night Shade Books in 2004, also included his essay, "A Few Notes on the Culture," which had been first published online in 1994.

There were Culture stories in the collection, though sometimes only obliquely. "Descendant," for instance, which reads like a variation on Arthur C. Clarke's story "Summertime on Icarus" (1960), is about a stranded space-man who has to keep walking around a moon in order to survive. Only in the last two pages does a knife missile appear, firmly fixing the story within the Culture. The best of the stories in the collection, though still slight com-pared to *The State of the Art* itself, is "A Gift from the Culture," which offers the same bleak weariness with the Culture that informs the novella. The luckless antihero, being blackmailed into acting as an assassin, talks of "my great adventure, my renunciation of what seemed to me sterile and lifeless to plunge into a more vital society" (*State* 11) and bemoans, "Oh the self-satisfied Culture: its imperialism of smugness" (*State* 13). The "imperialism of smugness" runs counter to the benevolent, liberal utopia, which is how the Culture is normally perceived, but it is as much a part of the society as its post-scarcity communism. When Banks himself talks of the Culture's "largely cooperative and—it would claim—fundamentally benign techno-cultural diplomatic policy" (Notes), that qualifying "it would claim" rather suggests the opposite.

"Piece," probably the last short story Banks wrote, was published in the *Observer* magazine in 1989 and was composed around the conjunction of the controversy surrounding Salman Rushdie's *The Satanic Verses* (1988; the fatwa was issued in February 1989) and the terrorist bombing of Pan Am flight 103 over Lockerbie in December 1988, though the first part of the story, which relates an encounter on an overnight bus and which seems to have been based on personal experience, originally formed the poem "Jack," which is dated March 1978 (*Poems*, 80–83). It is a story that explores the uneasy relationship between rationalism and faith, a topic that will become very prominent in

Banks's work. Despite his avowed atheism, Banks keeps returning to issues of religion and belief, particularly in his science fiction. But if the story opens up one direction his writing will take, it closes off another. From this point on he published only book-length fiction.

At last, in 1990, the earliest and the most troublesome of Banks's Culture novels appeared. Recalling the critique of traditional space operas that he and Ken MacLeod had absorbed from the criticism of John Clute and M. John Harrison, Banks said of *Use of Weapons* that "In a sense, the whole Culture came from the character Zakalwe [. . .]. I wanted to write about some sort of ultimate mercenary . . . [but] . . . I wanted to have him fighting on the side of genuine good. [. . .] That gave me the chance to answer all the questions I had about the right-wing American space opera I had been used to reading."[27] For instance, as Ken MacLeod has noted, "In this future there is none of the *Star Trek* nonsense of having a captain telling the crew, let alone 'the ship's computer,' what to do,"[28] thus emphasizing the difference from the traditional militaristically structured imperial model.

The idea seemed simple enough, but there were two problems: first, how to tell this particular story; and second, how to determine if the Culture is actually good. The first of these problems was immediate; the second has tended to be disguised, both by the structure of the novel and by straightforward assertions that the Culture is a utopia, but it is a deep-seated issue that has resonances in all of these early Culture novels.

The structural problem with the novel seems to have led Banks to drop the book. That *Use of Weapons* eventually appeared, and would become recognized as one of the most complex and rewarding of all of his novels, is down to Ken MacLeod. As Banks writes in the acknowledgments, "I blame Ken MacLeod for the whole thing. It was his idea to argue the old warrior out of retirement, and he suggested the fitness program, too" (*Use*, ix). MacLeod had been reading one of the Dumarest novels by E. C. Tubb (he no longer recalls which one) in which, in one passage, events happen in reverse chronological order, and he recognized that this device might provide the solution to Banks's structural problems. Hence, ten years after the first attempt to write *Use of Weapons*, and after *The Wasp Factory* had been published, MacLeod asked to see the manuscript of *Use of Weapons* again.

He read it and came back and told me there was a good novel in there struggling to get out. I told him he was mad again.

So he came up with two suggestions. First, putting the climax of the book at the end. It had been in the middle, because that's where the structure said it had to be, and such is my blinkeredness this idea of putting it where logic—and narrative drive—dictated it ought to go seemed totally radical when he suggested it, though of course also completely impossible, because of the all-important structure. But then he (second) suggested this two-stream idea, with one strand going forward in time and the other going back, both leading to their own climax, so that you'd get the identity revelation at the end—where it always had been—and the whole thing with the besieged battleship and so on at the end as well, where it belonged.[29]

The result is a story told primarily in two parts. In the chapters numbered in sequence, one to fourteen, we are told (in straightforward chronological order) how Diziet Sma and the drone Skaffen-Amtiskaw of Special Circumstances seek out the old mercenary Zakalwe for one last mission, and about the progress of that mission and something of its consequences. In alternating chapters, numbered XIII to I, we are given in reverse chronological order snapshots of Zakalwe's previous missions for Special Circumstances, coming back to the situation that led him to become a mercenary. Even this summary, however, simplifies the structure of the novel. The book opens with a poem, "Slight Mechanical Destruction" (written March 1978), then there is a prologue describing events that seem to take place somewhere between the two narrative strands but without actually providing the hinge that links them. At the end of the book there is an epilogue that seems to conclude the prologue rather than anything within the body of the novel, followed by another poem, "Zakalwe's Song" (written December 1973, an indication of the novel's long and complex gestation). Finally, there is a section headed "States of War," with another prologue and page numbering starting again at 1, as if we are reading the beginning of yet another novel. In a notoriously conservative genre when it comes to storytelling, this disorienting structure was instantly accepted by readers and applauded by the critics. "Banks assumes our trust and does not work for it," Kathleen Ann Goonan says, "although if we have read his other offerings he no doubt has it."[30] Indeed, it helped that Banks's "mainstream" novels provided a template; as Colin Greenland said, *Use of Weapons* is "very

Banks-without-the-M," and of the two strands of the novel, "The one that goes from front to back is another infuriatingly daft and anti-climactic secret agent thriller, but the one that's back to front has a screw like a gimlet."[31]

The story that screws like a gimlet is the story of Cheradenine Zakalwe, another of Banks's divided characters, like Frank, like Orr/Lennox, like the shape-shifting Horza. At first this division seems like the disconnect between how we see Zakalwe as a heroic figure and the brutal acts he carries out. But gradually we learn that there is another division, that Zakalwe is haunted by memories of something that happened in childhood. The central chapter, literally as well as figuratively, is the one where Zakalwe is injured and trapped on an island in the caldera of a volcano, a situation that recalls William Golding's *Pincher Martin*. As Zakalwe drags himself round and round his tightly circumscribed realm, always coming back to the same point (we learn later that he is inscribing on the ground itself a signal to his rescuers), so his thoughts keep coming back to the same point. This is where, as far as the reader is concerned, he starts to recall in detail the childhood events that are the key to the novel. But in a sense it is where he stops remembering, because the chapters before this point and therefore later in the story are much vaguer as to what is recalled. We learn that Zakalwe was the scion of a noble family, with two sisters, Darckense and Livueta, and a fourth child, Elethiomel, unrelated but from an allied family, whose father was "put to death because he killed lots of people" (*Use* 171). The four children are inseparable, helping to raise the alarm when the homestead is attacked, and when Darckense is injured, a fragment of her bone lodges itself in Zakalwe's chest. The scar remains as a constant reminder of his childhood until his body is completely rebuilt by the Culture following one near-fatal mission.

But, as ever in Banks's work (we think of *The Wasp Factory*, *The Crow Road*, *Whit* [1995], *Against a Dark Background*, and *Matter*, among others), the threat comes from within the family. When civil war splits the world of their childhood, Zakalwe and Elethiomel find themselves on opposite sides. Elethiomel, son of a mass murderer, proves to be a ruthless commander; he captures Darckense, kills her, and sends her bones back to Zakalwe made up into a chair, an horrific image that accounts for the curious obsession with chairs that has occupied Zakalwe throughout the novel. It is only at the very end, when Zakalwe, as payment for his final mission, has the Culture bring him face to face with Livueta, that we discover the truth. The man we (and the Culture) know as Zakalwe, who has convinced himself of that identity, is actually Elethiomel. It is the divided self, such a consistent feature of Banks's work, writ large.

The foreground of the novel is so taken up with the gothic tale of Zakalwe's identity, a tale marked by grotesquerie, excess, and bloodshed, that we barely notice what is going on in the background. Though Zakalwe is not himself of the Culture, and at the end very deliberately refuses the medical treatment that would extend his life (a refusal of the benefits of the Culture that is identical to that of Linter in *The State of the Art*), he proves to be the ideal representative of the Culture. We are constantly told of the goodness of the Culture, not least by Banks himself, as in this 1989 interview:

> I wanted to say, "Look, there is a possibility of something really good in the future. Here's a genuine, humanist, non-superstitious, nonreligious, functioning utopia where absolutely no-one is exploited; where they don't have money, where they don't have laws to speak of, my idea of a perfect society—and it's obviously not capitalist—but it's so communist it's beyond anything in a way. Something like the Culture could just about evolve from capitalism."[32]

Yet for all of this, Zakalwe's divisions, his uncertainties, and his brutality serve to stand for unstated aspects of the Culture. This is another book in which the perfect society is very carefully implied to be not so perfect after all.

Zakalwe's own view of the Culture, an outsider's view like that of Horza, is a strange mixture of antagonism and admiration. Early in the novel he tells the Ethnarch a fairy story that is clearly about the Culture: "They had no kings, no laws, no money and no property, but . . . everybody lived like a prince, was well-behaved and lacked for nothing. And these people lived in peace, but they were bored, because paradise can get that way after a time" (*Use* 29). "I hate the Culture's . . . tolerance" he says later (*Use* 104). Yet against this he notes: "I have never seen them be cruel [. . .]. It can make them seem cold, sometimes" (*Use* 243). He concludes that the Culture is "the most advanced—well, certainly the most *energetic*—humanoid civilization in the . . . Reality? (No.) Universe? (No.) Galaxy?" (*Use* 92)—the qualification is surely significant.

All of this, however, comes out in conversation with others who are outside the Culture. More significant is what emerges from Zakalwe's interactions with the Culture's representatives, Sma and Skaffen-Amtiskaw. There is, for instance, the same suggestion of duplicity that we encountered in *Consider Phlebas* and *The Player of Games*. Accepting that he can expect no immediate help from Special Circumstances, Zakalwe points out that "you have to stand off and be seen to be pure—fake though that might be" (*Use* 133). More damning is an exchange with Sma when she explains:

> "[I]n Special Circumstances we deal in the moral equivalent of black holes, where the normal laws—the rules of right and wrong that people imagine apply everywhere else in the universe—break down [. . .]." "To some people," he said, "that might sound like just a good excuse for bad behavior." (*Use* 261)

As Colin Greenland says, "Anyone who does not recognize the jazzy metaphor as pernicious cant is probably reading the wrong author."[33]

All of these early works about the Culture depend on an engagement with another society, specifically a society that is either actively (the Idirans in *Consider Phlebas*) or ideologically (the Azad Empire in *The Player of Games*) opposed to the Culture. It is an engagement in which whatever ideal is represented by the Culture is abandoned in the name of expediency or necessity. The Culture acts ruthlessly. It defeats the Idirans because the Idirans are tied to planets; though they are fighting a space war, it is essentially a war for territory. The Culture, on the other hand, is not tied to any territory at all; we see them happily evacuating and destroying one of their own orbitals simply to deny it to the enemy. This freedom of movement gives the Culture a built-in advantage over the Idirans, perhaps comparable to the advantage that England's small and maneuverable ships enjoyed over the large and lumbering ships of the Spanish Armada. But the freedom of movement would give no advantage at all if not accompanied by a willingness to use it without hesitation, without remorse. In *Consider Phlebas*, the Culture is glimpsed only peripherally, but what we do see, out of the corner of the eye, is a power prepared to be every bit as bloody as whoever opposes it.

Seven hundred years later, and in *The Player of Games*, the Culture has clearly lost none of that ruthlessness, none of that willingness to turn the enemy's morals and tactics against it. Except that the Azad Empire is not an enemy, it is not at war with the Culture. The Empire, we are assured, is cruel and expansive, but that expansion has not yet brought it into conflict with the Culture. Indeed, the Culture is so powerful and pervasive that one suspects that even an empire like Azad would hesitate before going up against it. This is the Culture—or specifically those organizations within the Culture, Contact and Special Circumstances—that do not see themselves bound by the prevailing morality of their own society; "the urge not to feel useless" (*Phlebas* 451) trumps the urge to do no harm. They may not always be efficient; the drone Flere-Imsaho, for instance, talks of the "Usual Contact snafu," and when Gurgeh says "I used to think Contact was so organized and efficient," the drone replies, "Nice to know something works" (*Player* 124). This may be misdirection by Contact, who are busy presenting themselves as less than efficient to the Azadians, but it also ties in with a persistent sense throughout Banks's work that no one is all powerful. Everyone, even the arch manipulators of Special Circumstances, is muddling through, without ever seeing the full picture. This means, of course, that we don't ever see the full picture either; when we watch Gurgeh beating the best of Azad at their own game, or Zakalwe being dropped into yet another conflict, we don't really know what ends Special Circumstances is working toward, or whether those ends are achieved or not. All we know is that the Culture's idea of diplomacy involves interfering in the internal affairs of societies that do not adhere to the same standards as the Culture, but that yet do not pose a direct threat either. At the very least, as Farah Mendlesohn suggests, the decadence of the Culture lies not in its pursuit of pleasure but "in its foreign policy: its expansionism, imperialism and attempts to 'civilise' the barbarians on its borders [. . .]. It has secured the good society for its members at the expense of others and at the price of abandoning its commitment to communism and to a related understanding of the dynamics of social change."[34]

For many commentators, however, the way the Culture engages with its neighbors is not just a sign of decadence: the Culture is itself an empire. For instance, as she considers the climax of *The Player of Games*, Patricia Kerslake poses a series of questions:

> Does the Culture's use of Machiavellian tactics render it morally reprehensible: a shell of techno-sophistication surrounding a vacuum of pure anarchy and cynicism? Or is Banks giving us another taste of authentic postcolonialism, by showing us that imperial behaviour does not require the frame of empire in order to accomplish its ends, but that imperialism is as much a single act as it is a mode of thought or philosophy?[35]

What she seems to be doing is viewing the Culture as imperial while at the same time representing the "very obsolescence of empire,"[36] a contradiction that lies at the heart of the counternarrative inherent in Banks's work, a counternarrative that makes the Culture not a utopia but the very essence of a critical utopia.

For William Hardesty, the stories are "old-fashioned adventure yarns" that "constitute portions of a master narrative of benevolent colonialism, showing the salutary effects of empire on both the rulers and, in theory at least, the ruled."[37] What makes the books interesting is that alongside the adventure there is an ironic "counter-narrative that interrogates, problematises, and criticises the myth of good will and good deeds that the master narrative promotes."[38] Thus, "[a]lthough on the surface the Culture's assessment of itself as the good guys seems defensible, the action and the formal structure of the text challenge that assessment."[39]

The Culture does not directly colonize anyone; rather, they maneuver a change of government to one that would be less oppressive for its people who are therefore more likely to choose to join the Culture, an indirect form of colonization. Beychae, in *Use of Weapons*, spells out precisely this sort of manipulation, the way the Culture's involvement in other worlds is not disinterested: "They want other people to be like them. . . . They don't terraform, so they don't want others to either. . . . The Culture believes profoundly in machine sentience, so it thinks everybody ought to. . . . [And on cross-species tolerance] . . . the Culture can sometimes appear to be insistent that deliberate intermixing is not just permissible but desirable" (*Use* 241). As Banks put it:

> I guess the difference between the Culture and the kind of interference we're used to is that the Culture isn't after anything, save some peace of mind. It's not looking for control over or access to natural resources, or to open up and exploit new markets, or to foist unwanted political systems on people who don't want them. The point is that the Culture can feasibly argue that, when it does interfere, it has the best interests of the populations it is interfering with at heart.[40]

That, of course, is an excuse used by those of every political stripe when they interfere in the affairs of others. That we see the Culture as a utopia would not make it any better, even if such interference did not lead to so many deaths.

But, vile as the Azad Empire might be, are those who fall under its sway any better off when the Culture interferes?

Mendlesohn is right when she says that Culture "diplomacy" indicates decadence, though the Culture is showing no overt signs of decay when, after the passage of centuries, we reach the events of *The Hydrogen Sonata*. But it is more than simply decadence that is on display here. We are clearly meant to question the disconnect between the avowed ideals of the Culture and their actual actions, between the insistence that the Culture is a communist utopia and the reality of that society.

On August 10, 1994, Ken MacLeod posted a long essay by Iain Banks on the newsgroup rec.arts.sf.written, derived from a talk Banks had given at science fiction conventions over the previous couple of years. Called "A Few Notes on the Culture," it was the longest and most detailed piece that Banks ever wrote to explain his creation, and is presumably based on the notes he kept while writing his earliest Culture novels. That the piece was published at all testifies to the popularity of the Culture, and of Banks's work in general. Though his publishing history in the United States was still intermittent, in Britain Banks's books regularly appeared in the bestseller lists. His Culture novels were particularly popular, contending for the major British science fiction awards; both *The Player of Games* and *Use of Weapons* had been short-listed for the British Science Fiction Association Award for Best Novel, and *Use of Weapons* had also been shortlisted for the Arthur C. Clarke Award. (*The Player of Games* lost to *Lavondyss* by Robert Holdstock; in both cases, *Use of Weapons* lost to *Take Back Plenty* by Colin Greenland.) And Banks's popularity was spreading through Europe as well. For three years running he had won Germany's Kurd Laßwitz Preis for Foreign Fiction: for *The Bridge* in 1991, *The Wasp Factory* in 1992, and *Use of Weapons* in 1993. It is interesting that all three novels seem to have been published in Germany as by Iain M. Banks, and that both *The Wasp Factory* and *The Bridge* were clearly considered science fiction. There was, then, a hunger for more about the Culture, even though Banks himself seemed at this point to be moving away from it (his most recent Iain M. Banks novel had been the non-Culture *Against a Dark Background*, and the next one, published in the same year that this essay appeared online, was *Feersum Endjinn*, another non-Culture story).

Although the essay contained some technological hand-waving ("switch to seven dimensions and even our four dimensional universe can be described as a circle. So [. . .] think of a doughnut [. . .] with only a very tiny hole in the middle. That hole is the Cosmic Centre, the singularity, the great initiating fireball, the place the universes come from" [Notes]), its main focus was on emphasizing the antireligious, anticapitalist utopianism of the Culture, which was what seemed to have most caught people's imaginations.

We are told that seven or eight space-going species formed a federation eight or nine thousand years ago, but this is no origin story. It tells us nothing about how or why such a federation would be the utopia that emerges in the books, and there is no King Utopus instituting a new rational order. The Culture is, thus, an odd utopia, not imposed or planned as utopias have typically been, not utopian by virtue of its structure, but precisely because of its lack of structure. It avoids the problems usually associated with utopias by being dynamic, ever changing. Although we are never told exactly how the Culture emerged—as Kerslake says, "Banks offers us a wholly new form of society, one that does not rise, phoenix-like, from the warm ashes of its recently deceased parent, but one which dispenses with the idea of 'parent' altogether"[41]—we may assume it was due to the circumstance of an end to scarcity as much as to any deliberate intent. As Hardesty puts it: "Because of abundance, the Culture has no need for competition or for all the devices, including governments and money, that humans have created to control or measure it. Hence, the regulations associated with all known societies or with other utopias simply don't need to exist, and therefore don't."[42]

Banks suggests that the Culture is "an expression of the idea that the nature of space itself determines the type of civilisations which will thrive there" (Notes), which would make sense if the other space-going civilizations that we witness, the Idirans, the Azad Empire, were not in their way inimical to the whole idea of the Culture. But these, he would argue, are young in terms of their expansion into space. The Idirans "believed themselves to be the arms and hands and fingers of God. But when the time came they would be able to assimilate the realisation [. . .] that it was not up to them to bring about the final order" (*Phlebas* 159). Or to put it another way: in time, the Idirans would grow up. And when the warmongers did become responsible adults, they would realize that "our current dominant power systems cannot long survive in space; beyond a certain technological level a degree of anarchy is arguably inevitable and anyway preferable" (Notes).

There is an economic aspect to this notion of anarchy in space. Underlying the Culture is the assumption that no society that spread across multiple star systems, that had the ships necessary to journey between the stars and the wherewithal to build orbitals that might be home to trillions, could emerge without having solved the problem of energy. The very fact of the Culture implies that they have managed to tap into a virtually infinite supply of free energy. And this basic underpinning will have a profound and necessary effect upon the nature of the society. Ken MacLeod sums it up thus:

> Matter is cheap. There is hydrogen to burn. This has consequences in the psychology of all the societies and individuals who swarm across this infinite plain. Their only scarcity is purpose. In their purposes, in the meanings they give to life, they are all in their own way in a realm of necessity, of ruthless and driven competition, of war and trade. Only life is finite.[43]

With all the energy you need on tap, you can effectively provide all of your citizens with anything and everything they may desire. Consequently, there is no want, no poverty, no need to work for a living. Since anyone may have whatever he or she desires at any time, the only issue facing people is how to make their lives interesting. Given that among the technological advantages of this world of plenty is an extended lifespan of several hundred years, this can be a very pertinent issue. Hence the number of Culture citizens we see engaged in extreme sports of one form or another (*Consider Phlebas*, *Look to Windward*), following different artistic pursuits (*Look to Windward*, *The Hydrogen Sonata*), playing games (*Consider Phlebas*, *The Player of Games*), partying (*The Player of Games*, *The Hydrogen Sonata*), or more likely joining Contact or Special Circumstances (just about every one of the novels). It would seem it is not imperialism that drives the Culture's approach to other civilizations but simply the need for something to do. Because "the galaxy is [. . .] an immensely, intrinsically, and inexhaustibly interesting place" (Notes) and interest is what life in the Culture is all about.

In fact, it becomes clear that for Banks utopia lies in the individual experience of those living in the Culture, but when it comes to interaction with others, particularly with other societies, therein lies anti-utopia. This is the counternarrative of Banks's books, the ambiguity that drives the stories. He has spelled out this difference between the personal and the social experience of utopia in a number of interviews. For instance, in the *New Musical Express*, he described the Culture as "my idea of heaven [. . .] People live for hundreds of years, it's a guilt-free society and also your orgasms last for minutes rather than seconds. F——! That's a Utopia to me!" But he went on to add:

> The rider to that is you could have Utopia at almost any stage of human exis-
> tence, but in a horrible sense what we produce is an expression of who we are
> as a species. The 20th Century is an expression of us as a species and that's quite
> frightening. Thank you, yes, the Holocaust, well, yes, ah, that was us . . . I think
> we may be temperamentally unsuited to Utopia, a bunch of nutters that any
> sensible galactic civilisation would corral off.[44]

Utopia, therefore, or at least the idea of the Culture as Utopia, is personal rather than social. This comes as no surprise; the conflict between the personal and the social is a theme that runs throughout Banks's fiction. In *Complicity*, for instance, Cameron says of his time in Iraq: "I just stood there, awestruck, horrorstruck, absorbing the ghastly force of it with my inadequate and un-prepared *private* humanity, not my public professional persona, not my skill, not the face I had laboured to prepare to face the sea of faces that is the world. And so I was humbled, scaled, down-sized" (*Complicity* 290, emphasis in the original). This clash between the personal and the public, between our differ-ent moralities, is something that affects all of Banks's protagonists. It therefore allows him to present, in the Culture, a place that is, at the least, his ideal place to live, "a fundamentally rational civilisation" (Notes), yet which still offers the conflicts, the irrationality, that make for drama. Thus, as Christopher Palmer says of *Consider Phlebas*, although this haven of peace and plenty and lots of sex is always hovering in the background, what we actually get is "a cocktail (with appropriately witty names) of destruction, decadence, nihilism, sadism, playfulness and irresponsibility, verve and juvenility."[45]

If you concentrate on the rough edges of the Culture, those places where it rubs awkwardly against other neighboring civilizations, then you don't have to spend too much time thinking how the center actually works. And Banks doesn't do so. In the four works that introduce the Culture, *Consider Phlebas*, *The Player of Games*, "The State of the Art," and *Use of Weapons*, we barely see the Culture itself. In *Consider Phlebas*, Horza visits an Orbital due for demolition, where he is captured by cannibals and witnesses the highly popular yet disturbing game of Damage, during which people die. This might reflect the liberality of the Culture, but it tells us nothing further, other than the fact that there are parts of the Culture where we probably wouldn't want to live. In "The State of the Art," the ship *Arbitrary* stands for the Culture, and those on board are seen living a hedonistic lifestyle and indulging in a feast that turns out to be of questionable taste. The ship that Sma joins in her quest for Zakalwe in *Use of Weapons* also stands for the Culture, and reflects, in the fashion for catching colds and in the orgies, something of the boredom we have already noted. Only *The Player of Games* spends any appreciable portion of its length picturing life in the Culture, but here, reflecting Gurgeh's own boredom with his life, what we see consists of tedious parties and uninspiring games.

Within the Culture, therefore, all we really know of life is that it is easy, very deliberately and specifically so. As Banks puts it: "Its easy hedonism is not some ground-state of nature, but something desirable, assiduously worked for in the past, not necessarily easily attained, and requiring appreciation and maintenance both in the present and the future" (Notes). There's no need to work because this is a post-scarcity society, so "human labour [is] restricted to something indistinguishable from play, or a hobby" (Notes). This is less a utopia than a land of Cockaigne, or a Big Rock Candy Mountain, a place notable for being the exact opposite of the hardships and difficulties of everyday life. As part of this hedonism, people in the Culture have drug-secreting glands that can eliminate pain or provide a chemical high. Given the amount of drug taking that occurs in Banks's other novels, from *Espedair Street* to *Complicity*, we should not be surprised that this is part of the good life. People in the Culture are able to change sex at will, and indeed it is unusual for anyone not to do so at least once during their life; on a social level this eliminates all forms of sexual discrimination, on a personal level it makes for great sex. Meanwhile, Horza's encounter with the cannibals is characterized by Francis Spufford as a "dandy cannibal satire on the Last Supper," which is one way of noting that the Culture is not just a secular society but is conceived as "a piece of sly, prolonged and magnificent anti-theism."[46] Again, coming from such an avowedly atheist writer, this is no surprise.

What is presented as utopian in the Culture, therefore, is wish fulfilment. This is a place where there is no need to work, where great drugs and wonderful sex are readily available and guilt free, and where Banks's most cherished ideals are shown to work. But we have not seen enough of the Culture to tell whether this wish fulfilment really does equate with utopia. The religious questioning implied here only really comes to the fore late in Banks's career. Before that, he would need to explore the Culture more directly, and in particular examine the relationship between human and machine sentience.

But for a time it seemed as if Banks wasn't interested in returning to the Culture at all.

## CHAPTER 3

## OUTSIDE CONTEXT PROBLEMS

Over Easter 1990, Iain Banks was a guest of honor at Eastcon, the British National Science Fiction Convention, held that year in Liverpool. Reading it today, his guest-of-honour speech is rambling and barely coherent, but one thing comes across clearly: writing "is actually quite good fun—I keep telling people that it is good fun, that I enjoy writing. I like putting words together on the word processor, on the keyboard or just scribbling them down" (Eastcon 5). It was the career Banks had set his mind on ever since he was at school, and now he was enjoying the fruits of his success. Now living in North Queensferry, a return to the environment of his childhood that speaks volumes for the imaginative importance of the Forth Rail Bridge, Banks and Annie Blackburn had got back together after a brief separation, and the pair would marry in Hawaii in 1992. He was now in a position to buy the expensive fast cars he had always loved, and before too long he had a fleet of them. And he had started to settle into the writing practice that, with a couple of interruptions, he would follow from then on: a science fiction novel by Iain M. Banks one year (in September 1990 it would be *Use of Weapons*) followed by a mainstream novel by Iain Banks the next year (in 1991 it would be *The Crow Road*). Writing after his death, his second wife, Adele Hartley, described the way Banks worked on a book, a routine that was already in place by 1990: "He would spend April through June thinking about thinking about a new book, July through September really thinking about it, September through Christmas plotting it out and making a detailed plan and then January through March actually sitting in front of this computer writing it."[1] A 1999 profile in the *Guardian* offered a slightly different version, beginning in mid-September, when Banks would write "roughly 3,000 words a day, eight hours a day, five days a week, till the book was finished—which had to be by December 23."[2] Then Banks would do revisions in the New Year, send the manuscript to James Hale, and at the beginning of February visit Hale in London to finish the job. Either way, it was a routine that allowed Banks considerable space for driving, for traveling and for socializing, all sorts of things that, he was well aware, did not look like hard work. Writing, he insisted, should be fun.

Above all, by Easter 1990 every one of the seven novels that had been published to date had been both a commercial and a critical success. Even his most recent book, *Canal Dreams*, reckoned by Banks himself to be one of his weakest, had been respectfully received. In *Vector*, Kev McVeigh had called it "a hard hitting piece of fiction" and "his most effective writing yet."[3] But despite the rich variety of the Iain Banks novels, Iain M. Banks was known only as the writer of the Culture novels. It was inevitable, therefore, that he would be asked during his guest-of-honor speech about future Culture novels, and it was probably a surprise when he replied that *Use of Weapons* would be "the last one for a couple of books. The book after that will be non-sf and the next sf due out in two years' time will be a non-'Culture' story" (Eastcon 6). Banks was preparing the ground for the fact that the next science fiction novel, and indeed the one after, would be a deliberate "digression from his main theme to see if he could in fact do without the Culture as a narrative element."[4] Or as Banks himself put it later: "I always enjoy writing Culture novels, I feel at home; it's my train set, I built it, I chewed that papier ma-che! I love writing Culture novels—it's almost too much of a self-indulgence. That's why I deliberately took two books away from the Culture to reassure myself that I wasn't so besotted with it that I couldn't write science fiction elsewhere."[5] The next science fiction novel (or, to be more precise, the next novel under the name "Iain M. Banks") would be *Against a Dark Background*. This was actually one of the earliest of Banks's novels, written immediately after his first attempt to write *Use of Weapons* but based on an idea developed even earlier, during his first year at university. It dates, therefore, from a time when Banks was simply trying to be a science fiction writer and when the Culture was the background for one novel only rather than the basis for a long-running and highly popular series. Now, given the fan base the Culture had already acquired, abandoning that setting was probably as radical a venture as the move into science fiction in the first place.

In fact, *Against a Dark Background* comes across as the complete opposite of the Culture. Where the Culture presents a post-scarcity utopia, where everything is freely available and it makes no sense to ask the value of anything, *Against a Dark Background* is set on an intensely, exaggeratedly capitalist world where everything and everyone has a price, a world where everything comes down to cost. Yet the story has the same high-octane pace, the same casual violence, the same propulsive quality, the same quirky humor that his fans had come to associate with the Culture novels. Would his readers accept Banks's science fiction away from the familiar universe of the Culture?

It is, perhaps, no coincidence that *Against a Dark Background* is, in terms of both plot and structure, the simplest of any Iain M. Banks novels, with the exception of *Consider Phlebas*. The complex chronological structure of *Use of Weapons* is replaced with a straightforward progression from beginning to end. The multiple viewpoints that are characteristic of the vast majority of Banks's novels are entirely absent; here, we follow one central character, Sharrow, and she remains our focus throughout the novel. And as in *Consider Phlebas*, the story is episodic, a series of adventures that build to an often violent climax before the story pauses, catches its breath, and moves to the next episode. Even so, it is possible to over-interpret the novel, as I believe Moira Martingale does in equating it to *Dracula* (1897) by Bram Stoker, largely on the strength of Sharrow biting the lip of her old family retainer to release the coded message he secretly holds, an act that results in his death. "This monstrous exercise of aristocratic power," Martingale says, "places Sharrow in the vampire's role of deathbringer in order to ensure her own survival."[6] It is, indeed, a monstrous exercise of power, something that is repeated throughout the book, but to suggest that it is a reimagining of *Dracula* on the strength of it is as plausible as comparing the book to *Hamlet* because everyone dies in the end. More likely progenitors, I would suggest, are any number of Hollywood action films, from *The Magnificent Seven* (1960) to *The Dirty Dozen* (1967), in which an unlikely team is assembled for a desperate mission from which most will not return.

In this instance, Sharrow, an aristocrat and one-time military leader, discovers that an idiosyncratic religious sect, the Huhsz, have declared a sort of fatwa against her. They believe that she has access to a Lazy Gun, which they claim as their own, and they will call off the hunt only if she returns the gun. Sharrow must then gather together her old gang, which involves, among other things, helping one of them, Miz, to steal an unstealable jewel, the Crownstar Addendum. Once the team is assembled, they travel to a remote and primitive realm, Pharpech, in order to find an ancient book, the *Universal Principles*, which has been lost for a millennium but which is rumored to hold a clue to where the last Lazy Gun might be. This in turn leads them to the city of androids, Vembyr, where Sharrow's grandfather's tomb is stored, the tombstone providing another clue in their hunt. From here they have to set out into the wilderness of the Embargoed Areas, a journey they hope will lead them to the Lazy Gun itself, but which instead, and inevitably, leads them into further peril, though it also sets up the ultimate solution of the mystery. The group is taken on a Cook's tour of different landscapes, peoples, and social systems, each of which brings its own particular dangers. At regular intervals throughout the novel an external group, the Solipsists, show up, first as saviors, later as enemies; and every so often Huhsz hunters put in an appearance, as a reminder of what set this rather ramshackle plot in motion.

In outline, it is a very familiar story: the gathering of the team of specialists, most of whom will be killed before the end of the novel; the search for clues, each of which sets our heroes rushing off to a totally different setting; and the final confrontation in which the real hidden enemy is revealed. We've seen it all countless times before, and to be fair, Banks never pretends it is anything other than a straightforward, bloody, and at times routine action adventure story. Of course, his flair for the big set-piece scene helps to carry the book, but what makes it a more interesting novel than this outline might suggest is the way persistent themes keep showing up, and the glimpses it offers, even through the later revisions, of a young would-be writer still learning his craft.

The most obvious of these themes is the way Golter, as an example of extreme capitalism, contrasts with the communistic Culture. On Golter, any land privately or corporately owned is outside the state system and owes allegiance not to any government but to "guilds, orders, scientific disciplines, linguistic groups, Corporations, clans and other organisations" (*Against* 46). It is notable, therefore, that while the legal profession plays little or no part in the Culture stories, and cost is of course irrelevant, here no description of the setting is complete without reference to expense, to legal disputes, to bid prices, and to the inconvenience and cost of interminable court cases. When the Brethren agree to release Sharrow's sister on recovery of the book, *Universal Principles*, it is a business deal: "We shall have a business agency draw up the contract itself; they will sort out the details with you or your lawyer" (*Against* 72). Zefla's description of Geis, Sharrow's cousin, places him squarely in this landscape: "He jumps out of the commercial equivalent of dark alleys, strips companies and fucks their employees. He's got no idea how real people work so he plays the market instead; he's a rich kid who thinks the banks and courts and Corps are his construction set and he doesn't want anybody else to play" (*Against* 52). This is what gives Geis the financial, and therefore political, clout to help Sharrow, as he offers to do at the beginning of the book; yet in a world that so lauds money making, the fact that he is so comprehensively portrayed in villainous terms, a thief lurking in dark alleys, is the first indication we are given that we should doubt his probity.

Every new setting is introduced in financial terms. Log-Jam, a city constructed of derelict, linked ships (that would later be echoed in Armada, the floating city at the center of China Miéville's *The Scar* [2002]), is initially described thus: "Like a lot of Golterian oddities, the Log-Jam was basically a tax dodge" (*Against* 64). Banks expands on this a few pages later: "a modest land boom [. . .] pushed property prices up and Piphram's historically punitive real-estate taxes exaggerated the effect. Then somebody [spotted] a loophole" (*Against* 68–69). The same primacy of cost over everything else keeps recurring throughout the novel. For instance, in the remote region of Pharpech, which the team must penetrate in order to find the *Universal Principles*, the king buys modern technology "to remove any monetary surplus from the country's economy [. . .] to keep the Kingdom stable by soaking up profit that might otherwise lead to progress and therefore instability" (*Against* 198). And when Sharrow negotiates for a submarine to get them to the Embargoed Areas, the captain refuses to do some things—not because of the danger but because, he says, "our underwriters have been blowing *very* cool in this last financial year" (*Against* 373, emphasis in the original).

And though the plot involves lots of death and destruction, Sharrow fleeing for her life from implacable hunters, narrow escapes, dramatic escapades and betrayal, nevertheless it comes down in the end to finance. The actor pretending to be Molgarin, the super-rich, super-powerful person who claims to be immortal and who captures Sharrow at the end, says he believes in "a more enterprising, more corporate style [. . .] one that releases the natural resourcefulness and entrepreneurial spirit of humanity" (*Against* 432). However, the fact that resourceful Sharrow is held prisoner at this point might suggest that "release" is hardly the apposite word. Meanwhile, Geis's own megalomaniac rant promises: "[T]hey might start a war. The insurance claims and the commercial disruption alone could wreck everything" (*Against* 472). Everything on Golter revolves around money.

There are, of course, negatives to the communistic utopia of the Culture, of which boredom appears to be the chief, but the Culture's citizens are invariably safe, long lived, and never in want of anything they might need. The opposite is true of this capitalist world. Though Sharrow comes from a wealthy family, the very peak of everything that Golter's economic and political system is geared toward, it gives her no particular power, no protection, no surety of safety, no guarantee that her needs might be met. Everything—life, liberty, and happiness—is for sale to the highest bidder. It is noticeable that whenever the Culture goes to war (for instance, in *Consider Phlebas* or *Excession*), it is with outside enemies; the vast majority of Culture citizens are unaffected by the conflict and remain in perfect safety throughout. But the war in which Sharrow and her team fought, and which ended only shortly before *Against a Dark Background* opens, was a civil war. Civil wars occur with remarkable frequency in Banks's work: with or without Culture interference they appear, for instance, in *Look to Windward* and *Matter*, not to mention *Feersum Endjinn* and *A Song of Stone*; and always they are presented as a form of social madness, a divided self on a cultural rather than a personal scale. The civil war in *Against a Dark Background*, therefore, indicates that the extreme capitalism of Golter makes for a failed state, a state incapable of fulfilling its most basic function, the protection of its own cultural and psychological integrity, and hence the protection of its own citizens. This is a theme that Banks would return to again and again, but it is never stated quite as baldly as it is here: where everything is for sale, everything is at risk.

But if the power of the check book is not enough to protect Sharrow from the threat of assassination, surely if everything is for sale, then it should be possible to buy off the hunters? So integral to every aspect of life is money that Miz's immediate response to the Huhsz hunting Sharrow is to ask this:

> "No, Miz. It's a matter of dogma; faith."
> "Yeah," he said, "So?" He looked genuinely puzzled.
> "The answer is no," Sharrow said patiently. "They can't be bought off." (*Against* 76)

Even the almighty check book fails when it comes up against religious extremism, which brings us to the second of the themes explored in this novel. From the sacrifice poles of *The Wasp Factory* to the suffocating community of *Whit*, Banks has repeatedly presented "the harm an over-commitment to religion and mystic superstitions can cause."[7] But since *Against a Dark Background* is one of the earliest and least sophisticated of his novels—as he said, it is "probably the one that's changed the least out of all the novels"[8]—these ideas are on display most boldly and baldly here. It is a novel that is filled with damaging sects whose rigidity and sense of their own infallibility also turn their society into one divided against itself, as destructive in their way as unfettered capitalism, if not more so. In an interview Banks described such cults as "symptomatic of the bigotry, calcification and imminent breakdown of our own society."[9] Such a breakdown is not so much social collapse as psychological disorder; unquestioned faith is a form of madness that can undermine an entire culture.

In the Culture novels, there is no need for religion, because the material plenty of this post-scarcity society offers, in Francis Spufford's words, "a completely secular version of heaven."[10] These novels, in other words, portray a cheerfully atheist universe in which the freedom to do as one wills is shown to contribute to a healthy society. But in the excessively capitalist universe of

*Against a Dark Background*, where scarcity is inherent in the system, religion flourishes as a means of control, of preventing people from doing what they might wish, and so contributes to a disordered and diseased society. This is most vividly illustrated by the Sea House, the religious community-cum-prison where Sharrow's half-sister, Breyguhn, is held. Here every monk and prisoner and visitor is enchained, their movements prescribed by the tracks set into the walls of this monumental structure. This physical entrapment serves to symbolize the mental entrapment that such religious orders represent. In the Sea House, where one goes, and, by extension, how one thinks, are laid out on strict and inescapable lines; symbolically, the need to think for oneself in an increasingly complex and demanding world is obviated. The attraction of this, the appeal of imprisonment, is demonstrated at the end of Sharrow's first visit to her half-sister. A monk "took one end of Breyguhn's chain and with a practised flick looped it over her head and round her arms, encircling her; he pulled tight, jerking her away from the great stone seat—her eyes closed, an expression of sudden joy on her pallid face" (*Against* 44). The tighter the restraint, the greater the release from responsibility, and so the greater the joy.

Another way in which religion disrupts social order and individual well-being is represented by the Solipsists, whose leader, Elson Roa, says, "[I] realised that I always had been God. God in the monotheistic sense that I am all that really exists" (*Against* 111). His followers, his "apparences," as he calls them, also believe themselves to be God, or rather, as he rather shamefacedly admits: "We all call ourselves God except for one apparence, who is an atheist" (*Against* 115). This denial of individuality, an expression of the way Banks feels that all religion entails the abnegation of the self, can have brutal consequences. When six of the Solipsists are killed at the Log-Jam, Roa considers it "an encouraging sign . . . [since it] indicates my will is becoming stronger" (*Against* 114). The Solipsists switch sides dramatically during the course of the novel, at first assisting Sharrow but later accepting a commission from the Huhsz. Their belief in their own individual divinity absolves them of any concern for, or even interest in, anyone else; being God paradoxically relieves them of any moral responsibility.

The Solipsists' insistence on their own divinity, and the prescribed track-ways of the Sea House, are examples of the false reasoning and rationalizations that Banks associates with religion. The Huhsz are, of course, the prime example of this: having determined that Sharrow must be sacrificed, they are immune to any rational argument, even when shown the falseness of their initial premise. In a space-based civilization such as the Culture, "the mutuality of dependence involved in an environment which is inherently hostile would necessitate an internal social coherence" (Notes); consequently, rationality and materialism are survival traits. The Culture is fundamentally atheist because religion would undermine the rational materialism that makes the Culture possible. In *Against a Dark Background*, Banks shows how dangerous religion is to the social cohesion of the world, how it divides the body politic and leads to an essentially schizophrenic society.

If these disordering forces of rampant capitalism and religion divide the social self, then the fracturing of the state continues down to the more personal level of the family. One of the reasons civil wars occur so often in Banks's work is that they famously pit brother against brother, parent against child, and his novels are full of instances in which R. D. Laing's notion of the divided self is writ large in the form of a divided family. It is there in *The Wasp Factory* and *The Quarry*, in *Use of Weapons* and *The Crow Road*, in *Complicity* and *Whit*, and it is clearly central to *Against a Dark Background*. It is no surprise when we learn that Sharrow and Geis were on opposite sides in the recent civil war.

The novel opens with images of family unity. While we are distracted by the violence in the opening scenes—the attack on Sharrow's mother in the cable car, the warning that the Huhsz are about to get a license to hunt Sharrow—what is actually happening is a mother saving her daughter with her dying breath, and a cousin, Geis, declaring himself willing to risk everything to protect her. So this is family as good and protective, to contrast with the betrayal to come. The sense of family unity quickly wears thin, however, when we encounter the antagonism of Sharrow's imprisoned sister, Breyguhn. By the time we come to Geis attempting to rape Sharrow—"There was an expression of predatory appraisal in his eyes that sent a chill through her. For the first time in her life she felt frightened of a man" (*Against* 274)—this is recognizable as a seriously dysfunctional family. In fact, Sharrow's own callous behavior toward the faithful old retainer, whose life blood she literally sucks from him to obtain information, suggests that the mutual antagonisms that constitute family relationships are a consequence of the aggressive capitalist structures within which they live. The self-sacrifice of Sharrow's mother now appears to be the aberration.

The fact that the final revelation, that all of this drama and mayhem is a direct consequence of family betrayal still comes as something of a shock, is testimony to how much we expect family unity to outweigh family division. But here division is central, whether of state or family or self. A year after the novel first appeared, Banks wrote an epilogue, which was published online. It seems to offer an image of reunion, turning the novel full circle to recreate the cable-car journey from the prologue. This time, Sharrow, looking "well, if rather older" (Epilogue), takes the part of her own mother; she is accompanied by an adopted daughter, and in place of the bodyguard there is Feril, her android ally, resurrected after his death at the end of the novel. Despite Sharrow's obvious nervousness, the journey passes without incident; there is no bloody attack, no self-sacrifice, all is now well. Except that this isn't Sharrow: "She had yet another new name now, and Feril supposed that in a sense, the lady Sharrow really had died" (Epilogue). Nor is this the same world:

> This four-year-old, kneeling on the seat of the cable car, staring intently out at the mists and architecture of the city, was just one of half a million orphans Golter's last spasm of self-abuse had produced. The signs that something good had come out of the Decamillenial War were still encouraging, but the correction had been severe, and any gain in social equality, any lessening in civilisation tension, had been bought at the expense of the millions of personal catastrophes. (Epilogue)

Sharrow's divided self hasn't been healed by her survival; her divided family hasn't been healed by the adoption of this little girl; the divided state hasn't been healed by these millions of personal catastrophes. All that the new name, the new family, the new state, offer is a fresh start; how they might turn out is ambiguous.

The subtle ambiguity of this epilogue sits slightly oddly at the end of *Against a Dark Background*. After all, one was written in the mid-1970s by a writer whose career had not yet properly got underway, and which was, as he told Andrew Wilson, little changed when he prepared it for subsequent and belated publication; the other was written more than a decade and a half later by a successful and sophisticated novelist. *Use of Weapons* was very extensively revised during its long gestation, so *Against a Dark Background* gives us our clearest view of the writer learning his trade. Banks has always used comedy, even in his darkest fiction, but here the comedy starts out very broad. The old automatic beachcomber, the incompetence of Geis's horseback arrival on the beach, the razzmatazz of Miz's welcome to Log-Jam; these are not just played for laughs, they are almost slapstick. And the Lazy Gun is cartoonish: fire it at someone and "a spear might suddenly materialise and pierce them through the chest, or some snake's spit fang might graze their neck, or a ship's anchor might appear falling above them, crushing them, or two enormous switch-electrodes would leap briefly into being on either side of the hapless target and vaporise him or her" (*Against* 107). But as the number of deaths increases and the mood of the story darkens, the use of comedy diminishes. It is interesting that when Banks talks of the Lazy Gun in the epilogue, it is not in terms of a piano falling from the sky but of a stealth cruise missile. And as the humor becomes more subtle, so the structure becomes more complex. At about the halfway mark in the novel Banks starts to introduce flashbacks, and as the story progresses from that point they become longer and more frequent, carrying more of the narrative burden. *Against a Dark Background* never gets to the multiple viewpoints and variant timelines that are a regular feature of Banks's other novels, but it does steadily become a richer and more rewarding book as it goes on.

Inevitably, the reviewers compared *Against a Dark Background* to the Culture novels and found it wanting, though one or two did simply assume it was set in a part of the galaxy not yet reached by the Culture, as if that made it more acceptable. Most noted the hell-for-leather plotting—John Clute called it "Demolition Derby shenanigans"[11]—and there was a general sense that it wasn't quite as good as people were used to—Chris Gilmore described it as "patchy, though far more is done well than not"[12]—but it was generally well-enough liked. If Banks had, indeed, been testing the water to see if he could move away from the Culture, then he had received the go-ahead.

*Against a Dark Background* was the last of the novels written during Banks's teens and twenties to see print. The adolescent novels, *Top of Poseidon*, *The Hungarian Lift-Jet*, and *The Tashkent Rambler*, were never going to see the light of day, and his later effort, *O*, had been cannibalized for *The Bridge*. If Banks was going to keep up his avowed aim of alternating science fiction and mainstream fiction, then he was going to have to write his first new science fiction novel in a decade. In such circumstances, one might have expected him to write another Culture novel, since that was the sort of science fiction he was used to writing and that had already proved remarkably successful. But Banks was not a writer to play safe.

His next science fiction novel was one of the most complex and daring of his career. *Feersum Endjinn* was the first (and by some counts the only) novel written under the name Iain M. Banks that was set entirely on Earth. Four different viewpoints take turns to carry the story, one of which begins her narrative with no knowledge of who or what she is, and one of which is told in the first person in a debased form of language that can be difficult to interpret. The four narrative strands come together at the end, but they appear to take different amounts of time to reach that point so that the timelines differ. And though it is a novel that revolves around a huge structure and that plays with notions of scale, it was not at all what was expected of an Iain M. Banks novel.

Everything that happens in the novel takes place in or around a building whose scale is practically impossible to comprehend. The fastness, as this immense building is called, is eventually revealed to be the base of the American continent space elevator, which had been designed to look like a castle. The elevator, along with others in Kalimantan and at Kilimanjaro, has long since been dismantled, meaning that those who remain on Earth no longer have the ability to get into space. This is a society in decline, and one thing the vastness of the building does is emphasize that its current inhabitants no longer understand the world that went before them. Nevertheless, there seems no real reason why the base of the space elevator should have been built on such a scale. As Bascule reports, in his distinctive and broken language: "Mr Zoliparia sez ov coarse ther wernt nevir no jiants & I bileev him but sumtymes u can luke owt ovir thi hall wif its mountins like cuboardz & mountins like seets & sofas set agenst thi wall & thi tabils & poofs & so on skaterd about thi playce & u fink, Whenz them big bags cummin bak then?" (*Feersum* 17). Assuming that humanity in this distant future has not indeed shrunk physically as well as in knowledge and aspiration, all that the size of the building does is intimidate.

Huge places and objects are, of course, a common device in Banks's fiction. The Culture novels go into great detail about the size of ships and Orbitals:

the General Systems Vehicle *Sleeper Service* in *Excession*, for instance, is ninety kilometers long by sixty kilometers wide and twenty kilometers high, while an Orbital would have "a surface area twenty times that of Earth" (Notes). But this emphasis on size is used to stress the wealth of the Culture, a wealth expressed in space. The citizens of the Culture are not overwhelmed by such monumental objects; rather, their extent gives people the liberty to live however they choose. The castle in *Walking on Glass* and the avatar of the Forth Bridge in *The Bridge* are more alienating in their bulk, but they are still built on a more or less human scale. Nothing within the fastness is on a human scale. Rather, we encounter "the ten-kilometre length of the Great Hall" (*Feersum* 8), while the clan of the Engineers is besieged in its headquarters "thirty kilometres away on the far side of the fastness, and three kilometre-high floors higher than the Great Hall" (*Feersum* 7). It is besieged because this is another civil war, another divided society. As part of that war, Sessine embarks on an expedition: "Here, though the snow-line was still a good kilometre above, the air was chill when not heated with the rotten smell of the semi-dormant volcano" (*Feersum* 12). Yet all this is within a room in the fastness. Repeatedly, just within the first dozen pages of the novel, we are made to feel tiny and insignificant within the inexplicable vastness of the setting, a place where the climate changes as it might if ascending a mountain, a place where there are volcanoes within rooms. When Gadfium later visits the observatory on the roof, air pressure is so low that observers need to be "able to operate without extra oxygen and pressurisation, which was much more than Gadfium felt able to do" (*Feersum* 35). If we think of the fastness as being like Erving Goffman's constructed defenses, then the protective walls have grown too big for those within its shelter. And since they no longer fit, they are no longer protected; the defenses themselves have become symptomatic of the hugeness and the terror of the world that surrounds them. In response, they fall apart, they fall into a civil war that seems to have been going on for longer than anyone can remember; they are divided.

Bascule, whose broken speech is often used to express the commonsense views of the author, puts it thus: "2 set iself up like dis in such a defeetinly vast & intimidaytinly inhumin structyir is meerly 2 anounce di cumin 2 rest ov is progress" (*Feersum* 22). This is a world without progress, without growth, a world that can thus only fall apart, and the huge, incomprehensible and largely ruinous nature of the fastness represents this. It is significant, therefore, that John Corbett traces the title to a passage in Havelock Ellis's *Impressions and Comments* (1914) where he writes of the "fearsome engine of modernity"[13] (Ellis uses the term to describe a motor bus); Banks's "feersum endjinn" brings, in the end, a sort of redemption in solving the problem of the Encroachment, but it would also seem to kick-start society into movement once more, which means the inhabitants of the fastness will at some point have to contend with what it is to be modern.

The fastness clearly stands for the world and for its society, and it is broken. Not only has the one-time space elevator been dismantled, closing off access to space, to the future, but what remains is now crumbling. Virtually every description of the fastness includes some reference to broken windows, falling walls, or other signs of decay. When we first meet chief scientist Hortis Gadfium III, she is supervising the construction of "the new oxygen works" (*Feersum* 5), which suggests breathable air is in short supply and must be manufactured, which in turn suggests environmental degradation. And that doesn't even include the destruction wrought by the ongoing war. At one point we follow a soldier, Tenblen, part of a unit working to cut through the floor on one of the upper storeys, directly above the enemy headquarters. The workings are a vision of hell "filled with a loud, fume-laden darkness pierced sporadically by flashes of intense, scarifying light, and permeated with a furious hissing sound punctuated by sudden screams and explosions" (*Feersum* 130). It is a place of stinking, corrosive fumes, of acid pools, of terror when the ground suddenly gives way beneath him and Tenblen plunges two kilometers down to the city below. The inhabitants of the fastness are actively engaged in the destruction of their world.

And against this backdrop of war and decay there is a greater destruction approaching. An Encroachment has been detected, a disorder in the universe that will block out the sun and end all life on Earth. In the absence of the space elevator, there is no escape; but rather than unite in the face of this greater threat and endeavor to find a solution, the King, his politicians, and advisors prefer to pursue the war with ever greater ferocity. *Feersum Endjinn* is not an overtly political novel; nevertheless, it is impossible to ignore the savagery of Banks's disdain for those who prefer enmities to alliances. This underlying political message is accompanied by more familiar Banksian positions, as when he declares: "money was all-powerful then and people said they made it work for them but money cannot work, only people and machines can work" (*Feersum* 115).

The plot of *Feersum Endjinn*, therefore, concerns those who, knowingly or not, work against this warmongering consensus. Of the four central characters whose stories form the bulk of the narrative, Gadfium is part of a conspiracy of senior scientists working secretly on the problem of the Encroachment. The soldier, Sessine, may have been assassinated because he was known to be sympathetic to them, then serves their cause in the afterlife of the crypt, the vast space where consciousness is stored in digital form through a prescribed number of afterlives. The nameless figure who appears as if from nowhere in the very first page of the novel turns out to carry a vital message from the crypt to the world above. And Bascule, the child who scours the deepest, darkest recesses of the fastness in search of his pet ant, turns out to be the unknowing link that ties all these strands together.

Bascule is the most interesting character in the novel, in large part because of his very distinctive narrative voice. There have been linguistic distortions before, of course. One thinks of "nadsat," the slang partly based on Russian criminal argot that Anthony Burgess created for *A Clockwork Orange* (1962), or the debased, post-apocalyptic language used by Russell Hoban in *Riddley Walker* (1980). In both novels the language is illustrative of the state of the society. Banks is clearly doing much the same, and the comparison with Hoban's novel in particular helps to emphasize *Feersum Endjinn*'s post-collapse setting. Banks had used phonetic spellings before, notably with the Scottish barbarian in *The Bridge*, and in both of the mainstream novels written immediately before *Feersum Endjinn*, *The Crow Road* and *Complicity*, he had brief passages in Scottish dialect. The barbarian's language is used for comic effect, but the dialect in the other two novels draws attention to the Scottishness of the subject. Although there is certainly a suggestion of a Scottish accent in Bascule's speech, it is not, as Christie March describes it, "the same phonetic Scottish dialect"[14] that the barbarian spoke in *The Bridge*.

Bascule's language is far more complex than March would suggest. Among other elements, it anticipates the way numbers substitute for words in text messaging: "duz she 1/2 a naim" (though text messaging as such was not introduced until after *Feersum Endjinn* had been published). This is combined with street argot: "Nuffink"; Scots dialect: "tho I doan xpect yule b able 2 here hir"; and homophones: "whot maid u call her that [. . .] itz her reel name" (*Feersum* 16). As with Russell Hoban's *Riddley Walker*, the language is far less off-putting read aloud than it appears on the page, and generally "Bascule's anti-language constructs him as that most alien of creatures, a young teenager."[15] The spelling aside, the language is generally grammatical, and Banks's invented orthography is sufficiently flexible to allow him to present a range of accents and vocal tics. Thus when Mr Zoliparia says: "Y, de dam tings litil betir than a hospis!" (*Feersum* 21) we identify him as West Indian. Dartlin speaks with a lisp: "I flu thwu 2 thi paliment ov thi cwows & pikd up sum gothip" (*Feersum* 76); while the sloth Gashton speaks with a Sean Conneryesque slur: "shtop being shilly" (*Feersum* 136). Right at the end, in the high great tower, we get a pure taste of Banks's own voice when Bascule says: "itz juss a totil hoot. Amazin views, 4 a start" and goes on to enthusiastically list "swimin bafs & flooms & ice rinx & a hooj & totily brilyint spyril skee sloap & a hoal bludy sqwadron ov space planes" (*Feersum* 278).

But though the inventive and brilliantly sustained voice of Bascule is the most eye-catching part of *Feersum Endjinn*, it is not the only example of Banks playing with language. On the very first page, long before we know that the viewpoint character is the asura, the messenger from the crypt, her broken sensations are conveyed in broken language:

> Noise of buzzing, something sliding again but not skin on skin; harder. Then light from behind/above. The small red light has disappeared. Then movement; darkness above/around sliding back, face neck shoulders chest/arms trunk/hands in light now; eyes blinking in light. Light grey-pink, shining down; blue-brightness through hole in curved cliff above/around. (*Feersum* 3)

The broken language is reminiscent of the impressionistic passage that opens *The Bridge*, but here it is specifically linked with broken identity, with "everything . . . stripped away" and then rebuilt, "a surfacing through layers of thought and development" (*Feersum* 3). There is a similar effect when Sessine wakes in the crypt. We have learned from Bascule that there is a "reincarnative prossess" (*Feersum* 18) that can give people up to eight lives (hence Hortis Gadfium III indicates that she is on her third reincarnation), and this is paralleled by eight reincarnations in the virtual reality of the crypt. When

he is assassinated, therefore, Sessine's enemies attempt to destroy him utterly by launching immediate and ruthless attacks upon him the moment he
awakens in the crypt. This rapid cycle of waking and dying is represented by
broken language:

He awoke.
"Ala——"
/He was in bed [. . .]
He awoke.
"Al——"
/He was in the nursery [. . .] (*Feersum* 46)

The progressively truncated form of the name Alandre, his own original name,
indicates the increasing rapidity of the cycle; the "/" before his location divides
him from it. In the cases of both Sessine and the asura the broken language is
connected to a stripping away of identity. These tiny people rattling around in
the fastness or in the crypt, both of which are far too big for any human scale
to apply, are thus divided from the reality of their world. It is only Bascule,
searching for the smallest of all creatures, his pet ant, who is eventually able
to ascend to the heights to discover the feersum endjinn that will end the mysterious Encroachment and presumably launch a new modernity, a new world
whose delights—"swimin bafs & flooms & ice rinx"—are on a human scale.

The underlying influences of Laing and Goffman run through all of
Banks's work, but they are most apparent in those stories not bound up in
the utopian enterprise of the Culture. Having brought these ideas center stage
once more in *Against a Dark Background* and *Feersum Endjinn*, it is perhaps no
coincidence that, in his next two mainstream novels, Banks turned back to
something like the Scottish fantastic that had begun his career. There was, at
this time, a rumor that Banks was intending to add the middle initial, M., to
all of his books, or conversely that he was going to remove the M. from his
science fiction novels. It was a rumor that Banks himself neither denied nor
supported. When asked about it directly, he only muddied the waters further:
"I've talked to my publishers and there's no problem about dropping the M—
or including the M for everything if I want—but I'm not really intending to
do it. I've thought about it but—och, I can't be bothered!"[16] Either way, it sug-

gests that Banks was less and less seeing any substantive difference between the work he wrote under the two different versions of his name. Certainly, throughout the rest of the decade, the supposedly mainstream novels all had an element of the fantastic.

The first of these Iain Banks novels, *Whit*, does not feature a castle (by now becoming a trademark location) as such, though the Luskentyrian Community at the heart of the novel does occupy a mansion house near Stirling, so there is a sense of that same troubled relationship with the past such buildings tend to signal in *Walking on Glass*, *The Crow Road*, and *Feersum Endjinn*. Victor Sage identifies the castle in Banks as a site of Scottish petrifaction, "a characteristic expression of Banks's political and moral skepticism. [. . .] [T]he Past haunts, critically, ironically, and embarrassingly, the Present."[17] Moreover, the whole Community is almost entirely surrounded by a river and is accessible only on foot and by an old and treacherous bridge, a setting that replicates the situation of Cauldhame Island in *The Wasp Factory*. More important, the novel is unequivocally about Scotland and reflects the same uneasy identity, the same divided self, that runs from *The Wasp Factory* to *Complicity*. The viewpoint character, Isis Whit, leaves the security of the Community on a mission to find her older cousin, Morag, and return her to the fold. But it is a journey that divides her, that reveals truths about her Community and herself, and thus undermines her previous certainties. In fact, there are few major characters in *Whit* who are not divided in some way. Morag is believed to be a successful musician but turns out to be a porn star. Grandfather Salvador Whit, who founded the Luskentyrian Community, turns out really to be Moray Black, an army deserter wanted on suspicion of theft. There is also, of course, the familiar betrayal from within the family; as so often in these novels, the division is on multiple levels of self, family, and society.

There are other ways, too, in which *Whit* conforms to the patterns we encounter in Banks's other works of the Scottish fantastic. The Community is a world of ritual: the reverse-buttoning ritual, the ban on technology, the requirement that the faithful wear secondhand clothes, the fact that members of the Community are forbidden to pay fares and are encouraged to travel indirectly. All of these rituals are as instinctive in shaping Isis's life and behavior as the various rituals that Frank devised in *The Wasp Factory*. And there's the role that language plays—for instance, in the ritual of singing in tongues, which, according to Isis, "sounds like nonsense, like babble, and yet through this glorious chaos we communicate" (*Whit* 47). There aren't many places in Banks's work where chaos is described as glorious. And in the end, much as Gurgeh had to become a barbarian in order to defend the values of civilization in *The Player of Games*, so Isis has to become like an outsider in order to save the Community and restore its moral purpose: "I had stolen, lied, deceived, dissembled and burgled, I had used the weakness of a relative to winkle information out of him, I had scarcely talked to my God for two weeks and I had used the works of the Unsaved almost as they did themselves" (*Whit* 368).

Banks, never entirely serious when discussing his work in progress, had at one point said of *Whit*: "It was going to be called *Whit*, then it was going to be called *Twenty-nine* . . . we might even be a bit cheeky and try to get away with calling it *Cult Novel*."[18] *Cult Novel* might at least have signaled that this, like the next supposedly mainstream novel, *A Song of Stone*, was not an entirely realist novel. In her study of Banks's mainstream fiction, Katarzyna Pisarska identifies *The Wasp Factory*, in which "the war-torn landscape of the island is a mirror image of the psychological landscape of the hero,"[19] as a blueprint for all of his novels. In *A Song of Stone* this paradigm is manifested as "a war cataclysm putting an end to society, the individual, and the very text."[20] Although the affect of the novel is very different, it can therefore be seen as a direct continuation of *Feersum Endjinn*. The war, whose aftermath brings the devastation that is central to *A Song of Stone*, is a civil war; the setting is a castle, not as grotesquely huge as the fastness but still a place that represents the whole of society, a physical and psychic protection that no longer pro-tects, a link with a past that is already being overturned. What's more, the importance of language in *Feersum Endjinn* is mirrored here. Bascule's broken and distorted speech is transformed into the "ornate, metaphysical, evasive"[21] speech of the narrator, Abel. As Banks said in an interview: "The only thing he has any control over is his language or how he expresses himself."[22]

Just as we can never be entirely sure where or when *Feersum Endjinn* takes place (the most precise thing we can say is that it is somewhere in the Americas, sometime in the distant future), so Banks is careful to deny us any chance to identify where and when *A Song of Stone* takes place. It would seem to be in Europe (the names Abel, Morgan, and Arthur might suggest an Anglophone country), and the military technology seems to indicate the middle years of the twentieth century. Banks himself said "it has a vaguely North European setting with the implication that the story is taking place during the second half of the Twentieth Century,"[23] though Alan MacGillivray is not alone in arguing that "the natural and social descriptions suggest a Scottish setting, poised between Lowlands and Highlands, in a possible post-disaster near-future."[24] This very careful imprecision is what makes the story work as a fable. After a devastating civil war, the old order has been overturned and no new order has yet replaced it; a state of affairs made concrete when aristocrats Abel and Morgan find their castle taken over by the lieutenant and her troops. Abel and Morgan, brother and sister and incestuous lovers (Banks here returning to a theme he has already used in *Walking on Glass* and that he will return to again in *The Steep Approach to Garbadale*), represent the decadence of the old order, out of touch even with their own immediate world. When the faithful old retainer Arthur dies, for instance, Abel cannot recall his surname. The lieutenant, nameless and at the head of a troop of nameless soldiers, brings with her violence and destruction. Pisarska notes how the soldiers are regularly compared to animals; one is like a faithful dog, another is as obedient as a hound. Even the dead medic was familiarly known as Vet. She points out how this dehumanizes but misses how it reverses the slaughter of animals in her blueprint text, *The Wasp Factory*. But the decadence of the past proves seductive to the brutality of the new: the lieutenant gradually usurps Abel's place, both in Morgan's bed and in control of the castle. Eventually, ineffectual Abel takes the lieutenant's place as the instigator of violence, killing her and unleashing the final destructive rampage of the troops that will lead to his own death. As Pisarska puts it, "The conflict which has wasted the country's body politic and its landscape has led to military chaos, disrupting previous social relationships and, as a result, obliterating all known axioms and points of reference."[25] And, as always, tearing apart the body politic is equated with tearing apart the body, literally, since Abel ends up tied to the mouth of a cannon. As he awaits his death, Abel muses: "Unless one's involvement is peripheral, nobody survives a war; the people who come out the other side are not those who went in" (*Song* 273).

As it was, despite the fact that the determinedly mainstream *The Crow Road*—"achingly well written, long but not long enough, fizzes like sherbet"[26]— and *Complicity*—"subtly constructed and brilliantly written"[27]—had both been reviewed in places like *Vector* and *The New York Review of Science Fiction*, neither *Whit* nor *A Song of Stone* were noticed by the sf press. Instead, all of the attention was on the book that came between them. This was *Excession*, Banks's return to the Culture. For readers, it was six years since *Use of Weapons*; but for Banks it was more than a decade since he had last written a new Culture novel from scratch. That had been *Consider Phlebas*, and I would argue that *Excession* and *Look to Windward* together serve as the concluding parts of a loose trilogy begun with *Consider Phlebas*, or, perhaps more accurately, as a diptych building on ideas first presented in *Phlebas*. Indeed, while *Use of Weapons* may be Banks's best individual science fiction novel, I think these two books together represent the high point of his science fiction career. Farah Mendlesohn, for instance, declares that *Excession* is "the most *classic*, the most archetypal in its revisioning of space opera; the most ambitious in its portrayal of a complex political society; and the most successful in its linguistic display and reconfiguration of the space opera baroque and in the immersive techniques of extrapolative fiction."[28] "Classic," one assumes, in the sense that the extravagance, the sense of scale, so typical of traditional space opera, is absolutely central to the book; and also in the sense that, more than any other Culture novel with the possible exception of *Consider Phlebas*, this is a story played out in space.

Iain M. Banks did not reinvent space opera singlehandedly; by the time *Consider Phlebas* was published, M. John Harrison's New Wave deconstruction of the form, *The Centauri Device* (1974), was more than ten years old. Nevertheless, the verve and invention of the Culture novels did much to establish what became known as the "New Space Opera." Banks kept the pace and scale, the limitless vistas of outer space as his venue, but subverted the politics, the imperialism, the hierarchies, the racism, and the casual assumptions that underlay space opera in its pomp. *Excession* is where this is most clearly displayed, as Banks's least classical space opera.

*Excession* is a novel replete with story. All of the science fiction novels originally written before the publication of *The Wasp Factory* tell essentially the story of one character: of Horza or Gurgeh or Zakalwe or Sharrow. *Feersum Endjinn* is more complex, with four narrative threads, but the four combine into one story, the race to save Earth from the Encroachment. In *Excession* there are several narrative threads that occasionally intersect with each other, but in the end combine not into one story but into several parallel stories. The mission that sends Byr Genar-Hofoen chasing across the galaxy ends up having nothing to do with the mysterious intrusion into our universe of the object identified as the Excession; the concern of the General Systems Vehicle *Sleeper Service* for its pregnant passenger, Dajeil Gelian, turns out to be only tangentially connected with the preparations for war against the Affront. Such multiple storylines would become a common feature of Banks's science fiction from this point on, though usually the strands of story intersect more closely than they do here. But that is because the central theme that ties all the disparate threads of this novel together is deception, and the reader is to be deceived as much as any of the characters.

What is expected of a space opera is that the story we read, the characters we follow, are central to some great occurrence. Banks undermined this expectation from *Consider Phlebas* onward, making it clear that the actions of Horza, as important as they may be to the individual concerned, in fact play no pivotal role in cosmic events. But in *Excession* he takes this approach a step further; not only do most of the characters play no significant part in the situation that occurs within the novel, but the majority of them have no knowledge of or interest in the grand scheme of things. Even the Big Dumb Object, the Excession itself, is mostly inert or inactive throughout the novel, an excuse for but not a participant in what is central to the novel. As Farah Mendlesohn puts it, *Excession* is a romance of "the day to day of lives lived through great events. Each of the main characters is much more concerned with their individualized futures than with the prospective end of the universe."[29] Thus as we follow each character, always expecting that through them we will glimpse some turn of the machinery that is the plot we sense working behind the scenes, we discover that even the character has been deceived, that what is revealed is less than we anticipated.

Outlining the stories that conspire to make up the novel is, therefore, a complex and often frustrating business. Take, as an example, one of the least of the storylines: Ulver Seich is an impressionable young woman who is recruited by Special Circumstances for one particular mission. For Ulver, working for Special Circumstances is the ultimate romantic attainment, a fairy story come true. While preparing for her mission she is privy to sobering information whose full import is beyond her comprehension (though it helps to provide the reader with a little extra detail on a different story line). But when the mission actually happens it is almost immediately revealed to be pointless; Ulver Seich contributes not one single step to the progress of any of the major storylines that make up the novel. Nor is she alone in this.

Yet the different plots do progress, rarely through the efforts of any one single character (though a couple of ship Minds do make a dramatic contribution to events), but more often by chance, by misdirection, by some combination of characters or circumstances beyond the ability even of a Mind to control.

The novel starts with Dajeil Gelian, who is "a little more than one hundred days into the fortieth year of her confinement" (*Excession* 3). She is pregnant, and throughout the rest of the novel Banks draws unsubtle attention to this fact by having her "tapping her belly gently" (*Excession* 310) whenever she appears; but the choice of word also suggests imprisonment. She lives in a "lonely tower overlooking the sea" (*Excession* 3), exactly the sort of situation in which a fairy tale princess is traditionally held in thrall, though the captivity is of her own choosing. The tower is located within the *Sleeper Service*, where she is free to come and go as she wishes and where she spends her days studying the other creatures that also occupy this ship. Nevertheless, she is Sleeping Beauty, a princess locked into a timeless stasis, her pregnancy never coming to term, her life never expanding beyond her own chosen limitations. It is worth noting, also, that she is the only living person aboard the *Sleeper Service*, which serves as a container for the recently dead who have chosen to remain in stasis until some future resurrection. Both the pregnancy and the stasis are echoed throughout the novel: for instance, the suspended animation tableaux created by the *Sleeper Service* become an artistic representation of the extended pregnancy; or Pittance, the "huge irregular lump of matter . . . [that was] . . . the remnant of a catastrophe which had occurred over four billion years earlier" (*Excession* 144), where a Culture war fleet is mothballed, tended by Gestra, who has taken the position precisely for the loneliness, the stasis of it; or the moment late in the novel when the *Sleeper Service* abruptly gives birth to a host of new Culture war ships. Everything in *Excession* would seem to be pregnant. The whole of the Culture is in a sort of suspended animation caused by its failure to sublime, a failure that becomes the central issue of the companion volume, *Look to Windward*.

Dajeil, therefore, is one of the central figures in the novel, but what is her story? The *Sleeper Service* is busy removing all of the beings, living or dead, that occupy its bulk, with the exception of Dajeil. It is clearing the decks for action, and we know there is a war coming, so it would seem that Dajeil is destined to play some part in this conflict. Meanwhile, the other major human character, Genar-Hofoen, is charged with getting to the *Sleeper Service* in order to speak with one of the dead held there in stasis, Zreyn Tramow, because she may have been a witness to the first appearance of the Excession. For much of the novel we are teased into assuming that Zreyn might be Dajeil: Zreyn and Genar-Hofoen knew each other, which is why he was chosen for the mission in the first place; Ulver Seich was chosen for her mission to distract him because she bears a resemblance to Dajeil. In fact, the body of Zreyn Tramow "was destroyed in an Idiran attack on the Orbital concerned half a millennium ago" (*Excession* 69), an aside that serves to date the events of this novel, and what remained of her mind-state had been removed from the *Sleeper Service* before Genar-Hofoen ever began his mission. It turns out that Dajeil and Genar-Hofoen are former lovers; he is the father of her child, but they split irrevocably, which is what prompted Dajeil to refuse to give birth. The *Sleeper Service* is playing cupid, trying to bring the two lovers back together again. It doesn't work out, but as is right and proper in any romance there is a happy ending for all concerned: Dajeil finds a new partner and has her baby, while Genar-Hofoen gets his wish of being remade as an Affront.

The novel's central characters, the ones we most engage with, turn out to be enacting an old story of star-crossed lovers whose actions and fate have nothing to do with the great events playing out in the background. Those great events, meanwhile, occur not at the instigation or under the direction of any individual, but by a series of chances or as a result of groups working together.

The Excession itself, for instance, an incursion into this universe by something from beyond, from outside, is first discovered by chance by an exploratory vessel of the Elench, a race that sometime before split from the Culture. The ship is destroyed in the encounter, except for one drone who, before its death, manages to send a desperate message. By chance, this message is seen by an agent of the Culture, who is able to understand something of its import and pass the news on. Thereafter, the issue of the Excession becomes the province of an ad hoc committee of ship Minds, whose own deliberations are usurped by an older group of Minds known as the Interesting Times Gang. Meanwhile the developing war between the Affront and the Culture seems to progress by a logic of its own, with no obvious cause or instigator until it ends just as abruptly when it is revealed that the war was fomented by a conspiracy of disaffected Culture Minds. There are no heroes or villains in this story, only individuals working, knowingly or not, as part of a group effort toward some end that none of them can fully grasp.

In an essay about Olaf Stapledon's *Star Maker*, Stanislaw Lem wrote:

> Certain magnificent civilizations, foreseeing the physical destruction brought on by the invasions of the "evil," "insane" worlds, don't even try to fend the threats off; they go to the slaughter serenely. Such civilizations, which are already capable of establishing spiritual contact with every mind in the universe, view themselves as leitmotifs in the gigantic symphony of the cosmos. By gaining an even greater distance from themselves, they understand that they are only single notes in the magnificent music—infinitesimal notes, but constitutive parts of the whole.[30]

Without suggesting that Banks was drawing on this image, or that he was even aware of Lem's essay on Stapledon, there is something in this passage that reflects the dashing attempt at self-sacrifice by the *Killing Time*, which perhaps comes as close as any character in the novel to being heroic. Having transmitted a copy of its mind-state, its soul, to another ship, "it then experienced a strange sense of release and of freedom while it completed its preparations for combat" (*Excession* 333). It dives upon the Affront battle fleet with a joy that comes of denying itself for the sake of the other Minds in its universe; and in fact it is the traitor ship, *Attitude Adjuster* (the closest thing to a villain, though it believes implicitly that it is acting for the good of the Culture), that suffers the crisis of conscience and destroys itself. Interestingly, this is the only battle in a book that is all about war; the war is shown to have been brought about by deception and ends with an overwhelming show of force by the *Sleeper Service*. It is as if the war happens only to provide this image of self-sacrifice, and to suggest that the cause of war is invariably betrayal (interesting how often betrayal is a key in Banks's novels)—a moral nicety that will be lost in later books. Lem's "gigantic symphony of the cosmos" perfectly captures the lyricism of Banks's description not of battle, but of the self-release that both the *Killing Time* and *Attitude Adjuster* experience. The war is not what matters here, as it is contrived and soon over; what matters is the contrivance of war, and this is one of the things that establishes the relationship between *Excession, Consider Phlebas*, and *Look to Windward*.

The Affront had been allies of the Idirans during the earlier war, and ever since, a faction of Culture Minds has believed that a renewal of war is inevitable, even necessary, in order to destroy the evil that they see in the Affront. And the Affront are clearly portrayed as evil: in our very first glimpse of them we see their regimental mess "adorned with plaques, company, battalion, division and regimental honour plaques and the heads, genitals, limbs or other acceptably distinctive body parts of old adversaries" (*Excession* 28). In fact, every description of the Affront concentrates on their cruelty, their disdain for the Culture's civilization, their sense of power and authority. Every bit as much as the Idirans in *Consider Phlebas*, the Affront are seen to be, literally, an affront to our sense of decency, a people fully deserving of being considered the enemy. Yet against this the Culture is positioned not as a nice liberal society but as one equally capable of cruelty and nastiness. In the face of genocide committed by a civilization known as the Race, for example, the *Grey Area* exacts a revenge that is violent and rather sickening, an action that calls to mind *Complicity*, in which morally indefensible crimes are committed against people who have themselves committed morally indefensible acts. Since the crimes in *Complicity* are described in the second person, the reader is implicated, making it ever more difficult to know whether to applaud or to decry the violence, a moral uncertainty that is meant to carry over into *Excession*. Such moral ambiguity is there also in the relish in the list of torture instruments that Ulver Seich finds aboard the *Grey Area*, where "some of the cabins and larger spaces had been fitted out to resemble torture chambers, slave holds, prison cells and death chambers" (*Excession* 339). Moreover, given that one faction of the Culture is prepared to lie and dissemble and betray in order to foment an unnecessary war, comfortable with the notion that millions would be likely to die as a result, it becomes less easy to discern who are the good guys and who are the bad guys in this conflict. The earlier Culture novels had subtly undermined the notion of the Culture as a utopia, but here and again in *Look to Windward*, Banks similarly makes us question the notion that the Culture has any moral superiority. It is worth remembering that *Excession* was written at the time of the Bosnian War, when the morality of NATO intervention and the passivity of UN peacekeepers in the face of events like the Srebrenica massacre raised issues that echo those examined in the novel. Banks's own later protests at Britain's involvement in questionable foreign wars would seem, therefore, to have the same roots as this novel.

The moral ambiguity thus presented is linked to the colonialist reading of the novel that is explicit in the text. This is specifically linked to the appearance of and response to the Excession. Two and a half thousand years before the novel opens, the General Contact Unit *Problem Child* happened upon a "dead star [that] was at least fifty times older than the universe" (*Excession* 65) and with it "a perfect black-body sphere fifty klicks across, in orbit around the unfeasibly ancient star" (*Excession* 67). Both of these subsequently vanished. Something very like that sphere has now reappeared, but without the dead star. It emits no signals, does not respond to messages, and seems to have been responsible for the destruction of the Elench ship that first happened upon it. It is, therefore, like the black monolith in Arthur C. Clarke's *2001: A Space Odyssey* (1968), a perfect and insoluble mystery.

What is known about the nature of the universe, as suggested in "A Few Notes on the Culture," is that there are levels of reality nested one within the other: "In the very centre of all the concentric, inflating universes lay the place they had each originated from, where every now and again a cosmic fireball blinked into existence, detonating once more to produce another universe" (*Excession* 270). It is an image that will find an echo in the nested worlds of *Matter*. Between these concentric universes are networks of energy that can, with caution, be used, but the black sphere seems to be plugged in to this energy grid more efficiently than has been possible for anyone else. It would seem that this Excession is an intrusion into this universe from a more advanced universe, though that is an explanation that really explains nothing. One way of talking about it, therefore, might be in terms of the intrusion of a three-dimensional object into a two-dimensional world, as in Edwin Abbott's novel, *Flatland* (1884). There is a suggestion of this, but the object is more frequently referred to as an Outside Context Problem, which is defined as "the sort of thing most civilisations encountered just once . . . rather in the same way a sentence encountered a full stop" (*Excession* 71). The usual way of talking about it is to imagine you are a tribe on a largish, fertile island; you'd tamed the land, invented the wheel or writing or whatever, the neighbours were cooperative or enslaved but at any rate peaceful . . . when suddenly this bristling lump of iron appears sailless and trailing steam in the bay and these guys carrying long funny-looking sticks come ashore and announce you've just been discovered, you're all subjects of the Emperor now, he's keen on presents called *tax* and these bright-eyed holy men would like a word with your priests. (*Excession* 71–72, emphasis in the original)

An Outside Context Problem is thus "the intellectual depressant of choice for those people and Minds in the Culture determined to find the threat of catastrophe even in utopia" (*Excession* 72).

All of this is, of course, explicitly colonial. The Culture apparently faces a situation in which its own General Systems Vehicles and Orbitals are as dugout canoes to the ironclads the Excession can presumably call upon. As Ulver Seich puts it to the drone Churt Lyne about the Excession: "'So this *thing* can do something the Culture can't?' 'Looks like it.'" (*Excession* 114, emphasis in the original). As a consequence, Robert Duggan argues, *Excession* "inaugurates a movement within the Culture novels toward the Culture being revealed as a smaller, younger and less powerful civilization than hitherto suspected."[31] I don't fully agree with this argument: the Culture is no younger or smaller than it was before, but we do see it situated upon a larger stage so that the extent of its power is now questioned. *Excession* doesn't so much open the Culture to the threat of being colonized as throw a sharp and revealing light upon the Culture's own colonizing impulse:

In a curiously puritanical way for a society seemingly so hell-bent on the ruthless pursuit of pleasure, the Culture . . . decided to attempt to accomplish what the gods, it seemed, could not be bothered with; discovering, judging and encouraging—or discouraging—the behaviour of those to whom its own powers were scarcely less than those of a deity. (*Excession* 82)

It scarcely needs spelling out that those godlike powers are the equivalent of the ironclads described only ten pages before. As Banks has said:

The Culture is aware that, in a sense, it's easy to have an internal utopia once you get beyond a certain technological stage and your aims are not too immodest (so that the Culture has Orbitals rather than Dyson spheres, for example). The tricky bit is trying to be externally helpful, even moral, without being hegemonistic; encouraging the spread of pan-cultural lessons without even accidentally imposing cultural sameness at the expense of diversity.[32]

In *Excession* we are explicitly told that the Culture is a colonizing power, and the moral ambiguities examined throughout the novel can often be traced back to this clash between the standards the Culture proclaims and those it actually upholds. We see this clash time and again; as the *Anticipation Of A New Lover's Arrival* says: "My fear—my terror!—is that our freedom from material concern has blinded us to our true, underlying nature; we have been good because we have never needed to make the choice between that and anything else" (*Excession* 160). In the face of the unknown "we may find that we are prepared to cheat and lie and scheme and plot like any bloody tyrant" (*Excession* 160). On a smaller scale the Culture is portrayed as a place of petty social jealousies where "the tiny [social] differences that did exist became all the more important" (*Excession* 198), and being an artist pointed to "a pitiably archaic form of insecurity and a rather childish desire to show off" (*Excession* 198). A post-scarcity utopia does nothing to change the essential pettiness of humanity; and in this, humanity applies as much to the supposedly superior Minds as to people. Thus the Interesting Times Gang, made up largely of entities so independent that many have not been heard of for centuries, constitute "a conspiracy of mostly very old craft which stepped in to take control of situations which might threaten the Culture's cozy proto-imperialist meta-hegemony" (*Excession* 171).

And if the Culture is more explicitly "proto-imperialist" than we have seen it before, it is also noticeably less powerful. Where the earliest Culture novels had presented an image of almost effortless omnicompetence, as in both *The Player of Games* and *Use of Weapons*, where it is able to interfere in other societies with ease, now, both here and in *Look to Windward*, it comes up against what it doesn't know. We are reminded that "for all that the galaxy had been penetrated by so many different explorers in all obvious primary directions to every periphery however distant, enormous volumes of that encompassing arena remained effectively unexplored by the current crop of in-play civilisations" (*Excession* 19). The Excession itself, appearing from nowhere, unmoving, silent, featureless, stands as a metaphor for how much the Culture still doesn't know. Or rather, does not choose to know. Hand in hand with the theme of deception that threads its way throughout the novel is the associated theme of willful ignorance, of shying away from certain knowledge. And the issue central to this unknown, the thing from which the Culture constantly looks away, is death.

Although death is more prominently the central issue of *Look to Windward*, it begins to emerge, somewhat less coherently, as a key theme in *Excession*. The key is in that phrase "the current crop of in-play civilisations," which begins to suggest that there is a natural lifespan to the galaxy's interstellar civilizations. At the end of that lifespan, civilizations sublime, they leave the material universe and move on into a pure energy state,[33] an existential variant on the nested universes that the Excession illustrates.

The Sublime was a notion that came to prominence particularly during the Romantic era, formulated in works by Immanuel Kant and Edmund Burke, among others. It placed mankind within the context of the natural world, a small figure overwhelmed by the vastness, the horror, the majesty of storms and mountains and the wonder of the heavens. We are humbled by the world around us rather than by God. As Edward James puts it, "The Sublime is a consequence of the liberation of humanity, by the Enlightenment, from the protection of revealed truth."[34] The Sublime was given literary expression in works as varied as *The Prelude* (1850) by William Wordsworth, *Wuthering Heights* (1847) by Emily Brontë, and, particularly relevant for our purposes, *Frankenstein* (1818) by Mary Shelley. In a direct line of descent from Shelley to the present day, science fiction has recast the Sublime as "sense of wonder" and identified it as one of the key concepts behind science fiction. Sense of wonder, generated by images of the gigantic, the mysterious, the strange, the alien, the terrifying, and the inspiring, is associated with a religious sensibility in a nonreligious age. As James says, "if the appeal of sf is in a combination of the rational and the miraculous, then we ought to think about the ways in which sf fulfils a role once fulfilled by religion in an age in which for many the power of traditional religion has disappeared totally."[35]

Banks's body of work is already replete with images and devices associated with a sense of wonder: there's the emphasis on the almost inconceivable size of everything from the Culture ships to the fastness of *Feersum Endjinn*; the constant appearance of the inexplicable, from the Excession to the Shell-worlds; the fact that throughout his books everything is crowded with the strange, the alien, the mysterious. As Jim Clarke says, the Culture Minds fulfill the sort of divine role that "provokes the feelings of awe, delight or fear which mark the sublime."[36] It is telling, therefore, that within this vast and crowded universe, where everything is designed to humble the individual, Banks chose to give the next stage in evolutionary development the name of "Sublime." This is not just a self-conscious reference to the science-fictionality of his books, but a very deliberate acknowledgment of the Romantic idea of the sublime. To take this next step is to enter a world whose very immensity swallows us up, makes us small and insignificant, fills us with awe and terror.

In the terminology of the books, to be one of the major galactic civilizations is to be "In Play," and the Culture distinctly wants to go on playing while avoiding the awfully big adventure of the Sublime. Because just as the Romantic Sublime was associated with thoughts of death, so the Banksian Sublime becomes a sort of death—one fear of the Sublime is "that we might simply die or be blown away like mist" (*Hydrogen* 387–88)—at least, to those in play it appears as unknowable and as terminal as death. Which is no doubt why the Culture consistently shies away from Subliming, even though it is a natural and welcome stage that every other major galactic civilization comes to, because it equates subliming with death, and the Culture's civilization is predicated on avoiding death.

On a personal level, Culture humans live 350 to 400 years, then face a choice:

> They could opt for rejuvenation and/or complete immortality, they could become part of a group mind, they could simply die when the time came, they could transfer out of the Culture altogether, bravely accepting one of the open but essentially inscrutable invitations left by certain Elder civilisations, or they could go into Storage, with whatever revival criterion they desired. (*Excession* 81)

The option to die is in there, but as only one option among many, and the other options are more attractive, particularly for people who, on a civilization-wide basis, have been putting off any decision on subliming for millennia:

"the bulk of the Culture had chosen not to, determining instead to surf a line across the ever-breaking wave of galactic life continuation" (*Excession* 82). But even this suggests indecision rather than dread.

(In fairness, I should note that not every commentator equates the Sublime with death. Jim Clarke, for instance, suggests that "the Sublime functions as a form of endgame to the process of evolution within the galactic context. Sublimation is an alternative to what we might term retirement,"[37] a view that is supported by statements like this: "The Sublime was where you went when you felt you had no more to contribute to the life of the great galactic meta-civilisation, and—sometimes more importantly, depending on the species—when in turn you felt that it had no more to offer you" [*Hydrogen* 63], though I would argue that it is less an endgame to evolution than another stage of evolution.) True, there are some remnant civilizations that seem to be still in touch with those on the other side, the Chelgrians in *Look to Windward*, the Zihdren-Remnant in *The Hydrogen Sonata*; and there are even those that have returned, if only temporarily, from the Sublime, such as the Culture Mind *Zoologist* in *The Hydrogen Sonata*; but these always seem vague, unclear, a sort of pan-galactic spiritualism rather than any direct contact between the realities.

The seed of the last three Culture novels, in which the Culture's resistance to subliming becomes central, is sown here, but there is a sea change in attitude between now and then. The option to "suddenly sublime off into Advanced Elderhood" (*Excession* 167) would seem to equate subliming more with growth than with death, but it is still a step into the unknown.

The whole of *Excession* is about presenting the Culture with barriers it is reluctant to cross: the barrier between the nested universes represented by the Excession, the barrier of subliming, Dajeil's refusing to cross the barrier of giving birth. We begin to get a picture of the Culture as a deeply conservative society, too attached to its comforts and plenty to be easy with the idea of risk or change. More of *Excession* is actually set within the Culture than in any previous novel, yet we see very little of it. Our viewpoint characters tend to be divorced from the life of the Culture, such as Dajeil isolated aboard the *Sleeper Service,* or Gestra, who has chosen to live totally alone upon Pittance; or they are disaffected, like Genar-Hofoen, who begins the novel serving as an ambassador to the Affront, and finds so much more life in their crude violence that he wishes to be remade as an Affront and to live among them permanently. They are not, in other words, perspectives from which we can reasonably expect to view the Culture.

We see the Culture perhaps more fully through the Minds, who play a more substantial role in this novel than in any previous. As Christie March says, *Excession*, "perhaps more so than Banks' other novels, explores in depth the technological dominance of the Culture Minds."[38] But where Oliver Morton adds that "Banks' machines save us from ourselves. They remake society in their own perfectable image,"[39] there are two problems. First, in *Excession* the humans are out of the loop, unaware of and unaffected by most of what is going on, so the machines are effectively saving us from ourselves by removing us from the equation. A more fundamental problem is that the machines prove to be no more perfect than humans; throughout the novel they lie, deceive, conspire, and foment war. In other words, in character they are as fallible as humans. If *Excession* shows us the dominance of the Minds in shaping and managing the Culture, once again we see that it is far less a utopia, far less perfect, than it likes to present itself.

But the Minds are of a different order of consciousness than the humans. Other than their wariness at the idea of subliming, a trait that seems to be shared equally by humans and by machines within the Culture, the Minds do not think as humans do. Their speed of thought, their virtual immortality, give them a huge amount of time, and as Banks has said, "I thought, what would they do with all this time? Inventing a world where you have different laws of physics,"[40] the sort of thing that is clearly meant to differentiate them from humans. Yet, in the same interview Banks likens this activity to "the ultimate version of [the game] Civilisation," so they are perhaps not all that different. Nevertheless, the distinction is such that, although we might share the point of view of a human character or even a drone, we do not actually see through their eyes, as it were; all we do is listen in on their conversations.

Their messages are laid out as a form of email, so that large portions of the book read as an epistolary novel, complete with codes and abbreviations that are incomprehensible to the general reader. For example, the very first exchange we witness begins thus:

(GCU *Grey Area* signal sequence file #n428857/119)

.

[swept-to-tight beam, M16.4, received @ n4.28.857.3644]
xGSV *Honest Mistake*
oGCU *Grey Area*
**Take a look at this:**
∞
(Signal sequence #n428855/1446, relay:)
∞
1) [skein broadcast, Mclear, received @ n4.28.855.0065+]:
**\*!c11505.\*** (*Excession* 15, italics, bold, and all other marks in the original)

Later, these codes and abbreviations are spelled out to Ulver Seich, but even without this gloss we can understand as much as we need to. The strings of numbers beginning "n" indicate a date, "x" means from, "o" means to, and so forth. Even so, this is mostly background stuff that it is not strictly necessary for us to understand. As Banks says:

> It was just me trying to work out how it would actually work, what the Ships would need—it's a sort of anorackish [*sic*] tendency in myself to want to get all these technical details right. You have to have something at the beginning to tell you who's talking to whom, so you do need that—a formalisation of the protocol that would have to go on anyway when a Ship talks to another Ship. I just like that stuff! I think it's neat, which is probably rather sad on my part but there you are![41]

What matters, of course, is what is actually communicated by the Minds, and a lot of that—"**\*!c11505.\***"—is oblique to say the least. The drone Churt Lyne has to act as a translator for Ulver Seich, and we sense that such translation is necessary for all interactions between humans and Minds. The *Sleeper Service* is no better at understanding its human passenger, Dajeil. Out of such misunderstandings arise, willed or unwilled, the deceptions that crowd the novel.

Against a vast backcloth, such subtlety can get lost. Although not universally negative, the initial critical response wasn't exactly ecstatic. "There's a mounting impression that the book isn't about anything much,"[42] Chris Gilmore wrote in *Foundation*, while Joseph Nicholas in *Vector* said: "All this action and at the end everything just evaporates?"[43] Later critics would rate the novel more highly and more unequivocally, perhaps because by then there would be the context of later Culture novels against which to set it. Although *Excession* neatly ties off all the major plotlines—happy endings for most of the human characters, the war concluded, the conspiracy unmasked, the Excession withdrawn—it remains a novel that feels unresolved. In the final page, the Excession itself concludes that the Culture is too undeveloped and unstable for contact, but, as Robert Duggan said, "at least some Culture minds already suspect this inadequacy and are aware but not necessarily complacent about how the encounter with the Excession has highlighted their own imperfection."[44] This is true but only part of the story, since we see time and again that the Culture actively embraces imperfection and resists sublimation. As Duggan puts it, "The novel ends with rejection of, almost amounting to a disbelief in, closure and finitude,"[45] and that fear of an end is more and more true of the Culture as a whole. It would take another novel, *Look to Windward*, to start to resolve some of the threads begun in *Excession*.

But before Banks got around to the concluding volume in this diptych, there was another science fiction novel, *Inversions*. This is something of an anomaly in Banks's science fiction. He has said that *Against a Dark Background* was originally meant "to be a fantasy novel with a totally rational scientific background,"[46] and to a large extent that's exactly what *Inversions* turned out to be.

The setting is a planet at a late medieval political and technological level. As is typical of Banks, the story is told by two different narrators in alternating chapters. In the powerful kingdom of Haspidus, a young medical assistant, Oelph, secretly reports on Dr. Vosill to his unnamed master. Vosill is a woman and a foreigner who is, therefore, trusted by no one, except King Quience, to whom she has become personal physician. Meanwhile, in a distant land that has recently undergone a civil war (yet another of the civil wars that proliferate in Banks's novels), an unnamed narrator tells the story of DeWar, a foreigner who has become the bodyguard of the realm's new "Protector." Through these reports we learn that Vosill and DeWar are more foreign than we might expect, with a variety of clues that suggest they "come from a society of benevolent spacefarers with an advanced technology indistinguishable from magic."[47] The novel, as Kathryn Morrow's review might suggest, makes concrete Arthur C. Clarke's famous dictum that any sufficiently advanced technology would be indistinguishable from magic.

Any further identification of these two spacefarers is never made explicit within the book (it is not even made specific that they are spacefarers). It is worth noting that both the Iain M. Banks novel before this, *Excession*, and the one after, *Look to Windward*, were emblazoned with the phrase "The new Culture novel." No such phrase appears on the cover of *Inversions*. Despite her reference to "benevolent spacefarers," Morrow makes no specific allusion to the Culture novels, though *Inversions* seems to have been identified as a Culture novel right from the start. Gary Dalkin notes how it "mischievously"[48] refers to "a different Culture" on the first page, while David Langford suggests that those in the know "will kick themselves on noticing one [. . .] word blandly planted near the beginning, plus a telltale two-word phrase in the epilogue."[49] In a later footnote to this review, Langford takes Banks to task for writing a

> Culture-sequence novel in disguise. What's naughty about this is that the ace in the hole which saves the Doctor *in extremis* appears to be a Culture "knife missile"—a semi-intelligent autonomous weapon—disguised as a jewel on her blunt old dagger, a point which isn't elucidated within *Inversions* itself. Familiarity with other Culture novels, such as *Consider Phlebas* or *Use of Weapons*, is required to make sense of it.[50]

It does nothing to blunt the force of Langford's criticism to note that there are many more hints and clues to its status as a Culture novel within the text than the two that Langford has picked up. This remains a novel that largely pretends not to be a Culture novel, yet whose pivotal moment can be fully understood only by those already familiar with other Culture novels. There is a sense, therefore, of teasing the fans rather than writing a fully independent novel. Nevertheless, for those happy to be teased, or for those content to let some references pass them by, it was still a good and very well-received novel: Dalkin said, "It seems to me to be as fine as anything he has written, and that is very fine indeed."[51]

The two clues that Langford picks up occur at the very beginning and the very end of the novel. The opening, "A Note on the Text," has been omitted from later paperback editions of the book; Simone Caroti, who does not share Langford's concerns about playing fair with the reader, concludes that this omission has "something to do with giving the game away at the outset."[52] The Note is written by Oelph's grandson, who found the two narratives among his grandfather's papers, and mentions that Vosill "may, or may not, have been from the distant Archipelago of Drezen but who was, without Argument, from a different Culture" (*Inversions* 1). The author of this brief note is given to capitalizing odd words, but this is clearly a nod to Banks's many Culture fans. In an epilogue at the end of the novel it is reported that Vosill disappeared at sea during her return to Drezen. A high wind and bright lights play about the ship, and when they clear, the doctor is no longer aboard. She "had been invited to dine with the vessel's captain that evening, but had sent a note declining the invitation, citing an indisposition due to special circumstances" (*Inversions* 341). The implication that she was picked up by a Culture ship from Special Circumstances is both playful and inescapable.

In between these bookends, a host of hints and suggestions keep those in the know alive to the fact that this is a Culture novel in disguise. DeWar, the bodyguard, tells a story about "a magical land where every man was a king, every woman a queen, every boy a prince and all girls princesses. In this land there were no hungry people and no crippled people" (*Inversions* 89). It's a story very similar to the one Zakalwe tells the Ethnarch in *Use of Weapons*, about a land that "had no kings, no laws, no money and no property, but . . . everybody lived like a prince" (*Use* 29). That story is overtly an oblique reference to the Culture; and the same is probably true here. As the concubine Perrund says: "This sounds a very equivocal land" (*Inversions* 90). We are, of course, meant to recognize Vosill and DeWar as Sechroom and Hiliti in these stories of Lavishia (presumably, though never explicitly, a Culture Orbital). We note, for instance, that Sechroom has a triangular scar above her left ear, and, sure enough, when the torturer Ralinge shaves Vosill's head, "at one place, over her left ear, his hands stopped and he looked more closely" (*Inversions* 300). Also Sechroom gives Hiliti a wooden ring, and in one version of the end of DeWar and Perrund's story their company's symbol is "a simple torus, a ring, such as might be cut from one end of a hollow pipe" (*Inversions* 345). The identification of Vosill and DeWar with Sechroom and Hiliti is, of course, a part of the novel's romance plot; a counterpoint to the romance of *Excession*, it is a story in which the separated lovers never reunite. But it also places the two protagonists within the fairytale realm we recognize as the Culture. Coincidentally, Vosill's talk of her supposed homeland, Drezen, is characterized by her enemy, Duke Walen, as "in such glowing terms that sometimes I thought you were describing a fairy-tale land" (*Inversions* 193). At one point, Vosill has a transcription of a conversation she could not have overheard, suggesting some listening device alien to this society. And when she criticizes the world map that Duke Quettil presents to the king, she does so in terms that suggest observation from space, speaking, for instance, of islands that are "more numerous, generally smaller, less regular and extend further to the north" (*Inversions* 140). When Nolieti the torturer is murdered, Vosill uses a medical terminology unknown to the other doctor present and can draw conclusions from the victim's wounds that are meaningless to everyone else. At the ball her gown is "unfashionably narrow" (*Inversions* 190) and "she was afraid of making some error of etiquette" (*Inversions* 191), suggestive of someone indeed from a different Culture, and she knows things about the Sequestered or Half-Hidden Kingdoms that are not common knowledge. More dramatically, when two scoundrels attempt to rape Vosill, they are knocked out by a force they do not know, and "the blades of their knives had been twisted, bent right round and made a knot of" (*Inversions* 244), something that requires a technology way beyond what is available on this planet. At the climax of the novel, when Ralinge is about to rape her, Vosill says something in "a different kind of language. [. . .] A language from nowhere" (*Inversions* 301–2), and the old knife she habitually carries presumably turns into a Culture knife missile, because that is the only thing that could have caused the mayhem while she was bound. But the mayhem is not witnessed, the knife missile is not named, and the book progresses by indirection and implication, not Banks's usual direct mode. If these features don't specifically mark Vosill as Culture, they certainly separate her from local mores and understandings.

Concluding that this is a Culture novel is pretty inescapable. It is less clear why it should be a Culture novel, and why that fact should be disguised. I would argue that, perhaps alone of all the Culture novels, *Inversions* presents Culture interference in other worlds in an entirely benevolent, even romantic light. It is an inversion of *Excession*, "the Culture from above, and then from below,"[53] as Nick Gevers put it in an interview; but here the Culture itself is the Outside Context Problem viewed entirely from the perspective of the less advanced civilization, (which is why the identity of the spacefarers needs to be disguised). One representative brings medicine and enlightened social views to the most advanced nation, while the other protects a new, relatively humane leader. In a sense, both fail: the doubt and suspicion that Vosill engenders among the aristocracy eventually prove too much, and she withdraws; DeWar is, in the end, unable to prevent the assassination of his charge and has to flee. Yet in both cases we get a sense that the seeds sown have taken root and the world will be a better place as a result. Every other novel moves between the Culture and one or more outside societies. We see the effects, for good or ill, of their engagement with other civilizations. We accept their self-presentation of being a utopia; yet always their motivations are open to question. Here, for one time only, we do not see inside the Culture, and perhaps as a consequence, we do not question their motives. Moreover, there is a frustrated, unfulfilled love story that links the two, another reason we see their actions as an unalloyed good.

As to whether it should have been disguised, there is, as I have indicated, a good reason those who perceive these visitors should remain unaware of their origin. Banks even draws attention to the disguise: we do not know until the final pages of the book who is receiving Oelph's reports on Vosill or who is relating the story of DeWar "after the fashion of the Jeritic fabulists" (*Inversions* 21–22), a style of "Closed Chronicle" that deliberately withholds the identity of the narrator. Moreover, as the invented "Closed Chronicle" suggests, there is the technical challenge also, in this case of writing a nonspecific Culture novel. Such varied works as *Walking on Glass*, *The Bridge*, *Use of Weapons*, and *Feersum Endjinn* indicate that Banks loved to set himself structural or linguistic challenges in his novels. As he put it to Nick Gevers: "*Inversions* was an attempt to write a Culture novel that wasn't. Also I enjoyed the discipline of writing about a non-historical time without instant communication and smart-ass machines (and also without enchanted swords and other assorted pixie-associated-stuff . . . though also with the capability of using an enchanted dagger if I chose to . . . )."[54] But that "enchanted dagger" remains the problem, as David Langford pointed out: when understanding a significant plot turn depends on knowledge of previous books, it is not exactly playing fair with the readers.

Curiously, playing fair is actually one of the themes of the novel. Of all of the Culture novels, perhaps because it is the least critical, *Inversions* is the one most directly concerned with morality. For instance, the whole of the prologue, written in old age by Oelph recalling the deeds of his youth, is an expatiation on the idea of selfishness as the core of all sin (as Jude Roberts notes, selfishness is an abiding interest that crops up again in such diverse works as *Surface Detail* and *Transition*[55]). The book consistently challenges notions of what is a sin and what is not, what is right and what is not. At one point, there is a discussion between Vosill and Oelph in which she suggests that things happen for "no reason beyond the workings of pure chance" (*Inversions* 108), a notion that horrifies him: "Do they not think that there is good and bad? And that one deserves to be emulated and the other not, but rather punished?" (*Inversions* 108). Vosill is a free thinker, which clearly marks her out from the society around her, as typified by Oelph's musing: "Did the Doctor really imagine that everybody went around believing different things? One believed what one was told to believe, what it made sense to believe" (*Inversions* 109). Vosill brings to a straitlaced society a freedom of speech, a directness of approach, that makes those around her uncomfortable. As Oelph says, she behaves with a "certain immodest forthrightness [. . .] plus the suspicion that while she pays flawless lip service to the facts of life which dictate the accepted and patent preeminence of the male, she does so with a sort of unwarranted humour, producing in us males the unsettling contrary feeling that she is indulging us" (*Inversions* 11).

Vosill's freedom, in dress and manner and thought, sets the aristocracy of Haspidus against her, which in turn generates conspiracies to destroy her, or at least her influence on the king. The conspiracies fail largely because she is more robust than they assume a woman to be. Thus, in practically our first glimpse of her, Vosill is summoned to the torture chamber where the chief torturer, Nolieti, wants her to preserve the life of a man he is putting to the question. Instead, secretly, she kills the man, robbing the torturer of his victim. Despite being a doctor sworn to preserve life, moral repugnance at torture trumps that. Thus when she herself is brought before Nolieti's successor, Ralinge, and is about to be raped, Vosill unleashes her knife missile, slaughtering Ralinge and his henchmen. Twice she visits the torture chamber, twice she brings death. (Parenthetically, I note that once again Banks employs both torture and rape as signifiers of moral wrong and as plot devices, a pattern that is already becoming questionable.) Physically, this is a woman who does not consent to her own subjugation or crumble in the face of violence; mentally she is also able to out-think her rivals. Thus when Walen springs his surprise by producing gaan Kuduhn from Drezen, an act which is supposed to catch her out in a lie about her origin, Vosill responds with joy and in fluent Drezeni, which even makes the reader momentarily conclude she is a native. This view of her mental agility is reinforced when, in her cups, she says: "I do believe that old bastard Walen thought he was setting me up" (*Inversions* 272).

In contrast (and the stories of Vosill and DeWar do often invert each other), in the Tassasen Protectorate DeWar's job of keeping General UrLeyn alive rarely involves killing anyone, and his most significant act is to work out how the general's son is being slowly poisoned and thus save his life. In fact, throughout these portions of the novel we most often encounter DeWar in the palace harem, telling his tales of Lavishia to the general's son and to the concubine, Perrund. Where Vosill's story consists of conspiracies and violence in a realm at peace, DeWar's is full of images of peace in a realm at war. In the end, when Perrund is herself revealed as UrLeyn's assassin, DeWar doesn't kill her but elopes with her, another reason to regard this novel as essentially a romance.

Both Vosill and DeWar act as irritants in the conservative societies slowly and often painfully emerging into what we would recognize as the modern world. Their very irritation has a progressive effect upon the world: for once, Culture interference works. But this has to be balanced with the next Culture novel, in which such interference emphatically does not work.

One way of looking at *Inversions* is as marking time before concluding the Culture sequence, which is what I believe *Look to Windward* was intended to do. It is, however, interesting to note that the theme of benevolent intervention played out in *Inversions* is also central to the next "mainstream" novel, another flirtation with the Scottish fantastic, *The Business* (1999). Here young Kate McGurk from a broken family in the Scottish slums is taken up by Mrs. Telman, who is identified by Pisarska as having "an aura of magic and the unknown about herself"[56] and whose benevolent interventions include finding Kate's mother higher-paying jobs so she can perform her maternal functions better. As a result of this, Kate's material circumstances improve, and she finds herself taken in by a massive, globe-spanning corporation, the Business of the title, that has been building its secret web since Roman times. At first the Business, a terrestrial Culture that incorporates many different peoples so long as they subscribe to the corporate ethos and abjure all religious and national loyalties, appears quasi-utopian, particularly as near-limitless wealth brings immense freedom. But as Kate rises in the hierarchy she finds its actions more and more open to question. Eventually she discovers that she herself is due to be traded in marriage to the ruler of a small Himalayan kingdom, which the Business plans to take over in order to gain a seat at the United Nations. Her life rotates among a series of Banksian castles—Blysecrag, the Gothic mansion in Yorkshire, the dreamlike Chateau d'Oex in Switzerland, and the Royal Palace in Thulahn—each of which emphasizes detachment from reality. (Interestingly, Katarzyna Pisarska compares Thulahn to Gatún Lake in *Canal Dreams*, where "the protagonist has meaningful dreams, and where her quest for self finds an (un)expected resolution,"[57] and sees Kate as resembling Isis Whit and Hisako Onoda.) By the end of the novel, Kate faces a choice between the modern, scientific, rational world of the Business and the traditional, natural world of Thulahn. Inevitably, since the Business is all the family Kate has, that is where the threat comes from, but like Isis in *Whit*, Kate eventually chooses community, though with an eye to modernization. Both worlds win, or at any rate achieve a measure of equilibrium.

Bringing the Culture down to Earth as the Business exposes some of the equivocation Banks seems to have been feeling about that aggressively rationalist civilization. At first it had been utopia, at least on a personal level: no money worries, great sex, the ability to be and do whatever you might want. But as he had shown in *The Player of Games*, in the face of barbarism it can become necessary to behave like a barbarian; and that notion, always implicit in Banks's fiction, returns to center stage in *Look to Windward* when the Masaq' Hub, talking about destroying Orbitals when it was a warship during the Idiran War, says: "War can alter your perceptions, change your sense of values. I didn't want to feel that what I was doing was anything other than momentous and horrific; even, in some first principles sense, barbaric" (*Look* 278). By the time of *Excession* that underlying sense of undermining moral principles had turned into open betrayal and treachery. Despite the last gasp of *Inversions*, which tries to insist that the Culture is truly good, really, on a corporate level the Culture was capable of behaving as well or as badly as any of the exaggeratedly cruel cultures he pitted against it. And there was the question, raised in *Excession* but not pursued, of what comes next. The natural life of all galactic civilizations is to flourish for a while and then sublime, but the Culture was consciously and deliberately bucking this trend, was shying away from subliming as much as anyone might shy from death. So where does the Culture go from here; how does it face a move into the unknown that clearly frightens it? That becomes the central question of what, I am convinced, was intended as the final Culture novel, *Look to Windward*.

The very title of the novel indicates that it completes a circle begun with *Consider Phlebas*. The two phrases appear consecutively in the "Death by Water" section of T.S. Eliot's "The Waste Land":

> Gentile or Jew
> O you who turn the wheel and look to windward,
> Consider Phlebas, who was once handsome and tall as you.[58]

The poem, set within a post–World War I urban landscape of "physical and spiritual decay, crumbling apart—a world of fragmentation,"[59] directs us to look for the rot below the surface, the skull beneath the skin. Felix Danczak, in an otherwise fascinating account of the immense influence this poem had on Banks's science fiction, curiously misinterprets the key line as "emphasising that we must take control of our fates. We must 'turn the wheel' for ourselves to survive."[60] A better interpretation would be that whoever takes the wheel of a sailing vessel will keep a weather eye to windward, for your fate comes from that direction, and your fate, ultimately, is inevitably that of "Phlebas the Phoenician, a fortnight dead."[61]

We might, crudely, identify Horza with Phlebas, and the consequences of his fate, that Idiran War, blows in from windward to affect the Masaq' Orbital in *Look to Windward*. In other words, this novel closes off the sequence initiated more than a decade before. And, as Eliot's poem implies, it tells how the Culture, once handsome and tall, must face the common fate of Phlebas.

As I have suggested, *Look to Windward* is the third of a loose trilogy of novels, including *Consider Phlebas* and *Excession*, in which the Culture and its enemies are shown to be shaped by the Idiran War. Although it is set eight hundred years after that war, *Look to Windward* still presents it as inescapable, an event that defines the Culture and that is the key event in Culture history: everything dates from that time. Exactly 803 years before, two suns had been induced to go nova by the Idirans, wiping out billions of people in their biospheres; now the light from those two novae is reaching Masaq' Orbital. The Mind that controls the Orbital has its own reasons for commemorating the battle and has declared the period between when the light from the first and the second nova reaches the Orbital as a period of mourning. The principal events of the novel take place within that period; in other words, the whole book is framed by death and by the response to death.

If the frame within which we must see the novel is shaped by one long-ago war, the events that precipitate the action are the consequence of another war—in fact, another civil war. In *Inversions* (and again, by analogy, in *The Business*), interference in the affairs of others is presented as beneficial, but in *Consider Phlebas* the Culture had been culpable in a long and costly war; in *Excession* elements of the Culture had attempted to initiate another war to complete unfinished business from the first war, and now, in *Look to Windward*, interference that had gone drastically wrong was again implicating the Culture in a costly war. The Culture had intruded into the politics on the planet Chel in order to end a brutal caste system that deformed Chelgrian society. Unfortunately, it miscalculated, and its chosen mouthpiece used his new position of power to launch a devastating war of revenge. Although the Culture had stepped in again to bring the war to an end, still billions had died, and the Culture was reviled as warmongers.

What is unusual about the Chelgrians is that a portion of their civilization had sublimed at a very early stage in their development and had then remained in contact with those who stayed behind. What the Chelgrians did with this was build a heaven very similar to Chelgrian mythology (prefiguring *Surface Detail*). The sublimed Chelgrians hold that those killed in war cannot enter heaven until an equal number of the enemy have been killed, and so a faction among the Chelgrians plot to destroy a Culture Orbital, Masaq', as an act of revenge and redemption. Their agent in this is Quilan, a Chelgrian soldier turned monk who is himself in profound mourning for the death of his wife during the war.

Every aspect of the novel, from broad plot points to individual motivation, is informed by death. Even the incidental encounters along the way, the scene-setting descriptions, hinge upon ways of dying, attitudes toward death, or types of mourning. To borrow an apposite analogy from *Excession*, death is an Outside Context Problem to be encountered as a sentence encounters a full stop.

The novel opens with a scene in a foxhole in the middle of the Chelgrian civil war. Worosei is on the point of having to abandon her husband, Quilan, who is trapped under a tank (here called a Land Destroyer, an obvious homage to H. G. Wells's Land Ironclads, but a tank nonetheless) and clearly beyond rescue. The marriage is tender and it adds piquancy to the generic battle scene. Here, for perhaps the last time in his science fiction (and war, which is commonplace in his sf, is vanishingly rare in his mainstream fiction), Banks presents war as messy, painful, and sad rather than grand and cruel, a significant change in his work. By a twist of fate, Quilan is rescued at the last minute, and it is Worosei who is killed. In one strand of the novel we follow Quilan as he recovers from his injuries, learns of his wife's fate, retreats into a monastery out of remorse, then is recruited and trained for the mission against Masaq' Orbital. By the time he arrives on the Orbital he has implanted in him the personality of Sholan Hadesh Huyler, an admiral-general of the Chelgrian Combined Forces who has been dead for eighty-six years, so there is a further sense of death being conquered. It is assumed that Huyler will ensure that Quilan sticks to his mission, but the details of that mission have been temporarily erased from Quilan's memory and will only gradually be recovered.

Counterpointing Quilan's story, we follow the Homomdan Ambassador on Masaq', Kabe Ischloear. Quilan's cover story in coming to Masaq' is to try to persuade the dissident Chelgrian composer, Ziller, to return to Chel. Ziller has been commissioned by Masaq' Hub to compose a major work to mark the end of the period of mourning, and he has no intention of even meeting Quilan, let alone of returning to Chel. As a friend of Ziller, and, not being of the Culture, as a presumed disinterested party, Kabe is asked by Masaq' Hub to liaise with Quilan and hopefully bring the two Chelgrians together. If *Excession* often takes the form of an epistolary novel relating the communications between the varying Culture ships, *Look to Windward* frequently takes the form of dialogues between Quilan and Huyler, and between Kabe and Ziller. What this means is that while more of *Look to Windward* is actually set in the Culture than just about any other novel in the sequence, we again see it exclusively through the eyes of outsiders, as this exchange between Kabe and Ziller makes plain:

> "You don't think I bait the humans too much, do you?" Ziller asked. He sucked on his pipe, frowning at it.
> "I think they enjoy it," Kabe said.
> "Really? Oh." Ziller sounded disappointed.
> "We help to define them. They like that."
> "Define them? Is that all?"
> "I don't think that's the only reason they like to have us here, certainly not in your case. But we give them an alien standard to calibrate themselves against." (*Look* 53)

And, of course, it gives Banks and his readers a position from which they can calibrate the Culture. In fact, only two Culture citizens play anything more than a fleeting role in the story; one is the avatar of Masaq' Hub, the other is Uagen, who is far from the Culture investigating the extraordinarily alien behemothaurs out toward the edge of the galaxy, and whose adventures impinge only tangentially upon the main story.

With occasional flashbacks to Quilan's preparations, the novel consists mostly of tours around Masaq' Orbital by Kabe along with either Ziller or Quilan, and these tours mostly illustrate attitudes toward death. This overarching theme of death is signaled early on when we learn that in the Culture people

> lived or died by whim! A few of their more famous people announced they would live once and die forever, and billions did likewise; then a new trend would start amongst opinion-formers for people to back-up and have their bodies wholly renewed or new ones regrown, or to have their personalities transferred into android replicas or some other more bizarre design, or . . . well, anything; there was really no limit. (*Look* 10)

Death is not meaningless, but there are so many ways of avoiding death that it becomes little more than a fashion statement. Indeed, since most people have their personalities recorded, they can be immediately reborn if ever they do die, or, as we saw in *Excession*, be stored somewhere for revival at a later date.

But if death has no reality, there is a suggestion that life itself loses its savor, which is why we repeatedly see Culture citizens taking part in extreme sports. For example, when Feli Vitrouv is about to fly with a wing suit above a dense forest, Kabe worries, "But you might die," to which she replies, "That's the whole point" (*Look* 43). Indeed, the point seems to be to come close to death, since we are told: "Feli Vitrouv was one of about half of the wing-fliers for whom no recording of her mind-state existed to revive them if they dived into the ground and were killed. It gave Kabe an unpleasant feeling just thinking about it. 'They call themselves the Disposables,' he said" (*Look* 52). Another extreme sport is rafting on lava: "'[M]ost of the people you saw there had lava-rafted before and had just as awful a time. [. . .] Though it has to be said that two of them have experienced temporary body-death when their lava canoe capsized and one of them—a one-timer, a Disposable—was crushed to death while glacier-caving.' 'Completely dead?' 'Very completely, and forever'" (*Look* 95). As they discuss the Culture penchant for extreme sports, Ziller argues: "They spend time travelling. The time weighs heavy on them because they lack any context, any valid framework for their lives. They persist in hoping that something they think they'll find in the place they're heading for will somehow provide them with a fulfilment they feel certain they deserve and yet have never come close to experiencing" (*Look* 98). To this, Kabe replies: "All naturally evolved sentient life is restless. At some scale or stage" (*Look* 99). Ziller is unconvinced: "[H]aving carefully constructed their paradise from first principles to remove all credible motives for conflict amongst themselves and all natural threats . . . these people then find their lives are so hollow they have to recreate false versions of just the sort of terrors untold generations of their ancestors spent their existences attempting to conquer" (*Look* 99). At one point, Ziller says to the hub avatar: "I'm becoming as thoughtlessly blasé about risk and death as your inhabitants" (*Look* 261), as if a careless disregard for death was one of the defining characteristics of Culture citizens. In fact, the issue is not so much death as a loss of interest in life. When Ziller and the Hub's avatar visit a dying man, he is quite content with his lot: "[I]t's time to change or move on or just stop . . . but really I can't be bothered living any more" (*Look* 267).

The dread of dying only really comes into the story in one extraordinary passage when the Hub describes the death of a Mind in battle: "It was over in a micro-second, but we felt it die bit by bit, area by distorted area, memory by disappearing memory [. . .]. [. . .] We experienced everything it experienced; all its bewilderment and terror, each iota of anger and pride, every last nuance of grief and anguish" (*Look* 279). This contrasts with the feelings the Hub describes when it talks of the destruction it was responsible for during the Idiran War, destruction that has fueled feelings of guilt ever since and that lies behind the period of mourning it has prescribed. It talks about feeling "Elated" (*Look* 278); behind the terror and pain of war and of death there is also elation. It is an ambiguity that is, I think, in Banks as much as in his fiction (the dedication of this novel, for instance, was "For the Gulf War Veterans" [*Look* vii]), and as Banks's own personal response to war became more pronounced over the next few years, so the sense of the fascination of war became more overt in his later fictions. However much he recognizes the terror of death in war, in that part of the Culture that remains Banks's personal utopia death's sting has been removed, because he has introduced so many ways to avoid it. Perhaps that is why he finds it such a compelling subject in this novel.

Death is equally the most consistent feature in Quilan's story. When Quilan comes to terms with the death of his wife, he thinks: "Gone utterly and forever. Gone in a way that was new, bereft of the comforts of ignorance, and without appeal" (*Look* 40), as if death is the novelty. On a monastic retreat he talks of his jealousy of Worosei's death in regard of the heaven that the sublimed Chelgrians have created:

> In the old days people died and that was that; you might hope to see them in heaven, but once they were dead they were dead. It was simple, it was definite. Now . . . Now people die but their Soulkeeper can revive them, or take them to a heaven we know exists, without any need for faith. We have clones, we have regrown bodies—most of me is regrown; I wake up sometimes and think, Am I still me? I know you're supposed to be your brain, your wits, your thoughts, but I don't believe it is that simple. (*Look* 142–43)

As the old monk says, "We live in a time when the dead can return" (*Look* 143). "They knew now that there came a time in the development of every civilisation—which lasted long enough—when its inhabitants could record their mind-state, effectively taking a reading of the person's personality which could be stored, duplicated, read, transmitted and, ultimately, installed into any suitable complex and enabled device or organism" (*Look* 143). Such technologies suggest a materialist universe, with more spiritually inclined societies, it is implied, turning away from the technology, though it might lead to their eclipse or extinction. Even heaven (or, as in *Surface Detail*, hell) is no more than a technological construct; the afterlife need be no more than a continuation of ordinary life for as long as people can be bothered to carry on. For Banks, therefore, this is a way of emphasizing the atheist nature of his vision even while building the whole structure around ideas of death and immortality.

But the death of the individual also stands for the death of the whole society, the subliming that the Culture has been putting off. In a long account of the phenomenon at, roughly, the midpoint of the novel, which shows how much the story pivots on this issue, we are told that "subliming was an accepted if still somewhat mysterious part of galactic life; it meant leaving the normal matter-based life of the universe behind and ascending to a higher state of existence based on pure energy" (*Look* 145). Generally, a whole society, species, or civilization tended to sublime together: "only the Culture was known to worry that such—to it—unlikely absoluteness implied a degree of coercion" (*Look* 145). To Sublime is the usual endpoint for most galactic civilizations; "to Sublime was to retire from the normal life of the galaxy" (*Look* 145). Ascending to such a nonmaterial phase of being would seem to be not just an invariable stage in the development of civilization, but generally a welcome one. For such a decidedly materialist society, however, the idea of the Sublime seems to contradict everything that the Culture has been built upon. Thus, the Culture had, in common with other advanced civilizations, attempted to build perfect AIs, unaffected by the character of their source species, but such perfect AIs invariably Sublimed, and "the Culture, more or less alone, seemed to find the phenomenon almost a personal insult" (*Look* 110). Something of the Culture's distrust of Subliming can be gleaned from a conversation at the start of chapter 11: nothing can happen in heaven because "if something *can* happen, then it doesn't represent eternity. [. . .] if you prevent the possibility of the alteration of an individual's circumstances [. . .] then you don't have life after death; you just have death" (*Look* 203–4). As for the technologically manufactured heavens: "These so-called heavens will not last. There will be war in them, or between them" (*Look* 204). The speaker is not identified, but the voice sounds like Ziller, though in this cynicism he is probably close to Culture thinking.

It is not unknown for elements of the Culture to Sublime; the Mind that previously controlled Masaq' Orbital had done so, for example. Yet when the Hub says of Culture Minds: "We are close to gods, and on the far side" (*Look* 280), we have to ask, the far side of what? Is it suggesting they have passed through death, that they have already effectively Sublimed? And during the Hub's final confrontation with Quilan, it says of the eight hundred years since the Idiran War that it's "a long time for an Involved to stay quite as determinedly in-play as we have. But our power may have peaked; we may be becoming complacent, even decadent" (*Look* 338). There is more than a suggestion in this that the Culture is reaching the end of the line. As I wrote at the time, "the Culture is dying. Not literally, not noticeably, but its hegemony has already lasted longer than any of its predecessors, and it is becoming notably decadent."[62] The novel was already "a meditation on loss,"[63] already in mourning for the passing of the Culture. After this, there was nowhere else to go.

## CHaPTeR 4

## APPROACHING THE WORLDGOD

It was more than a year after *Look to Windward* appeared in the United Kingdom before it was published by Pocket Books in the United States. Consequently, Gerald Jonas reviewed it in the immediate aftermath of the attack on the World Trade Center. Inevitably, he saw comparisons between the events of 9/11 and a novel that concerns a terrorist plot to kill billions, a plot intimately connected with the twin destruction of the two novas. "What Banks has to say about idealism, fanaticism, revenge, blame and forgiveness made as much sense to me as the news and analysis that blared nonstop from my television set," Jonas said, and "what's important in Banks's work is the subtext, which I take to be the idea that freedom is both necessary and dangerous, and that only by imagining the unimaginable, both in ourselves and others, can we hope to remain free."[1]

Any connection between *Look to Windward* and the events of 9/11 was, of course, no more than coincidence. Nevertheless, in a book written nearly two years before the fact, he seems to have caught the spirit of the times far more effectively than in books in which he consciously tried to reflect that moment. Banks's next mainstream novel, *Dead Air* (2002), for instance, specifically references the attack on the twin towers, and other recent news events, in the way he had in *The State of the Art*. Yet *Dead Air* was one of the least well-received of Banks's novels. Stephen Poole, writing in the *Guardian*, was typical. The attack on the twin towers looms over the book, he says, "but the novel does nothing with it; it is merely set-dressing. One of the few direct references—when Ken refers to 'the fundamentalist intensity of those who secretly guess they may well be wrong'—just seems spectacularly incorrect, the sort of comfortable liberal solipsism (no one can seriously think differently from the way we do, can they?) that a more sophisticated novel might have tried to anatomise."[2]

As it happened, *Dead Air* also marked the end of one stage of Banks's career. He took a one-year break from writing fiction, during which he produced *Raw Spirit*, ostensibly a travel book about the whisky distilleries of Scotland, though it was far more a hymn of praise to fast cars and old friends. He followed this with *The Algebraist*, and then there was nothing for three years. This stuttering final act was precipitated by a string of changes affecting, to very different degrees, both Banks's life and his writing. In the summer of 1998 he had been involved in a near-fatal car accident; "Typically, he emerged from the wreckage beaming, with cuts and bruises, to tell a horrified Italian couple who had stopped to help: 'Thank God for airbags!'"[3] By good fortune, he suffered no major injuries, but it is the sort of incident that prompts a reevaluation. On March 21, 2003, in protest at the way the government of Tony Blair was pushing the country into the Iraq War, he and his wife "cut [their] passports in half and sent the remains to Mr Blair's office in Downing Street" (*Raw* 6), an act that, temporarily at least, merely proved inconvenient when it came to trying to promote his books abroad. This did, however, mark the start of an increasingly vocal engagement in politics. More devastating was the state of his increasingly troubled marriage to Annie Blackburn. In 2006 Banks began a relationship with Adele Hartley, the following year he and Annie announced their separation, and they were divorced in 2009. It is undoubtedly this that lies behind the unusually long gap between the publication of *The Algebraist* in 2004 and the appearance of *The Steep Approach to Garbadale* in 2007. Perhaps an even longer-lasting effect on his fiction came with the death of James Hale in August 2003. To this point, Hale had edited every one of Banks's novels (with the sole and oft-regretted exception of *The State of the Art*), and so Banks lost the one voice he relied on above all others when it came to honing his work for publication. As he said in a 2010 interview, "I'm not as edited as I used to be, but that's really down to one guy, the very late and very great James Hale."[4] Subsequent science fiction novels in particular seem to be longer than their predecessors, more cluttered with info-dumps and subplots, asides and distractions, as if they are sorely in need of a sharp editorial scalpel.

Interestingly, in her *Guardian* review of *The Algebraist*, the first novel published after the death of James Hale, Justina Robson comments that "the lack of an editorial shepherd has left it to guzzle itself silly all over the paddock and get a bit fat and compulsive."[5] The novel is an overblown space opera set in the year 4034 A.D. in a universe in which humanity is the new kid on the block. It is a novel in which the age of the universe is constantly emphasized: races are billions of years old; we are told of a succession of wars, some fought long before humanity had even struggled out of the primeval swamp; travel, without the wormholes that are an essential plot device, is something that can take centuries. In the Culture novels we are perpetually reminded of the scale of everything we encounter, but here it feels as though we are being beaten over the head with hugeness, as if Banks is nervous that we won't recognize the space operatic nature of the work without intimations of immensity on every page. In one of the relatively few interviews Banks gave to promote the book, he described it as "very complicated, very baroque. It has loads of back-story. Basically, I had to write the entire history of the galaxy in which it's set. Ten million years. That took all of one Tuesday, as I recall."[6] Despite the typically self-deprecating jokiness of that final remark, this is pretty much what Banks does in far too many of the info-dumps that litter the work, and yet most of that backstory does not impinge directly on the action. We do not need details of an earlier war in order to understand the horrors of the war that is actually taking place now.

This may, in part, be down to the fact that Banks was doing something he hadn't done before. In the Culture novels he had created a left-leaning, nonhierarchical model for space opera, a reinvention of the form that fed into what became known as the New Space Opera. His earlier non-Culture space opera, *Against a Dark Background*, had contrasted an excessively capitalist society against the post-scarcity universe of the Culture, but he had not done that by reverting to the older form that he and Ken MacLeod had consciously worked against. In *The Algebraist*, however, Banks deliberately turns his back on all of the innovations he had helped pioneer, and he does not seem to be entirely comfortable in doing so.

In the beginning there is a suggestion that Banks is still holding to his fundamental idea that central characters in space operas cannot be major players in great events; that one individual cannot, through their actions, save the universe or hold the key to the future. This is grandiose, superhero thinking that has no place in the communal, socialistic approach that Banks takes to his fiction. Thus, in the prologue, the narrator tells us right at the start: "My own direct part in [the events of the novel] was vanishingly small and I have not thought even to introduce myself with anything as presumptuous as a proper name" (*Algebraist* 1). The nameless narrator, therefore, introduces himself as HG, for Head Gardener; he is a position not an individual (though one wonders if this is not also a tip of the hat to H. G. Wells?). But, having introduced himself, HG then disappears from the rest of the story, which in its structure and language betrays no hint of such an offscreen narrator. Only in a very brief epilogue does HG reappear, and his story clearly has no more than an oblique relationship to the events in the bulk of the novel.

Once the story proper starts, we are introduced to a central character, Fassin, who is summoned by the highest authority to take part in an expedition that could decide the fate of worlds; in other words, he is called upon to play the sort of world-saving "great man" role familiar from more conservative space operas. In keeping with this, the story is set within an aristocratic realm—"the monumental, bamboozling, hierarchic system that had surrounded them all since birth" (*Algebraist* 59)—a place of ritual, formality and extravagant titles. Thus, when Fassin visits his uncle, "he was aware that his attitude might be influenced by the fact that according to the customs of their family and the rules of their caste, the seniority and deference presently accorded his uncle would one day fall to him" (*Algebraist* 16). Throughout the novel, death and destruction are rained upon the hierarchic Mercatoria, the byzantine human society that governs this solar system, and we learn that Fassin is secretly an agent of the Beyonders, the anarchistic group snapping at the edges of the Mercatoria and perpetrating occasional terrorist outrages. Yet, at the end, when Fassin is restored as such hero figures must be, the hierarchy is back in place, the Beyonders are back on the edges of the system, and such changes as may be promised for the future are small and gradual. It is sometimes hard to accept that the political sensibility behind the early Culture novels also produced this.

Nor is the Mercatoria the only hierarchical society on display. Indeed, apart from the Beyonders, who are mentioned but barely glimpsed, there is no character in the novel who is not part of some highly structured society. The Beyonders have entered into an uneasy alliance with a violent dictator, the Archimandrite Luseferous, whose entire society, at least all that we see of it, is organized on strict military lines. And there are the Dwellers, "large creatures of immense age who lived within the deliriously complex and topologically vast civilisation of great antiquity" (*Algebraist* 21), suggestive of the behemothaurs in *Look to Windward*. The Dwellers make their home in the gas giant Nasqueron and hold the key that Fassin is commissioned to find. They have a complex series of divisions and subdivisions of the stages of life through which they pass—Adolescence, Youth, Adulthood, Prime, Cuspian, Sage, and ultimately "Childhood, the state of utter done-everythingness that was the absolute zenith of all Dweller existence" (*Algebraist* 325)—with consequent hierarchical degrees of authority and personal stature within the society. Indeed, the young of the Dwellers are held in such low esteem that they can be hunted by their elders and are regularly used to perform the most dangerous tasks. Wherever one looks, therefore, one sees a highly ordered society, with the actions of every character, of whichever race, dictated by and performed with full knowledge of their particular position upon the social ladder. The equality found in the Culture, even the social fluidity of *Against a Dark Background*, is entirely absent; and yet neither the social hierarchies nor the universal militarism are questioned, either by the characters themselves or within the structure of the book.

The story is actually played out as a simple action adventure, a series of episodes of peril and escape, mystery and solution, that is more straightforward in structure than anything Banks had written since *Consider Phlebas*. The entrance to the wormhole that connects this system with the rest of the galaxy was destroyed during the last war. A replacement is on its way, but it has to be towed there at sub-light speeds, leaving the system vulnerable, particularly to the terrorist depredations of the Beyonders and the expansionist plans of the Archimandrite Luseferous. Fassin is a Seer, an academic who enters the dense atmosphere of Nasqueron to study the Dwellers, a Slow species for whom "a billion years of nothing much happening was, they declared, merely like a long sabbatical to them" (*Algebraist* 19). The Dwellers have long since colonized gas giants throughout the galaxy, and it is rumored that they have their own secret network of wormholes. On one trip down to Nasqueron, Fassin discovers a portion of "The Algebraist," a three volume Dweller poem about "mathematics, navigation as a metaphor, duty, love, longing, honour, long voyages home . . . all that stuff" (*Algebraist* 166) that seemingly confirms that this network of Dweller wormholes really exists. As a result, Fassin is seconded to the Shrievalty Ocula, "an allegedly no-holds-barred intelligence unit answering to an Order and a discipline he knew no more about than any other lay person" (*Algebraist* 51), an operation that sounds suspiciously like Special Circumstances, and immediately dispatched back to Nasqueron to find the rest of the poem. The novel then follows Fassin as he is passed from one informer to the next, from one clue to the next, first in a series of set-piece scenes around Nasqueron, then visiting a number of different solar systems. Meanwhile, war is played out above the atmosphere of the gas giant.

This is not so much a war novel as a novel suffused with war. There are wars at every level, from the personal to the geopolitical; every relationship, between lovers, between a state and its citizens, between allies and between enemies, is marked by betrayals, violence, and abuse. The Dwellers are even conducting their own internal war as a sort of entertainment, attracting audiences from across the planet. (Y'sul, Fassin's guide among the Dwellers, doesn't know the cause of the war, "I'm sure there *is* one . . ." [*Algebraist* 253, emphasis in the original], and Fassin has to explain they are like duels, usually fought over some aesthetic dispute.) Although never spelled out, there is an underlying sense that war corrupts, that it seeps into every part of life and sours it. Yet, despite the fact that it must have been written around the time that Banks was cutting up his passport and writing letters to the newspapers in protest at the Iraq War, *The Algebraist* never feels like an anti-war novel, perhaps because the wound is too raw (as *Dead Air* was written too soon after the 9/11 attacks to do more than gesture toward the outrage), perhaps because the dictates of a traditional space opera mean that he too often gets the tone wrong.

This off-key tone is evident in small details. For instance, there is an awkward moment when Banks tries to make the reader empathize with the characters, when Fassin introduces the idea of Swim, which he defines as when "you suddenly think, 'Hey, I'm a human being but I'm twenty thousand light years from home and we're all living in the midst of mad-shit aliens and super-weapons and the whole fucking bizarre insane swirl of galactic history and politics!' That: isn't it *weird*?" (*Algebraist* 135, emphasis in the original). Except that Fassin has lived in exactly those circumstances all his life, and so have his parents, and his grandparents, and several generations before that. Why would he feel he is twenty thousand light years from home when this has always been his home? Why would it feel weird when this is normal for him? It is a defamiliarizing of the situation that the reader would feel, not the character. Such a clumsy shift in focus never occurs in the Culture novels, or in *Against a Dark Background*, or in *Feersum Endjinn*, because Banks is on surer ground, more confident that he is carrying the readers with him.

There is something disturbing and tonally wrong also in the detail and relish with which Banks describes the increasingly baroque violence and cruelty exhibited by his villains. The Archimandrite Luseferous, for instance, keeps the head of an enemy artificially alive to be used as a punchbag. "Stinausin, who had barely endured a month of such treatment before going completely mad, and whose mouth had been sewn up to stop him spitting at the Archimandrite, could not even kill himself; sensors, tubes, micropumps and biocircuitry prevented such an easy way out" (*Algebraist* 10). As we have seen, violence and torture are common in Banks's work, but in earlier books it tended to be brief and witty—for example, the man in *The Wasp Factory* who dies by jumping from a South African police cell and ripping his fingernails out on the way down, or Horza in *Consider Phlebas*, chained in a dungeon that is also a sewer. Here the violence is detailed and excessive, and it is certainly not witty.

The cumulative effect of such missteps is that the various wars that fill the novel seem strangely bloodless, as if the war in the background has no real meaning or effect. Death has always been a part of Banks's fiction, but this is the first novel in which mass death on this scale is central to the story. Previously, such mass deaths—for example, all those who died in the Chelgrian war in *Look to Windward*—have been prior to and a trigger for the action; here, they are part and parcel of what is happening. Even the Dwellers wipe out a whole fleet of ships, including many that were not engaged in the battle but may simply have witnessed it; and we are meant to believe that they are the good guys. There is a difference between writing of the horrors of war and writing to express one's horror at war, like the balance Banks struck between violence and comedy in his early novels, but here I think he gets the balance wrong. Only when Fassin learns that his entire Sept or extended family had been killed do we get any sense of a visceral opposition to war: "He had also realised that innocents died just as filthily and in equally great numbers in a just war as they did in an unjust one, and had known that war was to be avoided at almost all costs just because it magnified mistakes, exaggerated errors" (*Algebraist* 284). The "almost" is a revealing qualification in that sentence.

At the end of the novel, when the soldier Taince realizes that the enemy has fled and there will be no battle, she reflects: "I wanted death and destruction. I wanted the chance to die, the chance to kill, the chance to die . . ." (*Algebraist* 508). But when she kills herself and Sal shortly after, it is not a result of the brutalizing effects of war (she has in fact witnessed no conflict) but part of a private war, a long-planned revenge on a childhood friend she has discovered raped another friend (and hence this is yet another novel in which rape is a plot driver). The particular violence we see, as opposed to the generalized violence that goes on throughout the book, is always personal. The horror of war is shown not in scenes of high-tech battle or in bodies strewn across a ravaged field, but in the casual way that Luseferous has hostages thrown one by one from his spaceship. But all power relationships shown within the book are equally callous. When, before the war, Fassin gets caught up in a protest about the ownership of a habitat (there are no visible protests against war), the functionary who tortures him spends the time protesting that he doesn't like doing it; torture is just a bureaucratic routine. As a result of this, Fassin becomes a rather desultory agent of the Beyonders but displays no qualms at the widespread deaths caused by their terrorism. Violence, war, death, and destruction are constants throughout every strand, every subplot of the novel, yet they come across as rather mechanical, lacking in passion: the bad are too obviously bad, the good too obviously victims. Fassin emerges from it undamaged, and when war does come close, he proves to be quick, bold, and resourceful, the archetypal militaristic space opera hero. This is very much the sort of novel Banks once said he would never write.

If *The Algebraist* is not entirely satisfactory as a novel—"if some of the book's indulgences leaves [*sic*] you wishing a blue pencil had been more liberally employed it's probably because the detail sometimes seems either disconnected from the overarching story or, on occasion, appears out of step with what surrounds it"[7]—it is nevertheless of interest because of the way it prefigures some of the concerns that would emerge, more fully developed, in the final trilogy of Culture novels. In particular, this is the first of Banks's sf novels to touch significantly on religion as other than the threat it was in both *Consider Phlebas* and *Against a Dark Background*. In this case it is the Truth, the faith that underlies the Shrievalty, "the ultimate religion, the final faith, the last of all churches" (*Algebraist* 248), which holds that life is a simulation, a notion that has received a certain amount of scientific interest even today and that recurs in a passing mention in *Matter*. Followers of the Truth must evangelize because "once a sufficient proportion of the people within the simulation came to acknowledge that it was a simulation, the value of the simulation to those who had set it up would disappear and the whole thing would collapse" (*Algebraist* 248). The purpose of this religion, therefore, like the purpose of Subliming in the Culture, is to move beyond this reality. And as with the Sublime, there is hesitation because it could all lead not to another level of existence but to oblivion: when the simulation ended, "there might be no promotion, no release, no return to a bigger and better and finer outside: there might just be the ultimate mass extinction" (*Algebraist* 251).

Significantly, we learn that Luseferous, who does indeed play the part of Lucifer, was once a follower of the Truth. As part of the establishment he had been a favorite of the religious leaders, "a gifted evangelist and disputer, arguing, many times, with great force, logic and passion for the Church and its views. He had been often commended for this" (*Algebraist* 276). But when he abandoned the establishment, set up his own cruel realm of violence and torture, he had also abandoned the Truth. For him, faith became a way of controlling people, "a flaw [. . .] something which was wrong with others that was not wrong with him" (*Algebraist* 276). Thus, while religion may serve to control the masses (an idea that is not explored beyond this one brief reference), it is specifically not equated with evil, with those who are bent on war and destruction. On this reading, faith has started to shift from something that threatens galactic society to something that shapes it. Building on this, religious ideas will become an important underpinning of the next three Culture novels.

When Fassin contemplates suicide following the death of his family, it "seemed as pointless and futile as everything else in life. You needed desire, the desire for death, to kill yourself. When you seemed to have no desire, no emotions or drives of any sort left—just their shadows, habits—killing one-self became as impossible as falling in love" (*Algebraist* 291). This ties in with the Culture not Subliming because "Subliming ultimately [is] a selfish act."[8] And when Banks goes on to say, "People died. Even the immortal died. Gods died" (*Algebraist* 291), he is not only linking divinity with death, he is raising a concern about the place of death in a deathless universe that will be at the heart of the Culture novels he would go on to write.

If *The Algebraist* and *Dead Air* were too close to their inspirations to deal effectively with the state of the world, Banks would, five years later, produce a novel in which he was able to approach these same issues with the necessary distance. The result is one of his best books.

The status of *Transition* is questionable, largely because it was published in the United Kingdom as by Iain Banks (and therefore counts among his "mainstream" fiction) and in the United States as by Iain M. Banks (which makes it a science fiction novel). This could be an accident of timing: in 1994 Banks had told Andrew Wilson: "I have to remember whether it's an odd or even year to see whether the 'M' goes in this year or not."[9] But it is more likely to be the fact that the "M" represents not science fiction but, with the obvious and lonely exception of *Feersum Endjinn*, a very particular sort of science fiction, the broad vistas and gigantic scale of space opera. Everything else, ranging from the real to the surreal, is published without the "M." In an interview at the time, Banks was asked where he placed *Transition*, and he replied that "it sits in the same place that *The Bridge* sat," later adding that "*The Bridge* formed a template."[10] This, it should be noted, is not the same as saying, as Katharine Cox does, that "he links the settings to the world of *The Bridge*."[11] You are unlikely to encounter Orr in any of the many parallel worlds of *Transition*, because the world we encounter upon the Bridge is an ontological realization of the mind of Alexander Lennox in a coma. But the idea of shifting between worlds that reflect upon one another, first explored in *The Bridge*, provides a structural model for the shifting between worlds explored in *Transition*.

Linking *Transition* with *The Bridge* does, however, allow us to see it not as a straightforward mainstream novel but in the context of what I have called the Scottish fantastic, though without the Scottish setting. The characteristics of the Scottish fantastic I have adumbrated are all present in this novel. As Katarzyna Pisarska puts it, such novels contain "both the worlds semioticized by the characters as so-called empirical reality (which is empirical for them, even if it seems surreal or fantastic to the reader), and the worlds in which the laws of mimesis, as recognised by the characters, are variously disturbed or undermined."[12] Or to put it another way, such novels take us into both Glasgow and Unthank, into Edinburgh and the Bridge, into our world and Calbefraques; and the disturbed reality of one will affect our perception of the other. Moreover, the doubled reality of the world is reflected in, and very possibly a product of, the divided self of the characters. And *Transition* is a novel absolutely packed with divided characters. For a start, everyone who transitions from one reality into another flits from one body into another, which they take over for a while and then abandon as they go back to their original self. This implicitly divides identity from body, making the body no more than a vehicle within which the mind rides for a time.[13] In so doing, "Banks undermines our delusion of singularity and uniqueness, at the same time implying that the idea of humanity transcends that of individuality, and that in the many worlds of the multiverse everyone is simultaneously same and other."[14] That idea of the one and many is carried over into the plethora of narrative voices with which we are presented, some in first person, some in third, several of which will eventually resolve into the same voice. In differing ways there are no major characters in the novel who are whole; all are divided, sometimes literally, sometimes figuratively. Even the two characters who seem most complete, the principal baddie and the principal goodie, as it were, come across as mirror images of each other.

In the debate over whether to regard the book as mainstream or as science fiction, it is worth noting that, in the interview with Tim Haigh, which is perhaps the most revealing about this novel, Banks consistently talks of it in terms not of *Matter*, which is the book he wrote immediately beforehand, but in the context of the previous mainstream novel, *The Steep Approach to Garbadale*. That book, apparently, he had intended to be a far more complex work than it turned out to be. Banks likens it to scaffolding around the edifice that is needed to keep everything in place while he works on it, but once the building is finished there's no point in leaving the scaffolding there, "and with *Garbadale*, a lot of what I thought was narrative turned out to be scaffolding. So I ended up with a very conventional narrative, which isn't really what I meant it to be."[15] *Transition*, therefore, was planned from the start to be structurally complex, as a reaction to how *The Steep Approach to Garbadale* had turned out.

While *Transition* is set amid multiple parallel worlds, it is written in a way that most closely recalls Banks's mainstream fiction. The narrators and viewpoint characters in his science fiction are varied, generally have agendas of their own, and usually are not in full possession of the facts. We have to read between the lines, but we do not distrust what we are told; the narrative voice is assumed to be truthful. In *Transition* that is emphatically not the case. The very first words of the novel tell us: "Apparently I am what is known as an Unreliable Narrator, though of course if you believe everything you're told you deserve whatever you get" (*Transition* 1), though it is indicative of the symbiotic relationship between the two novels that this was originally intended to be the opening line of *The Steep Approach to Garbadale*. Even in Banks's mainstream novels unreliable narrators are not that common, but in books such as *The Wasp Factory* and *Complicity* we are invited to doubt or at least question the veracity of the narrator: that uncertainty does not occur in any other of his science fictions. There is also a knowingness about the writing that does not usually occur in Banks's sf, as when Oh explains his name as coming from a world where "the influence of the Mongolian Empires, especially in Europe, was more profound than the one in which you are reading these words" (*Transition* 84).

The novel is set within a multiverse—"we live not in one world—singular, settled and linear—but within a multitude of worlds, forever exponentially and explosively multiplying through time" (*Transition* 82)—in which certain individuals, with the aid of a drug known as septus, are able to transition between different worlds, some of which are radically different from each other, while others are virtually indistinguishable. Within the multiverse, control of septus and, through that, control of all of those able to transition, is in the hands of an organization known as the Concern, or sometimes as L'Expédience. Based in a reality in which the Earth is, uniquely, known as Calbefraques, this is a complex organization that "had many more levels than were immediately visible from the lowly strata where we existed in its tortuously convoluted hierarchy, and it was hard even to guess at how far beyond us it extended, given both the irredeemably complex nature of the many worlds themselves and the seemingly quite deliberate opacity of the organisation's structure" (*Transition* 212). It is, in other words, another example of the sort of power structure that is such a consistent feature in Banks's work, from the power play within families found in *The Wasp Factory*, *The Crow Road*, *Stonemouth*, and *The Quarry* to the antagonism toward Tory governments on display in *The Bridge* and *Complicity*. In his novels, any power structure puts the individual in explicit danger, but the greater the power structure, from the transnational corporation of *The Business* (which has a clear similarity to the Concern) to the authoritarian governments of *Feersum Endjinn* and *The Algebraist*, the greater the potential collateral damage. The power of the Concern to reach across an infinite number of realities, therefore, brings with it a consequent power to destroy worlds.

The plot of *Transition* concerns a war for the soul of the Concern. On the one hand there is Madame d'Ortolan, the only significant female villain in all of Banks's fiction, who is a ruthless opportunist who plots to assassinate all the members of the Concern's Board, leaving herself in absolute control. Against her is ranged Mrs. Mulverhill, an accomplished member of the Concern who has gone underground to foment a rebellion aimed at preventing Madame d'Ortolan's coup. But though these are major players in the action, they are relatively peripheral figures in the novel, for the burden of the story is carried by a range of other viewpoint characters, not all of whom are readily identifiable, and none of whom are anywhere near having a complete picture of what is happening. Moreover, most of the narrative voices do not provide a chronological account but rather dot backward and forward in time, and at least one of the voices alternates between first and third person, so there has to be an extra level of distrust in what we take from the account. As with all of Banks's structurally most interesting works, such as *The Bridge, Use of Weapons*, and *Feersum Endjinn*, the reader has to ferret out the real story from a variety of sources that are not necessarily coherent or reliable.

Of the chorus of voices telling the story, four are most prominent. Patient 8262 is hiding out in a hospital and in constant fear of attack. We do not know his name, we do not know what sort of hospital he is in or where it is, we do not know what he is supposedly suffering from or whether this is a real or a faked malady, though there are suggestions that this is some sort of mental illness, and we do not know what he might have done and to whom that might prompt the feared revenge attack. The Transitionary is Temudjin Oh, skilled at flitting between the worlds, who is initially employed by Madame d'Ortolan to carry out the assassinations she is plotting, but who is secretly in league with Mrs. Mulverhill. The Philosopher is a professional torturer. Torture has, of course, been a regular feature of Banks's work from *Inversions* to *The Algebraist*, but unusually, in the one novel in which the torturer is a leading character, he does not concentrate on grotesquely inventive ways of causing pain; the only means of torture the Philosopher describes in any detail involves paper cuts and lemon juice. Finally, there is Adrian, a wide boy in what is recognizably our own reality, who starts out as a drug dealer and works his way up to become a rich and ruthless player on the London financial markets, only to find himself employed by Mrs. Mulverhill. Adrian's enthusiastic description of heroin as "a drug that empties you out of one life and pours you wholesale into another one" (*Transition* 48) identifies heroin and septus as effectively the same thing and helps to tie this story of the many worlds down to being a story about this world now.

At the beginning of the book, the unnamed narrator refers to a golden age "between the fall of the Wall and the fall of the Towers," the first of which "ended an age of idiocy. The other ushered in a new one" (*Transition* 2). The events of the novel, so far as they can be dated in such terms, take place between this golden age and the financial crisis of 2008, a precision in setting that confirms the sense of this as a contemporary mainstream novel, though with the distortion and exaggeration associated with Banks's novels of the Scottish fantastic. The multiple conflicting narrative voices, the incoherent jumble of different worlds, the broken timelines, and the unknowable complexity of the Concern's hierarchy all suggest a novel about a world that has become disordered, fragmented, unencompassable. Certainly, such a departure from the real is signaled by the narrator's beginning with the end, with his anticipation of his own death. In fact, every one of the plot strands that make up the novel is neatly concluded in the prologue; all that follows is a way of spelling out just how unlikely such neat conclusions actually are.

The disorder that is built into the structure and the narrative voices of the book is also there in the often small details of the plot. We are constantly told, for example, that transitioning is simply a movement between worlds, not in time, yet there does seem to be an element of time travel in the mix. On a trivial level there can be displacement in space and time—"a few kilometres up or down, a few dozen laterally, and some hours later or earlier" (*Transition* 86)—when moving between worlds. More significant is the fact that Oh is employed to affect the course of events, such as when he has to delay a doctor on his way to an appointment, only for the building where the meeting was to take place to be destroyed moments later, or on other occasions to assassinate someone who would later become a dictator. This suggests that the Concern must have quite detailed knowledge of how things will turn out; it also doesn't make sense in a many-worlds scenario, because saving the doctor in one world will only mean he is killed in another. Note also the phenomenon known as "lag," "where otherwise near-identical worlds differ only in one being ahead or behind the other, by any interval up to several million years" (*Transition* 206), though Mrs. Mulverhill insists "it's not a real phenomenon" (*Transition* 206). Anyone who thinks about the premise of the novel must have doubts, but such doubts are not voiced within the novel until near the end, when Mrs. Mulverhill asks: "What is the point [. . .] of trying to do any good in the many worlds when there will always be an infinite number of realities where the horrors unfold unstopped?" (*Transition* 321).

The reason this doesn't make sense is that doing good has nothing to do with the purpose of the Concern, or with the subject of the novel come to that; it is rather, as with so many of Banks's novels, about control. Agents of the Concern "blindly obey orders without a second thought, even though there is no obvious immediate or even medium-term benefit to be observed, because they have come to trust that genuine good will always accrue in the fullness of time" (*Transition* 128). That blind obedience is at the heart of the matter. We encounter it constantly throughout the novel, where characters routinely disclaim any personal responsibility for what they do. The Philosopher, for instance, who illustrates this characteristic most vividly, says at one point: "I do no more than I am told to do and I would rather that the people I torture told the truth, or revealed the information that they carry and which we need to know, as quickly as possible, both to spare themselves and to spare me the unpleasantness of the task" (*Transition* 79). Again, when the Philosopher recalls torturing and killing the abusive father of GF, "I would even resist," he says, "the obvious conclusion that it was I who had done this to him. I had the nagging, perhaps illogical, but quite inescapable feeling that he was doing this to himself, that, despite my total and absolute control over him, he was still somehow responsible for his own torment" (*Transition* 173). With the (partial) exception of Madame d'Ortolan and perhaps Mrs. Mulverhill, the characters all present themselves as small cogs in a machine that is too vast for them to truly see or understand. This is existence as conspiracy.

Thus, in a novel set between the destruction of the Twin Towers and the destruction of the financial system, blame for the disordering of the world is squarely placed on the shoulders of those who blindly follow orders, of those concerns or businesses or centers of power that demand blind obedience without responsibility, of those who use heroin/septus to escape the consequences of what they have wrought. *Transition* is as complex and political a novel as *The Bridge* and deserves to be placed alongside *The Bridge* as one of the best things that Iain Banks wrote.

But the brilliance of *Transition* was a rare flash among Banks's later works. His return to the Culture after a break of eight years with *Matter* was widely celebrated: this was what his readership expected of Iain M. Banks. But in truth the final trilogy of Culture novels never quite rose to the levels of *Use of Weapons* or *Look to Windward*. In an interview he had given in 1998, before the publication of *Look to Windward*, Banks had said of the Culture: "I think there might be one more novel and that'll be it. In theory, you could write about it forever, but you'd end up going over the same ground."[16] In 1999, following the publication of *Look to Windward*, he made much the same point: "I could write Culture stories till the space cows come home, but they'd just be retreads of old ideas in a way. In a sense it's too easy for me to write

Culture stories. The stocks of other sf ideas are definitely going down—I don't seem to be having any fresh ones, which I find quite worrying."[17] These comments reinforce my sense that *Look to Windward*, with its emphasis on death, and a finale in which a Culture Mind Sublimes, which can be read as a synecdoche for the entire Culture Subliming, was intended as a closing off of the Culture sequence. If so, it was an idea Banks was quick to turn his back on. In an interview given shortly before his death he described continuing to write about the Culture as "a self-conscious decision; just like the Culture itself is determined to keep on going, refusing to sublimate or disappear off stage, so I think it would be too easy for me to lob in a series-ender."[18] It is interesting that Banks links the Culture's refusal to Sublime to his own refusal to give up on the sequence. But this self-conscious decision still feels a little like belated justification. Certainly, the late trilogy of what turned out to be the last Iain M. Banks novels does noticeably retread old ideas, as Banks, to a degree, acknowledged in an interview with Dave Golder in 2010. Although he talks emphatically about expanding the context of the Culture, he takes great pains to point out how he had laid the groundwork for the introductions in the earliest Culture novels, in effect saying how much he is going back to expand on earlier ideas.[19]

I read *Matter*, *Surface Detail*, and *The Hydrogen Sonata* as a trilogy (an approach shared, for instance, by Simone Caroti[20]) because the three novels are united in several ways, each of which set them at something of a tangent to previous Culture novels. Structurally, they are more straightforward works, with none of the divergent timelines, different timespans, narrative uncertainties, or other complexities found in earlier books, although, as with *The Algebraist*, each is given to frequent digressions and long explanations of things that would previously have warranted no more than a passing reference. Each uses multiple viewpoint characters, only one of which, usually one of the less significant players in the action, will be from the Culture. The focus is very much away from the Culture, looking out at a universe that is teeming with other races, and the Culture itself is never more than a peripheral or accidental participant in the action. The plots largely consist of various characters crisscrossing the galaxy on a journey that is destined to carry the story toward a violent climax; but what precipitates these journeys proves to be of little moment, tending to fizzle out or come to nothing. And the central theme of each of the novels is religious: the nature of God, the experience of afterlife, the truth of religious revelation. Each of these is approached cynically, of course—there is no such thing, there is always a rational, material explanation; yet there is also a sense of someone not able to put the issue aside, as if the vastness of the canvas has itself generated a religious awe that cannot be escaped.

In *Excession*, the appearance of the unknowable black object shows the Culture to be smaller, less significant, on a cosmic scale; there are inaccessible layers of existence beyond that which is known. Nevertheless, within that known universe, the Culture remains supreme, a force that cannot be seriously challenged by any of the other civilizations we encounter. Within the massively populated galaxy we begin to discover in *Matter*, however, this is no longer the case. In each volume of this last trilogy there is at least one other "Level 8" civilization, which puts it theoretically on a par with the Culture technologically and in terms of social development. The Culture is no longer the great power in the galaxy but one among many; it is probably first among equals, since the Culture comes out ahead in every conflict we see, able to out-think and out-fight all comers, but its preeminence can no longer be unquestioned. And with this readjustment in status comes increased fallibility. Already, in *Look to Windward*, we have seen the consequences of an ill-judged intervention in the affairs of others. But now such misjudgments are seen to be not rare events but commonplace.

Thus, in the opening pages of *Matter*, we see Djan Seriy Anaplian, whom we assume to be a Culture agent because she is accompanied by a drone, Turminder Xuss, stopping an army that was on its way "to take and burn and loot and rape and raze" (*Matter* 3). And she does it very deliberately, with minimal injury. However, as a knock-on effect, we subsequently learn that a city was attacked: "It was demonstrably not the worst that might have happened, but it was still an abomination, an atrocity, and she had had a hand in it" (*Matter* 77). In consequence, Anaplian rescues a child, which she intends to raise herself but ultimately passes on to others in Special Circumstances, as if what marks the Culture as the good guys is not so much the result of their actions as their feelings of guilt later. This is an example of the "ultimately dark art of always well-meaning, sometimes risky and just occasionally catastrophic interference in the affairs of other civilisations" (*Matter* 79). But then, that is practically all we see of the Culture in action. When Anaplian abandons her place in Special Circumstances to return home to the Shellworld Sursamen she necessarily sheds all of the physical enhancements she acquired upon joining the Culture: she goes as an individual, the actions she takes are her actions, not those of the Culture. She is better trained and better equipped than anyone else on Sursamen, and she is not abandoned by the Culture—she has help along the way—but this is not about Culture involvement in Sursamen.

The intrusion from another level of reality in *Excession* painted a picture of layers of existence. That image is recapitulated in *Matter*, made smaller and more concrete in the form of the Shellworld. A Shellworld was "mostly hollow. Each had a solid metallic core fourteen hundred kilometres in diameter. Beyond that, a concentric succession of spherical shells, supported by over a million massive, gently tapering towers never less than fourteen hundred metres in diameter, layered out to the final Surface" (*Matter* 63). The Shellworlds had been built by a race called Involucra or Veil a billion years before, then the Involucra had disappeared. (Sublimed? We are not told.) Sursamen is a typical Arithmetic Shellworld with fifteen interior surfaces, regularly spaced. Originally built as part of some inexplicable machine, the Shellworlds, when abandoned, had been populated by a variety of species under the auspices of a race that held part-ownership of the interior. In the case of Sursamen, the interior is jointly owned by the Oct and the Aultridia, who are rivals; these in turn are subservient to the Nariscene who have overall control of the world, and they in turn defer to the Morthanveld, in whose sphere of influence Sursamen is situated. The levels of authority that take us from the Sarl, the human race that occupies levels 8 and 9 of the Shellworld and which is the main focus of the novel, to the Oct, the Nariscene, and finally the Morthanveld, a level 8 civilization the equal of the Culture, is, of course, a mirror of the levels within the Shellworld. Wherever we look in this galaxy there are hierarchies.

The invention of the Shellworld provides an exotic setting for the action to come, but, more important, it provides for the mystery, the sense of awe, that runs right through this last trilogy. In each of the three volumes we are shown at least one structure whose origins, purpose, and meaning are unknown. There's the Girdlecity of Xown in *The Hydrogen Sonata*: "As far as anybody could tell, the Girdlecity of Xown had been built by the long-Sublimed Werpesh simply because they could" (*Hydrogen* 224). Or in *Surface Detail* there is the artificial mercury lake visited by Veppers, and the hole drilled below it to a magma chamber that kept the mercury simmering. "Nobody knew who had done this, or why. The best guesses were that it was either a religious thing or an artwork" (*Surface* 361). "Nobody knew" is one of the refrains of these late novels, turning the works away from the largely known and controlled universe that we first encountered toward a largely unknown and uncontrolled universe, one in which notions of God and the afterlife have consequently more space to flourish. This heavily populated galaxy is therefore full of wonders, and not the least wonderful thing about the Shellworlds is that they are home to gods. The WorldGod, "the God-beast in the basement" (*Matter* 59) as one Nariscene calls it, is a Xinthian: "They were the second or third largest airborne species in the galaxy and, for reasons known solely to themselves, sometimes one of them would take up solitary residence in the machine core of a Shellworld" (*Matter* 68). The Xinthia are apparently regarded with affection by other races; they are seen as "eccentric, bumbling, well-meaning, civilisationally exhausted—the joke was they hadn't the energy to Sublime" (*Matter* 214–15). However they are regarded by other races, they have turned themselves into gods, or at least into something worshipped as a god. The whole dynamic of the novel is a movement toward this WorldGod, though in the end it remains, as any god perhaps must, unseen and unknowable.

But the Xinthia are only the most overt manifestation of a fascination with the idea of godhood that runs throughout the novel. Recovering from a wound, which he compares to an afterlife, Ferbin, one of the central characters in the novel, contemplates religion in a galaxy of advanced races: "some had made thinking machines that had their own sets of imponderable and semi-godlike powers; some just were gods, like the WorldGod, for example, and some had Sublimed, which itself was arguably a form of ascension to Godhead" (*Matter* 206). This, the most positive view of Subliming in any of the novels, though it comes from outside the Culture, illustrates what underlies this interest in divinity. Development on a galactic scale means to become godlike if not actually to become a god, but it remains a step that the atheistic Culture and its atheistic author are reluctant to take. The Sublime is, rather, something to be avoided; it is considered to be "selfish self-promotion" (*Matter* 174), though this view comes from the Culture, which regards itself as "not just in itself completely spiffing and marvellous and a credit to all concerned, it somehow represented a sort of climactic stage for all civilisations, or at least for all those which chose to avoid heading straight for Sublimation" (*Matter* 173–74). Echoing a phrase from "A Gift from the Culture" about the "imperialism of smugness" (*State* 13), the Culture is here seen as the result of "millennia of smug self-regard" (*Matter* 174); it would seem to regard itself as too good to Sublime.

Of course, to understand the role and nature of god it is necessary to be somewhat less developed; as Ferbin's father believed, "only the very poor and downtrodden really needed religion, to make their laborious lives more bearable" (*Matter* 206), which implies that atheism is a luxury for the rich and leisured, or at least for those who might themselves be gods. The focus of the novel, therefore, is upon the Sarl, a race at a transitional stage somewhere between medieval and early modern (a situation not unlike that seen in *Inversions*), who occupy two adjoining levels within the Shellworld, though over time the race has split and the two levels are at war with each other. Here, Prince Ferbin, the wastrel son of a strong king, flees the battlefield and, in hiding, witnesses the murder of his father, the king, by Mertis tyl Loesp, the king's most trusted advisor and best friend, who is staging a coup. Loesp kills the wounded monarch by plunging his hand into the wound and squeezing the heart, which can perhaps be read as a symbolic rape. The king had clearly been preparing for a more peaceful future. Ferbin had been trained for diplomacy, not battle, and as Ferbin's younger brother Oramen mused: "War itself was becoming old-fashioned and outmoded. Inefficient, wasteful, fundamentally destructive, it would have no part in the glitteringly pragmatic future the greatest minds of the kingdom foresaw" (*Matter* 33). Loesp, however, plans a more martial future; rather than ending the war, he wants to extend it, leading to complete conquest of the next level.

Understandably fearing for his life, Ferbin concludes that his only option is to flee out of the Shellworld, contact his sister who had left years before to join the Culture, and through her recruit the help of more powerful races in avenging this affront to the natural order of things. The journey that Ferbin and his servant, Holse, take is a typical learning process. As they encounter successive levels of alien civilization, approaching the godlike, technologically advanced level 8 civilizations of the Morthanveld and the Culture, so

Ferbin becomes less self-centered and more self-aware, while Holse acquires greater independence and authority. But what they learn from these increasingly godlike beings is that they are indifferent. They may feel sympathy for Ferbin's lot, but they have no desire or right to intervene. However, Ferbin does meet up with his sister, Anaplian, who gave up her coveted place in Special Circumstances when she heard of her father's death, and though she has had to give up most of her augmentations, she does at least arrive accompanied by a drone, Turminder Xuss, and by a ship's avatar, Hippinse.

Meanwhile, back in the Shellworld we follow the adventures of Anaplian's other brother, Oramen; young, naïve, untrained, and having to learn of the danger he now faces from Mertis tyl Loesp, who has assumed the title of regent. But we also start to piece together the true explanation for these events. Ferbin's home level, level 8, is in the domain of the Oct, a race that grandiosely claims to be the descendant of the Involucra who built the Shellworlds. The next level down, however, is in the domain of the Oct's rivals, the Aultridia, and on that level a major archaeological discovery is in the process of being exposed. This site is known as the Nameless City, an ancient alien metropolis that is being revealed by the scouring of a mighty cataract. At the heart of the city is a building known as the Sarcophagus, with "a gigantic, elongated formal entrance a hundred metres across and forty high, flanked by a dozen soaring sculptures of cut-away Shellworlds" (*Matter* 492). This, the Oct believe, will confirm their heritage and bring with it the increased respect among space-faring races that they believe is their due. They have thus fomented the war, and Loesp's usurpation, in order to gain access to the Nameless City; and for a moment it seems as if their efforts will pay off when a grey cube is unearthed at the center of the Sarcophagus, within which is something that claims to be a member of the Involucra. Once released, however, it turns out the thing is an Iln, another long-dead race that was devoted to destroying Shellworlds, so as Ferbin, Anaplian, and their companions arrive for the climax of the novel, all comes down to a conflict between the WorldGod Xinthia and the devil Iln.

Given that the novel has overtones of an overarching battle between good and evil, the sense of small figures caught up in a conflict that is vaster than they can comprehend, it is not surprising that Gwyneth Jones, for instance, found echoes of *The Lord of the Rings* in the book. She points in particular to "soft-headed prince Ferbin and his servant Choubris Holse, whose resemblance to Frodo Baggins and Sam Gamgee gets beyond parody—I mean, gets beyond anything *but* parody—long before we hit the no-kidding straight-steal of the Epilogue."[21] Certainly, Holse's return home to hearth and pipe is inescapably reminiscent of *The Lord of the Rings*, but even if we don't go quite this far, there is still the sense of this being a Culture novel by numbers. There are details designed to appeal to fans of the series, but made jokey or even, in Jones's terms, parodic, as in the character of Jerle Batra, who has adopted the form of "a small, rootless, spherical bush made from tubes and wires" (*Matter* 81). But too often there are slips or inconsistencies: as when the Culture's interference in other societies is excused on the grounds of the terrible things people do which are likened to a disease for which "the Culture represented the hospital, or perhaps a whole caring society, Contact was the physician and SC (Special Circumstances) the anaesthetic and the medicine. Sometimes the scalpel" (*Matter* 169). This doesn't quite fit with the reasons for Culture interference given in earlier novels, though it does fit with the sort of rationalization we find in Banks's next novel, *Transition*. There is a disconnect also when Anaplian thinks of her personality backup that could be downloaded into a clone, and muses: "[T]o be an SC agent was to be owned by SC. The compensation was that even death was just a temporary operational glitch, soon overcome" (*Matter* 179). But from every other Culture novel we have seen that this is true for all Culture citizens; death is always a choice; this opportunity for rebirth is not confined to Special Circumstances. And when did the people working with SC start being called agents? (Come to that, this is the first novel where Subliming is referred to as "Sublimation.") When Anaplian is aboard the Medium Systems Vehicle *Don't Try This At Home* she plays a game with "one of the ship's officers" (*Matter* 224), yet Li's ludicrous, not to say embarrassing, antics in *The State of the Art* have shown us that this term is meaningless on Culture ships. Throughout the novel there is a sense that Banks's attention has wandered away from the Culture, and as a result is missing the nuances he had so effectively created before.

This sense that the Culture is no longer the focus of the novel but has become instead a setting or a bystander for a trilogy musing on issues relating to death and the afterlife is even more apparent in the next Iain M. Banks novel. As Simone Caroti suggests, the fact that nothing in this trilogy has any direct impact on the Culture raises moral problems: "The moral conundrums in [*Surface Detail*] are, from a critical utopian perspective, a lot less problematic than they'd ever been before,"[22] largely because, as in all three of these late novels, the Culture is not directly or intimately involved. The various horrors conjured up—and these novels feature a massive accumulation of horrors—are not contingent on and do not impact on the utopian character of the Culture. Therefore, there is a sense that they are observed rather than experienced, a moral entertainment rather than a moral lesson. Which is why the rape and violence involved become ever more questionable.

Dealing with the godlike character of advanced galactic civilizations in *Matter* edges around the central concern of this last trilogy, which is the Sublime. Banks moves fractionally closer to the topic in *Surface Detail*, in which he consistently explores notions of life after death, though he dodges the issue quite spectacularly by suggesting there is no such thing as death. Every one of the viewpoint characters in the novel dies, and in every case they are either brought back to life, or death is shown to have not been real after all. By the end of the novel, the only named characters who genuinely die are the baddies, a moral simplicity that seems at odds with the complex worldview found in *The Player of Games* or *Excession*.

*Surface Detail* opens with an extended scene in which Lededje is hunted and killed by Veppers. She is his slave, owned since birth as a result of a family debt, her status marked by a complex network of tattoos that cover not just the surface of her skin but every part of her, down to her bones. When this particular bid for freedom is ended, Veppers is on the point of raping her when she bites off the tip of his nose (a symbolic castration?), prompting him to kill her at once. But she does not die: at some point in the past a visitor from the Culture had given her a neural lace, and in the moment of her killing her mind state is instantaneously transmitted to a Culture ship. The neural lace thus allows Lededje to be reborn aboard the *Sense Amid Madness, Wit Amidst Folly*, so accurately that "there is almost certainly less of a difference between the you that died and the you that you are now than there would be between your selves at one end of a night's sleep and the other" (*Surface* 78). Significantly, the reborn body has none of the tattoos; identity is all in the mind, not in the body, though Lededje regrets the loss of the tattoos that are so intimately tied up in how she sees herself.

The scene shifts to Vatueil, an insubordinate soldier involved in tunneling under a castle during a medieval siege. He finds a secret way into the castle, but the way is booby-trapped, and he is captured, tortured, and killed in a gruesome fashion. But Vatueil is a mercenary in a digital war where "Everything, including dying, happened within a meticulously overseen simulation where the backed-up self was allowed to know everything that had happened to each of its earlier iterations" (*Surface* 255). He is soon engaged in another battle scenario.

The scene shifts again, to a Culture Orbital where Yime Nsokyi is desperately trying to fight off an all-out attack, only to be one of the last to die when the Orbital is destroyed—at which point everything is reset and the attack is revealed to have been an exercise, "a punishment drill, a simulation for masochists" (*Surface* 36), as she calls it.

Other not-quite-real deaths occur regularly throughout the novel. Even the small incidental stories are full of death, as for instance with Nopri, who is killed and recreated every time he tries to talk to the enigmatic alien Bulbitian (a story that calls to mind *Rogue Moon* [1960] by Algis Budrys). And when we come to Auppi fighting what she thinks is a smatter outbreak, knowing that her mind state is safely stored, she compares herself to warriors of old who "thought they were effectively backed up too, sure in themselves that they were bound for some glorious martial heaven" (*Surface* 431). After Yime's false death, however, the novel shifts to the most important postmortem scenario in the book.

Prin and Chay are two Pavuleans in their version of Hell, which is designed to ensure that those who are consigned to Hell "suffer with every sinew, cell and structure of their body, no matter how atomised it might have become and how impossible such suffering would have been with an utterly shredded nervous central system in the Real" (*Surface* 47). It is a digital construct: as Prin says, "we are code, we are ghosts in the substrate, we are both real and unreal" (*Surface* 49), but the suffering is real enough, and Prin and Chay are there to discover the truth about the place and report back to their fellow campaigners in the Real. In fact, Prin manages to escape, taking a powerful anti-hell message to the Pavuleans, but Chay gets stuck. If the central invention of *Matter* was the Shellworld, inspired by the layered realities of *Excession*, this central invention of *Surface Detail* is clearly modeled on the Heaven of the Chelgrians in *Look to Windward*.

Heavens, such as that of the Chelgrians, do exist, though the afterlife as Heaven tends to be fairly restricted to "boundless sex, adventure, sport, games, study, exploration, shopping, hunting or whatever" (*Surface* 127), which sounds remarkably like the Culture for the majority of its citizens. It would seem that our imagination of what might constitute Paradise is profoundly limited, and hence most such Afterlives featured a final death because "it was quite a rare species that naturally generated individuals capable of being able, or wanting, to live indefinitely, and those who had lived for a really long time in Afterlives were prone to becoming profoundly, gravely bored, or going catatonically—or screaming—mad" (*Surface* 128). However, in parallel with these Heavens, and judging from this novel far outnumbering them, there are also Hells, which "existed because some faiths insisted on them, and some societies too, even without the excuse of over-indulged religiosity" (*Surface* 132).

The reason for the Hells, as given by a Pavulean conservative, is that "we need the threat of punishment in the afterlife to keep us from behaving like mere beasts in this existence" (*Surface* 258). This allows Banks to separate Heaven or Hell from religious faith; asked in 2010 if it was a comment on Catholic theology, Banks replied: "Absolutely . . . [but] . . . [i]t's certainly not just aimed at the Catholic Church, of course—but at superstition in general."[23] Such afterlives are simply a technological achievement. Something like the neural lace that saved Lededje has been invented time and again by different races throughout the history of the galaxy, and "once it was possible to copy a creature's mind-state you could, as a rule, if you had the relevant background and the motivation, start to make at least part of your religion real" (*Surface* 120). In this instance, religion is indistinguishable from a socially imposed set of moral principles. Thus, the Pavulean conservative can go on to say, without irony, "I have no idea if there really is a God" (*Surface* 258), because God has no part to play in this idea of religion. But this is a transparently false argument, and I think we are meant to realize that. Separated from the notion of God, from the moral dictates of religion, the Hells become no more than an exercise in sadism. This is the view of many advanced societies that object to the Hells because Virtual Environments "devoted to inflicting pain and suffering on sentient creatures seemed not just wrong but perverse, sadistic, genuinely evil and shameful, disgracefully cruel. Uncivilised, in fact" (*Surface* 132). Chief among such protestors, of course, is the Culture, whose "atypically inflexible attitude probably had shifted the whole meta-civilisational moral debate on such matters slightly but significantly to the liberal, altruistic end of the ethical spectrum" (*Surface* 133). We are surely meant to read the Culture here as standing for Banks's own moral position, although we cannot forget the overt fascination with forms of hell and with torture that is displayed in all of his fiction. Indeed, this uneasy balance between fascination and disgust is neatly caught by Chel, who realizes that "there was a perverse beauty about it, an almost celebratory fecundity about the depths of creativity which must have been plumbed to produce such imaginative cruelty" (*Surface* 277). We have seen such perverse beauty, and at times comic delight in pain, in Banks's novels ever since *The Wasp Factory*, though the balance does seem to have shifted more toward the perverse than the beautiful since *The Algebraist*. As Vatueil puts it when captured by the Nauptre, "Why did so much of everything have to come down to pain? We are creatures of pain, creatures of suffering" (*Surface* 481).

The fact that the moral complexities surrounding pain and torture are trumped by the more simplistic moral position that Hell is wrong is part of the flattening of moral affect noted earlier. The Hells represent an excess of suffering and therefore are obviously wrong, and that's an end to it. All the good races in the galaxy oppose the Hells. Chief among these, as we have seen, is the Culture; yet when the two sides in the Hell debate went to war—a war "amongst the Heavens, between the Afterlives, if you wanted to be pedantic about it. And it was over the Hells" (*Surface* 117)—the Culture stayed out of it. Why this might be so is necessary for the plot of the novel, but is not explained in any way that really makes sense. I think in this we get an echo of Banks's vehement opposition to the wars in Afghanistan and Iraq, a feeling that a powerful Western nation should not be interfering in the affairs of another state simply because they are strong enough to do so. But what holds true in Iraq, where the reasons given for war are questionable, does not necessarily hold true in the Culture. Banks has so loaded the scales, making the Hells so unquestionably terrible, having the war fought out in simulation rather than in the Real, that the failure of the Culture to join the coalition in support of their most deeply held moral beliefs comes across as perverse rather than principled.

And it is not as if the Culture itself is beyond question. Demeisen, the avatar of the *Falling Outside The Normal Moral Constraints*, allows himself to be occupied by someone who won a competition: "No control over either body or ship whatsoever, obviously, but the full experience in other respects—sensations, for example" (*Surface* 207). The avatar then proceeds to torture his own body: "He suffers his pain and learns his lesson while I . . . well, I gain some small amusement" (*Surface* 207). So we get torture, the imposition of a little personal hell, purely for pleasure. And this from a member of the Culture, which is supposed to be vehemently opposed to the Hells and the suffering they entail. Nothing more clearly demonstrates the ethical dilemma presented by Banks's books: on the one hand, there is the moralist who makes a point of arguing that violence and suffering are wrong; on the other hand, there is what would seem to be an ever more blunted sensibility, so that violence becomes increasingly grotesque and gruesome, while rape and torture are convenient plot devices. The cruelty of Demeisen is presumably meant to recall the shocking wit of the early novels, but somehow, as with Luseferous in *The Algebraist*, the wit is less adept.

Thus the novel progresses. Within their digital construct, where the war of the Hells is being fought out, the anti-Hell side is losing. Vatueil, who has now risen through the ranks to become one of the leaders, is among those pushing to extend the war into the Real, and to do so in a way that compromises the Culture so that it is forced to bring its superior forces into the struggle. Meanwhile, Prin is winning the moral argument against the Hells among the Pavuleans, so much so that the conservatives are trying to bribe him by promising to arrange the release of Chay. They argue that the Hells are mere pretense: "All that matters is that people are frightened into behaving properly while they are alive. What happens after they are dead is really no concern of the living. Nor should it ever be" (*Surface* 259). Of course, the Hells do not feel like a pretense to those who are in them, as Chay is. She survives because, right from the start, she had lost faith that the Real exists, that there might be anything outside the Hell, and therefore she has lost all hope of escape. Hope, it turns out, is the necessary ingredient that turns the various horrendous physical pains of Hell into genuine existential torment, so the

Pavulean equivalent of Satan spends time trying to restore her hope, without success. In the end, she is granted the ability to permanently kill one resident of Hell every day, at the cost of a small increment in her own physical pain; she becomes, in effect, an Angel of Death. It is interesting that both Heaven and Hell are ended by death, as if the afterlife is not really postmortem but just an interlude before the real thing. In a novel apparently filled with visions of what comes after death, they all come down to a delay before the actual and unknowable cessation.

In counterpoint to these stories, Lededje and Yime are both crisscrossing the galaxy. Lededje wants revenge on Veppers, and though the Culture in general doesn't approve and isn't prepared to help, it is not exactly hindering her either. And the rather madcap ship, *Falling Outside The Normal Moral Constraints*, chooses to accompany her on her quest. Yime, on the other hand, is an agent of Quietus. *Surface Detail* is set five hundred years later than any other Culture novel, and in the meantime Contact divisions seem to have multiplied. Since "the dead outnumbered the living in the greater galaxy" (*Surface* 166–67) (or perhaps it might be fairer to say those who are no longer living but not yet actually dead), Quietus has been established to deal with them. In this instance, however, Yime's main interest would seem to be with the living, since she is tasked with stopping Lededje from killing Veppers. It turns out that Veppers made his immense fortune by providing the substrate in which most of the galaxy's Hells are located, but no one knows where this might be. So the various plot strands of the novel all come together in the collision of Lededje and Veppers, a climax marked with explosions, hair's-breadth escapes and sudden reversals of fortune, and in the end all the good guys live or are restored to life, and all the bad guys are killed, with no talk of an afterlife for them.

As a final grace note, in what Simone Caroti considers an "easter egg," the little extra slipped in at the end of the credits of far too many films as a treat for the fans, after contriving all of his happy endings, Banks turns his attention back to the mercenary, Vatueil. Now, back in the Real, he is "using what he liked to think of as his original name—even though it wasn't" (*Surface* 625). In the very last word of the book we discover that name is Zakalwe. I cannot see this as an "easter egg," but rather as a slip, another indication that Banks had grown careless with his own creation. *Surface Detail* is set nearly eight hundred years after the events of *Use of Weapons*, and at the end of that novel Zakalwe deliberately refused the treatment that would have extended his life. It was an embrace of death that was a necessary consequence of his being confronted with his own true identity, his own past. To put Zakalwe into a situation where he suffers death over and over again makes a certain amount of sense; but to suggest that he is still on the scene, still a mercenary, eight hundred years later, is to undermine everything that *Use of Weapons* worked toward both structurally and artistically. It suggests that someone who welcomed death is still avoiding it—though that does, of course, make Zakalwe an ideal avatar for all the dodging that Banks and the Culture both exhibit when it comes to facing the Sublime.

The central role that the Sublime played in the Culture novels reached a sort of climax in *Look to Windward*, but in the end Banks stepped back from the brink. Instead, in this late trilogy, he approached the idea of the Sublime tangentially and noncommittally, through notions of godhood and the after-life. It was only in what would be his last science fiction novel, *The Hydrogen Sonata*, that he came anywhere close to directly confronting the issue, though once more, fear of death wins out over dying.

In *The Algebraist*, Banks introduced the idea of a religion, simply known as The Truth, based on the idea that we inhabit a simulation. This idea, that "life was *very* like a game or simulation where every possible course and outcome has already been played out" (*Matter* 386, emphasis in the original), is raised again in *Matter*, only to be dismissed by Hyrlis on the grounds that "only reality—produced, ultimately, by matter in the raw—can be so un-thinkingly cruel" (*Matter* 340). Nevertheless, the idea persists: the translation of Chay from Hell back into the Real at the end of *Surface Detail* is both an actualization of this belief and an undermining of Hyrlis's argument. All religions need some version of heaven, some promise that life is not the end and there will be a reward for putting up with it: the idea that we live within a simulation is unique in that heaven is thus equated with ordinary, everyday life. The problem for a secular, non-faith-based religion, which is how we might regard the Culture, is what form such a heaven might take. The digital heavens described in *Surface Detail*, for example (see *Surface* 127–28), are, as I have noted, indistinguishable from what is already everyday life within the

Culture, which is why I find it much easier to regard the Culture as a personal heaven rather than a social or political utopia. If you cannot imagine a heaven that is any better than what you have on a day-to-day basis, what incentive do you have to go there? Hence, the Culture's version of heaven, the Sublime, is literally unimaginable; and it is hard to think of any reason why the Culture might choose to go there.

Therefore, in *The Hydrogen Sonata*, the whole issue is approached obliquely, by way of another religion known as The Truth. In this instance a race at an early stage in its development is in receipt of a holy book that is not composed of culture-specific homilies and vague moral precepts but actually serves as a remarkably accurate blueprint for social and technological development right up to becoming a part of galactic society. Over time, as the Gzilt grow to become a level 8 civilization, one of the races involved in the original establishment of the Culture though they then choose not to join the group themselves, the Book of Truth becomes less relevant. Nevertheless, it was of immense importance in the early centuries of the civilization, and the Gzilt retain great affection for the Book of Truth and regard it as fundamentally shaping who they are.

As the novel opens the Gzilt are twenty-four days from Subliming. We are never quite clear why they have chosen to Sublime; it seems to have been the result of political maneuvering by one person, and everyone else we encounter seems to be going along with it, not having strong feelings one way or the other. At such a time, it is traditional for other races to send messages, which may include apologies for past wrongs. It is in such a spirit that an unarmed diplomatic ship from the Zihdren-Remnant, the survivors of a race that Sublimed long before, meets up with a Gzilt warship to deliver a representative for the Subliming ceremony. But the Gzilt ship behaves with great suspicion and ends up destroying the other vessel for no apparent reason. This sets in motion a plot of byzantine complexity but surprising inconsequentiality in which "a variegated cast of highly kinetic characters describ[e] hyperspace doodles entangled in such a mess that the whole thing would be infuriating if the proceedings weren't this much fun."[24]

It quickly becomes apparent that the Zihdren-Remnant message concerned the fabrication of the Book of Truth—"Mistake, accident, prank, deliberate interference?" (*Hydrogen* 72)—and, as we eventually are not surprised to learn, it was concocted by "a tiny faction within the Zihdren: a solitary university faculty, a small renegade research team with a single dissident individual at its head. We are, and always have been since the Book was put together, an experiment" (*Hydrogen* 112). For Cossont, the Gzilt who is our main viewpoint character: "Personally, she wasn't sure it really mattered whether the Book of Truth had been based on a lie; a lot of people had long half assumed that" (*Hydrogen* 192). A development of Banks's belief that space opera heroes cannot really save the world is that, increasingly, plot strands in his novels are initiated by trivial points or lead to unsatisfactory resolutions or are not really resolved at all. This is one example: since we are repeatedly told that the Book of Truth is generally assumed to be based on a lie and that such a popular assumption has led to no apparent societal problems, why are extreme measures taken to prevent the confirmation of this coming out, and why bother at such a late stage in proceedings when it is likely to have no conceivable impact on the Subliming? As two of the Culture ships involved in the business discuss the matter, *Contents May Differ* suggests that even if they discover the truth, it would be inclined to say nothing. To which the *Just The Washing Instruction Chip In Life's Rich Tapestry* replies: "Which begs the question, why, then, are we bothering to hunt down this truth at all?" (*Hydrogen* 202). The closest we get to an answer to this question comes when the *You Call This Clean* tells Scoaliera Tefwe the reason for their interest: "Just in case it turns out to be something we should have bothered about. Always try to avoid setting up future opportunities for kicking yourself" (*Hydrogen* 207). This point is repeated several times in the novel; for instance, when Tefwe finally catches up with Ngaroe QiRia he asks, "But how much difference might it make? [. . .] Knowing the truth of it, if it is true?" to which Tefwe replies, "I don't know, Ngaroe, I'm not sure anybody knows. But we can't just let it go" (*Hydrogen* 334). When, right at the end, QiRia confirms what we've known throughout the novel, that the Book of Truth was indeed a fake, it comes as no surprise to anyone, either character or reader. Moreover, it doesn't matter. As QiRia says: "Though it was a . . . I don't know; a faith-shaking secret . . . that's just in theory. In practice, people don't believe for good reasons anyway, they just believe and that's it" (*Hydrogen* 500). So the question of whether the Book of Truth is fake or not is ultimately irrelevant, faith trumps reason. Furthermore, the truth is revealed only on the last day as the Gzilt are about to Sublime, so the revelation can have no substantial effect on the progress of the Subliming. Indeed, the Sublime has, to a certain extent, already taken the place of religion; as the Gzilt president puts it, "The Subliming makes all of us sound like religious zealots" (*Hydrogen* 51).

But in order to get to the idea that reason and faith are two different things, and that one cannot affect the other, an awful lot of people have to be killed. And if we don't understand why Cossont and the Culture are devoting so much energy to tracking down the truth, still less do we understand why Septame Banstegeyn, the politician who steered the Gzilt to Subliming, is so violently opposed to the truth coming out. John Clute supposes that he is "terrified that this revelation will so unbalance Gzilt civilization that its citizens will eschew Sublimation,"[25] though I'm not sure that at this late stage anyone other than, perhaps, Banstegeyn himself really cares that much. I suspect that, even at a time when it can have no lasting impact, it is simply a power play. Certainly, in the dying days before Banstegeyn and everyone else Sublimes, he authorizes the destruction of a Gzilt military base because it may have received a message from the Zihdren-Remnant ship, and he arranges the assassination of the president and kills his own lover in the process. It's not a good explanation, but it's just enough to keep the plot moving. In this, I agree with Clute that "the McGuffin in this novel is an even more blatant damp squib than usual; but then that, as I've suggested, may be the point of *The Hydrogen Sonata*: which means to be all journey and no arrival."[26] The damp squib is, to a degree, the tutelary deity of this final trilogy, but hold on to that "no arrival"; in this novel, as in all the Culture novels from *Look to Windward* onward, arrival would be Subliming.

All of this scene setting is designed to set the hyperkinetic plot in motion. Like every member of the Gzilt, Vyr Cossont has served in the military—as one ship notes, for all its militaristic surface, everyone a member of a regiment, a love of uniforms, the Gzilt are essentially unmartial, while the Culture, though pretending to be peaceful, has actually been in a major war, the Idiran War, that a thousand years later continues to haunt it—but she is now a musician. In particular, she is spending the time before Subliming trying to master the Hydrogen Sonata, which is the popular name for T. C. Vilabier's "26th String-Specific Sonata For An Instrument Yet To Be Invented, MW 1211" (*Hydrogen* 11), which is played on an instrument specifically developed for the piece and known as an "Antagonistic Undecagonstring—or elevenstring" (*Hydrogen* 11). The joke is that the music is very difficult to play but not very pleasant to hear: "As a challenge, without peer. As music, without merit" (*Hydrogen* 33), one critic describes it. Millennia after it was composed, it is still the one thing for which Vilabier is known, but from long-lived QiRia, who knew him, we learn he would have hated this, since he wrote it as a joke, out of anger. Typically, what lends the novel its name is neither serious nor significant.

Unexpectedly, Cossont is called back into service for one special mission. Given the timing, she is, more than anything else, irritated by this and doesn't take it seriously, until her regimental headquarters is attacked and destroyed during her briefing. She alone escapes, thanks to a passing Culture ship. The attack makes her mission suddenly serious. Years before she had briefly met a Culture citizen, QiRia, who claimed to be ten thousand years old, and who may know the truth about the Book of Truth: her task is to find him, or at least his memory. Her mission, aided by the Culture ship *Mistake Not . . .,* and chased by a Gzilt vessel intent on stopping her, occupies the bulk of the novel and takes her on a zigzag course filled with dead ends, false leads, last-minute escapes, and other incidents designed to keep the tension high. Meanwhile, a group of Culture ships reminiscent of the Interesting Times Gang from *Excession*—and the prevalence of long passages of dialogue involving these ships suggests that *Excession* was deliberately intended as a model for this book—try to keep a finger on the multifarious strands of action. All of this, the chasing down of QiRia, the ships' dialogue, is designed to provide a platform for discussions about and alternatives to Subliming.

Cossont "wondered what it would really be like to be Sublimed, to have gone through with it, to be living on this reputedly fabulously and unarguably real Other Side" (*Hydrogen* 16). Like death, Subliming seems inevitable, yet no one knows what it is like. "Exactly what it was like in there was debatable: very, very few came back and none came back less than profoundly altered. These few returnees were also seemingly incapable of describing the realm they had left, however recently, in any detail at all" (*Hydrogen* 64). Thus, the ship *Caconym* is carrying within it another Mind, the *Zoologist*, which once Sublimed all by itself, then, "later it had done something for which the term 'unusual' was woefully inadequate: it had come back again" (*Hydrogen* 136).

But this provides no useful information about the Sublime because "the ship's memories were abstracted, beyond vague; effectively useless. The Mind itself was basically a mess; self-restructured (presumably) along lines it was impossible to see the logic behind" (*Hydrogen* 137). As the *Zoologist* explains, "When you come back from the Sublime, it is as though you leave all but one of your senses behind, as though you have all the rest removed, torn away— and you have become used to having hundreds" (*Hydrogen* 150). Yet from the Chelgrians to the Zihdren-Remnant there seem to be races who retain contact with the Sublimed, and Subliming is always presented as a choice, indeed as an informed choice, so the Gzilt "regarded taking a child with you as something close to abuse" (*Hydrogen* 22). Therefore, something of the nature of the Sublime must surely be known. Yet the whole thing is subject to variation: for instance, we learn that "in theory an individual could Sublime, but in practice only solitary AIs ever did, successfully" (*Hydrogen* 16). I don't think the prospect of not Subliming successfully has been raised before, but now we are told that "to do it properly required serious numbers—preferably a whole civilisation" (*Hydrogen* 16). This is because "you just evaporated in there. . . . [only] [c]ivilisations, and the individuals within those civilisations, survived and flourished in the Sublime over galactically significant periods of time, though they gradually changed beyond comprehension" (*Hydrogen* 16). Though this is immediately undermined by the suggestion that an even greater and more rapid change would happen anyway in the Real, and the Sublime is actually more stable.

One possible alternative to Subliming is Elderhood, but "opting for Elderhood just looked like a sort of failure of nerve, given what the Sublime realm offered: a space of infinite flourishing without threat or danger" (*Hydrogen* 64). A better alternative, however, is represented by the ten-thousand-year-old QiRia, who was present at the creation of the Culture: instead of moving to a new state of existence, a form of heaven (and hence, effectively postmortem), there is the option of simply not dying. QiRia is a rather shadowy figure—immortality is as mysterious and hard to encompass as the afterlife—but I suspect we are meant to see QiRia as the more rational choice: better to not die than to move on to something that seems ideal but is essentially unknown. And even this extended life acquires its religious aspect when QiRia's mind state notes that "one develops a certain god-like indifference to it all, intellectually"

(*Hydrogen* 317). In the end we learn that the reason QiRia has continued to live for so long is because he once held a secret that was neither particularly secret nor of any great moment, but in a novel filled with insubstantial rationalizations, this feels particularly feeble. In *Look to Windward* we were introduced to a host of ways that Culture citizens avoided death, some of which, at least, are still extant in this novel, since Tefwe, for instance, has her mind state stored aboard a ship, ready to be decanted into a new body whenever needed. QiRia's refusal to take any of these options looks like another failure of nerve, and in this he stands for the Culture as a whole.

An even more telling stand-in for the Culture is Cossont herself. As the novel opens, she is prepared to Sublime. Not unnaturally, she wonders what it will be like, how it will feel to occupy this curious new fold in reality, but she does not fear the process. She is ready and willing to go with her fellows into "this reputedly fabulously and unarguably real Other Side" (*Hydrogen* 16). During the course of the novel she is repeatedly attacked, suffers terrible injuries, and has to flee for her life on more than one occasion; at one point, in a curious echo of the opening of the first Culture novel, she and Berdle, the avatar of the *Mistake Not . . .*, are displaced into "the stern ventral waste disposal semi-solids holding tank" (*Hydrogen* 459), in other words, into the shit. Yet, when all of this is over, when the Gzilt finally go ahead and Sublime, she chooses to stay in the Real. The twenty or so days she spends with the *Mistake Not . . .* are filled with peril, but they are also filled with life, and life always wins out whatever the alternatives.

By the end of the novel, the Culture has once again looked upon the Sublime, then turned away. The question of what comes next clearly continues to fascinate while remaining unresolved. Unfortunately, as things turned out, there never would be a resolution.

## CHAPTER 5

## AFTERMATH

Iain Banks died on June 9, 2013. At his request, the publication date of his last novel, *The Quarry*, had been brought forward; but his death was still earlier than anyone had anticipated, and it would be nearly two weeks before the book actually appeared, on June 20.

The central character in *The Quarry*, Guy, is dying of terminal cancer, an eerie coincidence. On the day that Banks learned the news about his own condition, he had already "written 90% of the novel; 87,000 words out of 97,000. Luckily," he said, "even though I'd done my words for the day, I'd taken a laptop into the hospital in Kirkaldy, and once I'd been given the prognosis, I wrote the bit where Guy says, 'I shall not be disappointed to leave all you bastards behind.' It was an exaggeration of what I was feeling."[1]

Perhaps inevitably, most reviewers focused on the coincidence of life following art, but in many ways that is the least interesting aspect of the book. It was, as Banks readily admitted, not the sort of book he would have chosen to go out on: "Let's face it; in the end the real best way to sign off would have been with a great big rollicking Culture novel."[2] But it was a novel that provided a very neat conclusion to Banks's career because of the way it echoed and reiterated some of the key themes of his first published novel, *The Wasp Factory*. As Katarzyna Pisarska illustrates, the resemblances between the two books include "the father/son relationship, the secluded northern locus, the quest for the feminine, the conflict between rationality and superstition, or the real and the imaginary, and the narrative derived from the perspective of a socially inhibited youth."[3] I would add the way that, in common with just about every book Banks wrote, the key to the main power relationship, the most significant threat, lies within the family.

Two years after his death, the very last Iain Banks book appeared. *Poems*, by Iain Banks and Ken MacLeod, contained a majority of the poetry he wrote between 1973, when he went to university, and 1981, when he stopped writing poetry, at the same time that he began writing *The Wasp Factory*. The collection includes some fifty poems, plus a further thirty-two by MacLeod, who has written poetry throughout his career. Poetry clearly played an important part in Banks's development as a writer: lines from his poetry were incorporated as song lyrics in *Espedair Street*; *Song of Stone* started with one of his poems (which is not included in the collection), and *Use of Weapons* begins and ends with two poems that are included. *Poems*, therefore, makes apparent many of the influences on his writing, from the poetry of T. S. Eliot to the songs of Pete Atkin and Clive James. At the same time that *Poems* appeared, a rumor that there would be one more Culture novel completed by Ken MacLeod was finally scotched when MacLeod revealed that Banks had died too early to leave anything but the most rough and incomplete notes for such a project. Given how emphatic Banks was that what we might consider his juvenilia, from *The Hungarian Lift-Jet* to *O*, should not be published (if they even still exist), his posthumous publishing career has been more curtailed than many other popular and successful writers. Which is probably to the good.

Iain Banks, with or without the "M," was a writer who inspired a devoted and enthusiastic following precisely because of the unpredictable variety of his work. In his interview with Stuart Kelly he lamented the low-key nature of his last novel: "It's a fairly simple book as well; not many characters, there's only really one location and it doesn't muck around with flashbacks or narrative order."[4] But that in itself makes *The Quarry* something of an exception among his novels. More usually, Banks's work revealed a dizzying, exuberant variety of styles, devices, and effects. He moved fluently from the gothic grotesqueries of *The Wasp Factory* to the chilly postmodern games of *Walking on Glass*; he took extraordinary liberties with the structure of works such as *The Bridge*, *Use of Weapons*, and *Transition*; he injected startling linguistic invention into *Feersum Endjinn*; there were vivid and convincing family dramas such as *The Crow Road* or *Stonemouth*, brutal crime stories such as *Complicity*, oddly detached fables such as *Song of Stone* or *Whit*. Above all there was the regular back-and-forth movement between the overtly science fictional and the allegedly mainstream. Yet even within something as apparently coherent as the Culture novels, Banks introduced huge differences in style and perspective, from the almost epistolary manner of *Excession* to the oblique allusions of *Inversions*. All of which was conducted with a wit, flair, and style that swept his readers up in the sheer fun of his books. As Adam Roberts said, "It is exactly for the witty, cynical and urbane tone of Banks's writing that people love his books so much."[5]

So far, I have attempted to show that within all of this diversity there are continuities, resonances, references, and links, that ideas raised in a mainstream novel will be further explored in a science fiction novel, that there are issues that crop up again and again. But it is also important to celebrate this range and variety. The plethora of obituaries that greeted Banks's death, for instance, reveal an amazing variation in approaches to his life and work.

Writing in *The Humanist*, for example (Banks was "an Honorary Associate of the National Secular Society and a Distinguished Supporter of the Humanist Society Scotland"[6]), Francis Spufford notes that Banks "engaged, with the creation of the Culture, in a piece of sly, prolonged and magnificent anti-theism."[7] Spufford goes on to say: "Where religion, on the Marxist reading of it, is a kind of comprehensible counsel of despair, the heart of the heartless world, Banks supplies a counsel of optimism . . . [he] . . . wants to demonstrate that a materialist imagination can reach just as far as a religious one."[8]

This atheism is something that is implicit in practically all of Banks's work, and explicit in most of it. Our first experience of the Culture shows it at war with a theocratic society, and we see the same ideas at play in *The Crow Road* and in *Whit*, in *Matter* and in *The Hydrogen Sonata*. In these works and others, "Banks constructed a fictional world that seemed to feature an undeniably supernatural element—faith healing, Gods, prophetic religious texts—only to rationally deconstruct and debunk them."[9] But the attack is mostly directed not so much at god as at religion; it is not the god that is debunked but the religion that worships that god. The difference is subtle but important. Religion, Banks has said, is "a set of hypotheses arrived at by very primitive people two thousand years ago and it's not fit for purpose, it doesn't describe reality, it's that simple."[10]

Thus, in *The Crow Road*, a novel filled with ideas and images of community, the one community that does not make sense, that disconnects its members from the world around them, is the bizarre sect created by Uncle Hamish. The fact that Hamish has only a single follower is an indication that this is not genuinely a community, not really a way of belonging in the world. In *Whit*, Hamish's sect is transmuted into the Luskentyrian Community, but it is a community that is based on a lie and that consequently lives at a tangent to the real world; Isis Whit can make her way in the world only by abandoning the fundamental precepts upon which her whole life has been based. In 1996 Banks aptly summed up *Whit* as "a book about religion and culture written by a dedicated evangelical atheist—I thought I was very kind to them. [. . .] Essentially, Isis makes the recognition that the value of the Luskentyrian cult is in their community values rather than their religious ones."[11]

It is, therefore, in the way that religion dictates our interactions with each other, with the world around us, that the problem lies. About the belief systems underlying religion, so long as they are not imposed, Banks is somewhat more equivocal. He has joked that "each of us is just a solitary smart ape on a piffling little planet in an ungraspable big universe, and the sheer bleeding obviousness of there being no supreme deity could itself be a huge cosmic joke on the part of a particularly annoying and mischievous god."[12] Even without believing in a god, the question of what a god might be became more and more important in Banks's work. His novels continued throughout his career to promote a rational universe, but he cannot escape the fact that, the more technologically powerful the Culture, or any other In Play civilization, may become, the more its powers resemble those we associate with gods. Increasingly, therefore, the questions that come to dominate the novels, particularly the last Culture trilogy, concern religion. They do not necessarily give credence to religion—they remain the works of an evangelical atheist, as he described himself—but they are nonetheless religious questions. If races have acquired abilities indistinguishable from those of gods, how are they not gods? If there are, therefore, godlike beings, is not religion a rational behavior? And if, as Banks promised from very early in the sequence, there is another order of being toward which even the most advanced civilizations aspire, is not this a form of heaven? What we find, therefore, is that the very rationality of the universe Banks created makes religious questions inescapable.

Because religions shape the communities we make, the social structures we organize, the antireligious stance Banks adopted throughout his work is necessarily a political stance also. This is a point that is at the heart of Timothy Baker's observation about the Culture that "the utopia is already corrupt; it continually engages in a religious self-undermining in which its values collapse upon themselves."[13] As I have said throughout this book, the Culture is a personal utopia, but it is not a political or a social one. There is a worm of corruption that comes out repeatedly through the Culture's interactions with other societies. Nevertheless, I disagree with Baker's more general point that the Culture's interference in the affairs of other species is compared to a Crusade in which "the zeal with which the Culture attempts to perpetuate itself is akin to the fundamentalist religiosity it wishes to replace."[14] This is a misreading triggered, I suspect, by the fact that *Consider Phlebas* can be (mis)aligned with the Crusades on Earth (see chapter 2), but in fact, even in the religious war against the Idirans (the only conflict in the sequence that can seriously be equated with the Culture attempting to perpetuate itself) I think its involvement cannot sensibly be likened to a Crusade.

Even so, this brings us to another important perspective on Banks's work that is highlighted by the different obituaries. Thus, for Robert Stafford of the Socialist Party of Great Britain, Banks was "a precocious writer of visionary socialist science fiction."[15] Despite Banks's own protestations that he was not a political writer, his political views suffused everything he wrote. In chapter 1 I looked at how Banks was part of a new generation of politicized Scottish writers who emerged in the wake of the failed referendum of 1979. For some commentators, like Jerome Winter, this is a key moment in Banks's political awakening. The failure of the 1979 referendum was "for many Scottish citizens a state of governance tantamount to abject recolonization,"[16] and consequently Banks projected onto his "galactic canvases a radical left-wing politics extrapolated from living in a postcolonial, globalized Scotland."[17] Frank's violence in *The Wasp Factory*, for instance, "is not just part of his desire for rigid control and coherence,—and an exaggerated form of masculine behaviour, but is also the result of a symbolic instability inherent in his identity,"[18] and that instability of identity, that divided self, is as much political, the instability of being a Scot in the United Kingdom, as it is personal. Thus Banks is identified as a writer who "dramatizes a break with [the] sort of neoliberal regime"[19] exemplified by the government of Margaret Thatcher, a prime minister whom Banks excoriated both privately and in novels such as *Walking On Glass* and *The Bridge*. To be honest, I find this too narrow a view of Banks's political writing; he had been politically engaged long before the 1979 referendum (his visit to London in 1977 during which he researched and wrote *The State of the Art* had been to take part in a demonstration), and by the end of the century his views were even more pronounced. Still, it is undeniable that detestation of Mrs. Thatcher and all she stood for is present in a lot of his writing, from *The Wasp Factory*, which satirized "both the draconian policies and increasingly libertarian stance of the Thatcher government,"[20] to *Complicity*, which "was letting off steam, a way of getting out all the anger and bitterness I felt about the '80s and the Thatcher years."[21]

But this brand of politics, negative and party political, is only a fraction of the story. Time and again, views that are broadly conservative and capitalist come in for attack—for instance, in *The Crow Road* and *Against a Dark Background*, *Transition* and *The Hydrogen Sonata*. But these views are usually offset by more positive communal ideas. This is best exemplified, of course, by the Culture, which is typically described as "a sprawling, intergalactic left-libertarian thought experiment [. . .,] a functioning anarchist society with no government, no laws, and no money."[22] The Culture regularly comes up against authoritarian regimes that rule by inflicting pain and restricting freedom: the Azad empire in *The Player of Games*, the Affront in *Excession*, the proponents of Hells in *Surface Detail*. In such circumstances, it is all too easy to see who are supposed to be the good guys and who are the baddies. In the example of the Culture as it is presented to us we see that the Culture is "[d]esigned to bring out the best in human beings, and [is] organized in such a manner that we could live together harmoniously whilst maintaining individual freedom

[ . . .,] the ultimate creation of a rational, secular humanity."[23] It is a model, a hope, a heaven, a form of living that is good for everyone who falls within its embrace. When he was asked in 2010 if *Surface Detail*, which pitted the Culture against religious fundamentalism, was a reflection of current affairs, Banks replied: "I wanted to put across my sense of what a fully developed society would actually be like, and I'm trying to make the argument that we are still behaving in a relatively barbaric way at the moment."[24] However, at the same time, "I'm not convinced," he says, "that humanity is capable of becoming the Culture because I think people in the Culture are just too nice—altering their genetic inheritance to make themselves relatively sane and rational and not the genocidal, murdering bastards that we seem to be half the time."[25]

The point is that, looked at communally, the Culture is undeniably good for everyone; but look below the surface, at the level of the individual, and it's not always so clear. Individuals, like Gurgeh in *The Player of Games*, have to become like the barbarians in order to defeat the barbarians. In *The State of the Art*, Linter chooses to abandon the Culture for the crudity, danger, and disadvantages of life on Earth because life within the Culture can be stifling. The diplomat, Genar-Hofoen, in *Excession*, wants to become like the Affront, a brutal and militaristic race. Masaq' Orbital in *Look to Windward* appears to be crowded with people who choose to pursue life-endangering sports without the usual Culture supports of backup that would see them revived if the worst happened. En masse, as a community, the Culture appears very like heaven, a place, as we have seen, of great sex, extended lifespan, absence of worries, and there are machines to take care of everything from the massively complex to the tediously mundane. Who wouldn't want to live there? No wonder it is acclaimed as the great modern utopia of the political left. And yet, as in Ursula K. Le Guin's story, there are those who walk away from Omelas.

And in Banks's political writing, it is always the individual that matters, more than the party, more than the community, more than the family. Authority, kings and dictators, market forces, and one-party states are invariably wrong because they can only operate by restricting the individual. Families are so frequently the source of danger and disturbance in his novels (*The Wasp Factory*, *Against a Dark Background*, *The Quarry*) because they are themselves power structures. Get things right for the individual, and other things follow, but the freedom to choose your own way must take precedence. One thing that does allow the Culture to be seen as something of a utopia is that those who disagree, those who feel discomforted, those who feel constricted, are enabled to leave: it is a utopia only in so far as it recognizes that it is not utopian for everyone.

One indication of the primacy of the individual over familial, social, political, or cultural norms is the prominence of women in Banks's work. Leaving aside the liminal case of *The Wasp Factory*, women have been viewpoint characters or leading players in an unusual number of novels for a male writer of Banks's generation, including *Canal Dreams*, *Against a Dark Background*, *Feersum Endjinn*, *Song of Stone*, *Whit*, *Inversions*, *The Business*, *Matter*, *Surface Detail*, and *The Hydrogen Sonata*, but a woman has been the villain in only one of his books, *Transition*. (In his interview with Tim Haigh[26] Banks said that he had tried to make the grandmother in *The Steep Approach to Garbadale* into the villain, but it hadn't worked; yet again *Transition* is seen in terms of what he didn't do in *Garbadale*.) This isn't exactly good feminism; the women can often be victims. After all, rapes or attempted rapes drive significant plot elements in *Canal Dreams*, *Against a Dark Background*, *Inversions*, *The Algebraist*, and *Surface Detail*. But Banks's female characters are at least as likely to be strong, competent, and effective as any of his male characters. He has said, "It should be relatively easy to write a female character because you spend your time in the same society,"[27] and elsewhere in the same interview he added: "In a sense it's easy to be blind to the sexism that's still around and somehow manage to ignore the other elements of society that still are unequitable in terms of gender or whatever." Banks pauses and then laughs, "But it's only stupid or ignorant people who do that."[28] Women play significant roles in his novels not to make a point about equality but because not to do so would be stupid or ignorant.

But that doesn't mean there are no troubling issues around this. Women, as I have noted, are liable to be the victims of sexual violence, but then, there is an inordinate amount of violence all the way through his work. Banks had no qualms about the violence in his writing: "In principle, anything's OK, as long as I've got an excuse to put it in—which is a more honest way of saying, 'Is it artistically justified?' You shouldn't self-censor yourself just because you have a gut reaction that an idea is too horrible. If there's a reason for it, it has to be done. There's a moral point to that ghastliness, pain and anguish."[29] And this moral point is summed up by Peter Suderman:

Banks made many of his Culture antagonists into torturers, either directly or indirectly. It was how he defined the true monsters of his world. For Banks, there was no clearer sign of an individual's seething villainy than his willingness to methodically inflict physical pain on another intelligent being. Torture, in all its gruesome variations—and Banks was a master at describing it in great and horrific detail—was the ultimate form of coercion and the greatest abuse of power.[30]

True, there are an unusual number of torturers in his books—Ralinge in *Inversions*, the Philosopher in *Transition*, Luseferous in *The Algebraist*—not to mention scenes relating to torture in *Use of Weapons*, *Excession*, and *Surface Detail*. But it is not just the bad who torture. When Frank in *The Wasp Factory* torments small animals, it is a reflection of his divided and damaged personality; when Demeisen, the avatar of the *Falling Outside The Normal Moral Constraints*, tortures the person who is riding inside him, it is an indication of the ship's wild and unpredictable character. And if gruesome is an indication of villainy, what are we to make of Banks's lovingly detailed descriptions of cruelty, some of which, at least, are meant to make us laugh?

If we allow the individual freedom from constraint—that is the most consistent political message throughout Banks's work—then how are we to cope with the fact that each individual contains his own villain? That is a question raised but never answered in these novels. Like the idea of the Sublime it is something that must always remain just out of reach. And that is why I believe that the personal political aspect of Banks's work is far more complicated than most utopian accounts allow.

One of the things that keeps being mentioned about Banks's work is how visual it is. In the final interview in the *Guardian*, Stuart Kelly notes, in passing, that Banks said "he'd love there to be a film of *Consider Phlebas*."[31] No such film exists, of course, but then there has been little in the way of adaptations of his books to other media. In 1996 the BBC produced a four-part dramatization of *The Crow Road* directed by Gavin Miller with a screenplay by Brian Elsley, and three years later the same pairing of screenwriter and director produced a film of *Complicity*. Since Banks's death the BBC has also broadcast a two-part adaptation of *Stonemouth*. Other than that, *The Wasp Factory* was quickly snapped up for filming, but by the mid-1990s the production company was so mired in legal problems that nothing happened. A script for *Espedair Street*, on which Banks collaborated, was completed in the late 1990s but not produced. And in 2009 the *Hollywood Reporter* published an article suggesting that the short story "A Gift From the Culture" was being developed for director Dominic Murphy, though at the time of writing this is still, supposedly, in development.

Banks has fared a little better in other media. In 1998 *Espedair Street* was dramatized on BBC Radio 4 in the style of a Radio 1 rock documentary; and in 2009 Radio 4 also broadcast an adaptation of *The State of the Art* written by Paul Cornell, the only one of Banks's overtly science fiction books to have been successfully dramatized. A play, "The Curse of Iain Banks" by Maxton Walker, was produced at the Edinburgh Fringe in 1999, in which "the characters meet a gruesome death every time Banks writes a novel."[32] And in October 2013 an opera of *The Wasp Factory* composed by Ben Frost, with a libretto by David Pountney, was produced at the Royal Opera House in London. The staging of the production was powerful: "As in the book, Frank is the narrator, but Frost has him represented by three female singers, a device that not only enhances the musical possibilities but also vividly displays Frank's descent into insanity: there are always other voices in his head,"[33] though the opera seems to have been let down by the quality of the music.

But if adaptations, perhaps surprisingly given the verve and visual impact of Banks's fiction, do not provide another avenue by which to appreciate his work, the very fact of the opera suggests there is another route: music. Music has always played a vital role in Banks's work and seems to be, in a sense, almost symbiotic with the fiction. In the 1999 *Guardian* profile, we are told that "he's been writing rock songs for as long as he's been writing novels," and therefore, "he wouldn't let *Espedair Street* be filmed unless the songs used in the film were his own."[34] Banks continued to compose music throughout his life, latterly using a complex program on his Apple computer. He also collaborated with musician Gary Lloyd, whom he met in the 1980s when Lloyd composed a CD of music inspired by *The Bridge*.

But it is not just *Espedair Street*, in which Banks effectively imagines himself into the role of a rock star, in which music is vital. Contemporary novels such as *The Crow Road* and *Complicity* reference so many songs that they effectively have their own soundtrack. A 1993 interview for *New Musical Express* begins with a discussion of the relative merits of Deacon Blue—"they're Scottish and you can forgive them more"[35]—and Runrig. It is important that the central character in *Canal Dreams* is a cellist, and both *Look to Windward* and *The Hydrogen Sonata* are centered on musical compositions. Apart from *Espedair Street* itself, music is not the driver in any of these books, but it is always there, part of the air that the characters breathe, and an essential aspect of what makes them.

Perhaps because of his popularity, or maybe because of the overt division in his work between science fiction and mainstream (several obituarists acclaimed his mainstream novels but of course had not read the science fiction), or even his somewhat cavalier approach to genre, by the time of his death his fiction had received considerably less critical attention than might have been expected. Even a magazine like *Vector*, the critical journal of the British Science Fiction Association, which normally provides fairly comprehensive coverage of science fiction published in the United Kingdom, did not review all of his Iain M. Banks novels. At the more academic end of the field, *Foundation* had a special issue on Banks in 1999, but other than that you could count on the fingers of one hand the number of critical essays on his work published during his lifetime in such journals as *Science Fiction Studies*, *Extrapolation*, and the *Journal of the Fantastic in the Arts*. And I can find only two books about Banks published before his death: a reader's guide to *Complicity* by Cairns Craig, and a reader's guide to *The Wasp Factory*, *The Crow Road*, and *Whit* by Alan MacGillivray.

That's not exactly critical neglect, but neither is it the enthusiastic embrace of a major, not to say canonical, writer. But that situation was starting to change. In 2006 there was a two-day conference on his work at the University of Westminster, and this was followed in September 2013, three months after Iain Banks died, by a one-day symposium devoted to the Culture held at Brunel University in Uxbridge. The questions that emerged several times during the Brunel conference were: Would Banks's work survive? Would it still be read in a hundred years' time? At the time of his death, the answer to that question might not have been obvious. His books were still in print, a thirtieth-anniversary edition of *The Wasp Factory* had appeared with a new preface by Banks, and his work attracted an eager popular audience—though none of that was necessarily a guarantee of longevity.

But the Brunel conference itself was a symptom of change. Two new books about Banks, both obviously written before his death, made an appearance at the conference. *The Transgressive Iain Banks*, edited by Martyn Colebrook and Katharine Cox (organizers of the Westminster conference), was a collection of essays that largely, though not exclusively, covered the books by Iain rather than Iain M. Banks; while *Gothic Dimensions* by Moira Martingale, concentrating mostly on *The Wasp Factory* and *The Bridge*, argued that these works should be read as Gothic fiction and seen through a Freudian lens, arguments that I found not entirely convincing. If nothing else, the two books together signaled that Banks's work was at last being seen as worthy of serious critical attention. More books have followed. *Mediating the World in the Novels of Iain Banks* by Katarzyna Pisarska is a fascinating analysis of recurring themes and patterns in his mainstream books; while *The Culture Series of Iain M. Banks* by Simone Caroti is an enthusiastic if not always very analytical take on the ten Culture books.

These books, with more on the way, mean that all at once there is a critical infrastructure for students of Banks, and the very fact that there is this body of work may well mean that in the future more people will choose to study him, one way of keeping his work alive. But what is of most interest is that each book takes such a different approach to Banks's fiction: even when laid out for study, it is a body of work that refuses to be restricted to neat categories. These are novels that, by their very nature, open up rather than close down possibilities for readers, critics, and students alike.

Even more important than the critical response to his work, however, is the long-term effect Banks has had on science fiction. This legacy is threefold: there is the direct influence he had on other writers, emerging from this is his formative role in the New Space Opera, and, as an expansion of that, his centrality to the British Renaissance around the turn of the century.

The most obvious and immediate influence Banks had was upon his life-long friend, Ken MacLeod. Banks had a talent for friendship, and many of those he met at school remained close throughout his life, but MacLeod was the one who shared his interest in science fiction and in writing; MacLeod was the one who helped to shape his ideas and his fiction, especially in the case of *Use of Weapons*. MacLeod, a Trotskyist with direct knowledge of the various sectarian divides of the European left, was more politically active than Banks and thus was, initially at least, less single minded in his writing. It was Banks's encouragement that finally led him to produce his first novel, *The Star Fraction* (1995). Since then he has written a string of highly successful novels that often turn upon his political interests and knowledge (*Cosmonaut Keep*, 2000; *The Execution Channel*, 2007; *Descent*, 2014), but which, in their broad vistas, the readiness to turn to Scottish landscapes, and their humor, contain clear echoes of Banks's work.

There is an intriguing feedback loop between Banks and M. John Harrison. Harrison's criticism played a vital role in shaping Banks's approach to science fiction (see chapter 1), and the way he subverted the familiar tropes of space opera in his early novel, *The Centauri Device*, makes it an important precursor to the Culture. After this, however, it was the example of Banks's work that was one of the things that lay behind Harrison's belated return to science fiction in the Kefahuchi Tract trilogy (*Light*, 2002; *Nova Swing*, 2006; *Empty Space: A Haunting*, 2012). Though these three novels pursue themes and ideas typical of Harrison's other work and contain overt references to a variety of science fictions including *The Ship Who Sang* (1969) by Anne McCaffrey, *Clans of the Alphane Moon* (1964) by Philip K. Dick, and *Stalker* (1979), directed by Andrei Tarkovsky, the overriding influence of Banks is evident in the way Harrison approaches the scenes set in space, with their half-understood mysteries, alien plenty, and huge vistas all dwarfing the petty and often inconsequential acts of the human characters.

Among others who have admitted his influence are Stephen Baxter, Paul McAuley and, perhaps more surprising, China Miéville, but it is writers of space opera who owe Banks the most. The writer who is closest in affect to Banks may be the Scottish writer Michael Cobley, whose Humanity's Fire sequence, beginning with *Seeds of Earth* (2009), can at times feel as if he is deliberately trying to emulate Banks's work. However, the natural inheritor of Banks's mantle is probably Alastair Reynolds, whose debut, *Revelation Space* (2000), gave notice of a writer as comfortable with the necessary scale and pace of a story told against the galactic immensity of space as Banks ever was.

Space opera is important here, because in creating the Culture Banks had wrested the subgenre away from its traditional roots. In the late 1960s and 1970s the familiar conservative character of space opera had been given a boost first by the appearance of the original series of *Star Trek* (1966–69), whose apparent utopian impulse was offset by its military hierarchies and its insistence that a few men (practically all men) were able to change the fate of entire worlds, and then by *Star Wars* (1977), with its space empires and a plot hinging on the restoration of an aristocratic order. Banks reversed all that: the utopian character was, as I have shown, complex and questionable, to say the least; there are no military hierarchies; empires are unfailingly bad; and order is not aristocratic but anarchistic. In thus reimagining space opera, Banks laid the groundwork for what would become the New Space Opera, which appropriated the scale and color of the old form while jettisoning its political baggage in favor of a more left-leaning, humanistic vision of our future in space. Key exponents of the New Space Opera, a list that might include Catherine Asaro and Peter F. Hamilton, Charles Stross and John C. Wright, along with Baxter, McAuley, Reynolds, and many others, may come from the political left or the right, but all owe a debt to Iain M. Banks.

Alongside the emergence of the New Space Opera during the 1990s, another shift was occurring in the sf firmament, variously known as the British Renaissance or the British Boom. The New Wave in Britain during the 1960s had established a new generation of writers who rejected the traditional forms of science fiction in favor of a new form that hybridized ideas of "inner space" with literary techniques borrowed from modernism. But when the magazine central to the New Wave, *New Worlds*, collapsed at the end of the decade, science fiction in Britain entered a decade of stagnation. The new writers of any significance who emerged during the 1970s can be counted on the fingers of one hand. A new magazine, *Interzone*, appeared in the early 1980s, but the uneasy mixture of warmed-over new wave fiction with American cyberpunk in the early issues failed to revitalize British science fiction. Then came *Consider Phlebas*, a reimagining of the hoariest of sf forms from one of the most popular and most controversial of mainstream novelists.

There are many origin stories for the British Boom,[36] but the name Iain M. Banks features prominently in all of them. It is no coincidence that many of the most exciting writers of the New Space Opera are British. Banks showed that treating the oldest forms of science fiction in a cavalier manner can give them a new lease on life; he showed that wit and humor are not inappropriate, whether the work is one of searing intent or soaring imagination; he showed that science fiction and literary ambition are compatible—in fact, they are necessary companions. The British Renaissance lasted little more than a decade at its height, but it introduced a host of new writers, it encouraged established writers to take their work in new and more challenging directions, and it effectively reinvented science fiction in Britain, a sea change whose effects are still being felt. Banks did not bring this about on his own (he would have decried any such suggestion), but he was undoubtedly one of those who helped to create it.

What I have tried to do in this book is suggest how varied Banks's work is, how many different approaches he took in exploring the key themes and ideas in his novels, and how many different approaches there are for the reader in unearthing and analyzing and enjoying those themes. He is a writer who uses violence to decry violence, who divides his characters in order to suggest political divisions, a writer who presents religious ideas from a humanist standpoint (or who presents atheist ideas from a religious standpoint), a writer in love with epic-scale and small-scale wit, a writer who can make us laugh out loud at gothic horror yet shiver at jokes. He is a clever writer who does not come across as demanding, a great storyteller who infuses his work with serious ideas, a writer who is equally at home with the most baroque science fiction and the most recognizable realist fiction (though he so eschews genre boundaries that each informs and is informed by the other).

But there is one aspect of his work that I have touched on only tangentially so far, even though it may be the most important part of it. It is something that is, perhaps, captured by his friend of twenty-five years, Michelle Hodgson, who began her obituary: "Iain Banks didn't laugh—he guffawed. Alongside his hearty intellect and appetite for politics, Iain knew how to appreciate the simple pleasures of life, from food to fireworks to friendships."[37] Laughter is one thing that everyone who knew him recalls. He was a man with a tremendous appetite for life. Ken MacLeod remembers the Iain Banks who would fall backward off his barstool without spilling a drop and continue his peroration from the floor.[38] Everything he did should be fun, and that included his writing. As Banks said in one interview: "You do have the whole galaxy to play with, and you have the full panoply of types of planets to play with, not just rocky watery planets. You've got no excuse for getting bored with it!"[39]

Banks's books are scattered with jokes, with ridiculous inventions that are there simply because he enjoyed inventing them. A book should be fun to write, or there was little point in doing it; and it should be fun to read for the same reason. And he succeeded. His books could be many things—politically informed, philosophically challenging, colorful, spectacular—but the one quality they all share, science fiction or mainstream or the many that don't quite belong in either category, is that they are fun to read.

# A FEW QUESTIONS ON THE CULTURE
by Jude Roberts

This interview with Iain Banks was conducted by email between April and June 2010 as part of Jude Roberts's PhD on the Culture. It draws on the extraordinary way Banks's writing investigates and interrogates language, the body, the relationship between the self and society, and the relationship between the self and the other, to consider what it is to be a person. The full, strident, and often playful answers he gives here are entirely characteristic of his writing and persona more generally. A version of the interview was published at *Strange Horizons* on November 3, 2014; this extended version is published here for the first time with the permission of the interviewer.

JUDE ROBERTS: When did you first start to imagine the Culture? Was it in response to any particular event or influence?

IAIN M. BANKS: Long ago. In the '70s, at least. Partly it was in reaction to a lot of the sf I was reading at the time. The British stuff mostly seemed a bit miserablist and the US's too right wing. I wanted sf that combined what I regarded as the best of both; the thoughtfulness and sense of proportion of the UK's and the energy and optimism of the US brand.

The way the Culture came about initially was as—I thought at the time—a single-use solution to a particular problem. I was getting ready to write *Use of Weapons* and I knew that Zakalwe was this sort of ultimate warrior guy, just very martially able, but I wanted him to be on the side of the good guys somehow. Squaring that circle was the problem, so I came up with the idea of the Culture as his ultimate employers: a society basically on the side of the angels but willing to use people like Zakalwe (utopia spawning few warriors, as the later-written poem says) to do its dirty but justified work. The "justified" bit always having something to do with statistics; from the beginning the Culture had to be able to prove—rather than simply assert—that it was generally doing the right thing, even when it interfered without permission in other societies. That was it, initially, but then the Culture proved to be the nucleus around which all my other until then rather nebulous ideas started to cluster and take shape, and it just developed—naturally, it felt—by itself, from there.

JR: In *Look to Windward* you give an example of the Culture bringing into being, however unintentionally, precisely the kind of situation it is trying to avoid and/or resolve. Doesn't this suggest that the statistical approach is fundamentally flawed?

IMB: No, I think it just proves that you'll never get it right every time, even if you do your best and have really good statistics which you use properly and with the best of intentions. The Chelgrian civil/intercaste war is the Culture getting it wrong, but at least they admit it, and that lesson goes into the statistics and changes them, making subsequent interventions less risk-keen and more likely to work better. I hope it's obvious from the novel just how horrified and guilty the Culture feels about this, and how near-unique it is.

JR: Do any books in particular stand out in your memory as examples of being "a bit miserablist" (UK) or "too right wing" (US)?

IMB: Good question. Annoyingly, no. Maybe I've repressed the details . . . Oh dear. I'd make a rubbish academic, plus I hate it when people can't give examples of what they're complaining about. I may actually have to do some research here. Or at least remembering. I suspect a lot of the stuff I was finding worthy of objection was in the form of short stories, individual examples of which have long since sunk into the morass of generalisation and averaging that is my mushy memory.

JR: You have previously mentioned Alistair MacLean as an early influence on your writing. To what extent do you think your writing challenges the lone male hero image of masculinity in MacLean's writing?

IMB: That's a good question. Would that I were sufficiently self-analytical to have an answer as interesting. I don't know, is the short answer. I guess it's possible. Perhaps being an only child has an influence here.

JR: I've just been reading M. John Harrison's *The Centauri Device*. How much do you feel you have been influenced by his work?

IMB: A great deal, though possibly less than I'd have liked. I can't recall consciously invoking Mike or *The Centauri Device* when I was thinking about *Consider Phlebas*, but I'd like to think it was somewhere at the back of my mind at the time.

JR: Are there any feminist science fiction writers whose work you admire and/ or consider to be an influence on your writing?

IMB: I admire pretty much any female sf writer just because they have to have an extra dose of self-belief to tackle such a male-dominated genre. Singling people out I'd have to mention Le Guin, C. J. Cherryh, Octavia Butler, Alice Sheldon/James Tiptree Jr., Gwyneth Jones, and Joanna Russ, though probably only Le Guin could have been any sort of influence on me, and I don't know that she actually was.

JR: How concerned are you with the way you represent female characters?

IMB: Very, though it's not something I fret over; it's kind of built-in, by now. It depends a lot on what sort of story I'm writing, though. With the Culture stories it's generally a given that women will play a large (and symbolically important) part in the narrative.

Elsewhere, I'm a bit more conscious of always trying to help redress the (im)balance I find in so much other fiction and other fictive media.

JR: Have you read any work by Michel Foucault, Jacques Derrida, or Emmanuel Levinas (or any other continental philosophers)? If you have, what did you think?

IMB: The little I've read I mostly didn't understand, and the little I understood of the little I've read seemed to consist either of rather banal points made difficult to understand by deliberately opaque and obstructive language (this might have been the translation, though I doubt it), or just plain nonsense. Or it could be I'm just not up to the mark intellectually, of course.

JR: How much of the history of the Culture do you have worked out? In "A Few Notes on the Culture" you said that it emerged from seven or eight societies coming together. What happens after that? What I'm interested in is how much conflict is in the Culture's history?

IMB: A lot, probably. I've never worked it out. I've left it fairly open in case I ever want to set a story there. Though I suspect it's only the Culture as it exists, fully formed, from the time of the Idiran War onwards, that truly interests me. The Culture in its pomp is what attracts.

JR: What was the motivation/inspiration for creating Marain (both yours and the Culture's)?

IMB: The Culture's motivation was attempting to make a universal language, free from cultural bias, but embodying what you might call encouragements to think clearly and rationally—even humanely (so not really culturally neutral at all, then).

I was doing it as a laugh, as a sort of tiny hobby, for a brief while. It was quite fun working out how much information you could pack into a nonary grid and I did start work on a Culture-English dictionary, but it was always going to be too big a job, and it all felt rather arbitrary, just pulling phonemes out of the air and deciding: Right, that's what General Contact Unit is in Marain (something like Wukoorth Sapoot-Jeerd, if memory serves) . . . I've recently had an offer to do this properly, as it were, but I doubt I'll take it up.

JR: In *The Bridge* there is a scene where aeroplanes fly by. It struck me as being reminiscent of the sky-writing scene in *Mrs. Dalloway*. Was that intentional? Also, later on Orr is told that the planes were writing in Braille. Given that the Culture already existed at the time you were writing *The Bridge* it occurred to me that the writing might actually be Marain—is it?

IMB: I haven't read *Mrs. Dalloway*, and until now didn't know there was sky-writing in it, so no conscious influence there. I think the idea of sky-writing in Braille as an image of pointlessness had been around in my notes for a while before it was used in *The Bridge*, so might just have predated the Culture. Probably not, though. Oddly, I don't recall thinking then or until now that the two ideas were similar, but you're right; they are, of course.

JR: To what extent do you think your political perspectives and attitudes inform your writing about the Culture?

IMB: A lot. The Culture stories are me at my most didactic, though it's largely hidden under all the funny names, action and general bluster.

The Culture represents the place we might hope to get to after we've dealt with all our stupidities. Maybe. I have said before, and will doubtless say again, that maybe we—that is, homo sapiens—are just too determinedly stupid and aggressive to have any hope of becoming like the Culture, unless we somehow find and isolate/destroy the genes that code for xenophobia, should they exist. Plus we'd have to develop AIs and let them be themselves; another big ask.

JR: While you have often been resistant to attempts to characterise your writing as distinctively or definitely Scottish, would you be prepared to acknowledge the politics of your Culture novels as Scottish—as opposed to English or American?

IMB: A bit of all the above. I am conscious of being Scottish, British, European, English-speaking Anglo-Saxon-Celt, and what you might call Western. Also a citizen of the world, and all that. A humanist. I would like to think that the politics of the Culture novels is more kind of generally socialist or communitarian, rather than specifically Scottish.

JR: Many critics and reviewers have claimed that the Culture represents the American Libertarian ideal. Given that this is clearly not the case, how do you characterise the politics of the Culture?

IMB: Really? I had no idea. Obviously I haven't read the output of the relevant critics and reviewers. Let's be clear: unless I have profoundly misunderstood its position, I pretty much despise American Libertarianism. Have these people seriously looked at the problems of the world and thought, "Hmm, what we need here is a bit more selfishness"? . . . I beg to differ. This is not to say that Libertarianism can't represent a progressive force, in the right circumstances, and I don't doubt there will be significant areas where I would agree with Libertarianism. But, really; which bit of not having private property, and the absence of money in the Culture novels, have these people missed? The Culture is hippy commies with hyper-weapons and a deep distrust of both Marketolatry and Greedism. One rests one's case.

JR: To what extent does your writing about the Culture endorse the Culture's point of view?

IMB: Probably too much. I started out bending over backwards to present the opposite point of view in *Consider Phlebas*, making it look like the Culture represented the bad guys, at the start, at least, but, let's face it: *La Culture: c'est moi.*

JR: In "A Few Notes on the Culture" you said that the ship body fulfils the same function as the human body, i.e.: it's just a transportation system. You also said that being able to physically change the sex of your body is important to maintaining gender equality. These two statements seem to contradict one another, the first saying that the body isn't important at all and the second saying it's crucial. How important is the body in the Culture?

IMB: I don't think the two statements do contradict each other. Without a body you're helpless; without a ship or something similar, so is a Mind. What I meant in the first instance was that the ship was not there to be commanded in the *Star Trek* manner; the Mind, the AI, was what really mattered, not the thing it inhabited. Of course the ship/body/housing is important, but what holds the personality is the entity at its centre. In the same way, it's our mind—housed within our human body—that contains the essence of who and what we are; we can imagine—with the appropriate future medical technology—regrowing a lost limb, or major organ, without that changing who we really are, but regrowing the brain (without the information that the original brain held) would make us a totally different person. Same with a Mind and a ship. That does not mean that embodiment and context are not important; they are, vitally, but ultimately what matters is where all the information is held. In the end, the body matters quite a lot in the Culture, which is why it's made quite clear that despite having gone through periods when non-human bodies were highly fashionable, the vast majority of people in the Culture in the novels (all of which take place when the Culture is in a stable, cruise-phase, mature-technology state, many thousands of years after its inception) are mostly human in their form, albeit with significant modifications.

JR: Have you considered giving Culture humans the ability to abandon gender altogether?

IMB: Yes, and there is mention of people who have done just that, I think, in the novels. At the very least it's implied, I believe. In the new one, *Surface Detail*, there is a fairly major character we follow throughout the novel who is effectively neuter.

JR: In "A Few Notes" you said that Culture-humans can turn off their pain receptors. In *Consider Phlebas* when Fal falls while mountain climbing it says that she lay in pain for a day. What level of control over pain and other bodily stimuli do Culture-humans have?

IMB: It varies; not everybody has the full works, as it were. Also, not everybody chooses to use what they have, plus the whole system is not perfect in every individual. Generally, though—in theory—everybody has full control. You can turn off pain at will. Though it's a bit like ignoring the red warning message on your car's instrumentation; it's a signal something's wrong and you need to power down and get some repair work done. And for some people the warning signal itself is almost as distressing as raw pain itself.

JR: You have said that you consider yourself to be a humanist. Could you elaborate on what that means to you?

IMB: I think I fit the dictionary definition of a humanist pretty well: non-religious, non-superstitious, basing morality on shared human values of decency, tolerance, reason, justice, the search for truth, and so on. My personal take on this goes a little further—as any serious sf writer's would kind of have to unless they reject the very idea of both AI and aliens—to encompass the rights both of these (as it were, still potential) categories, but other than that I'm probably fairly typical.

JR: Given that there are (I assume?) no gods in the Culture universe, what does Subliming mean? Does it differ from transcendence? If so, how? Why doesn't the Culture sublime?

IMB: Subliming means leaving the matter-based universe and ascending/disappearing into the pure-energy state represented by the compressed dimensions string and brane theory talk about. I haven't made this entirely clear yet in the novels, though I still might in the second draft of *Surface Detail*. Still scientific, still materialist, in a sense; definitely not any sort of religious nonsense. The Culture has decided to forgo Sublimation, for a while at least, in order to stick around in the physical universe, in the Real, and do what it can to make it a better place, Subliming ultimately being a selfish act.

JR: How much does your concept of Subliming have to do with the chemical process of subliming?

IMB: It's just a symbolic word, really; indicative of the process of the tangible seemingly vanishing into thin air.

JR: You say Subliming is ultimately a selfish act? Also, *Transition* is clearly all about selfishness. Is this a central concern for you at the moment, both creatively and politically?

IMB: Absolutely. We live in a Greedist culture; we are ruled by Greedists, in the grip of Marketolatory. Selfishness is the new black and I despise it. And I really do blame Margaret F. Thatcher; she did everything in her considerable power to turn selfishness from a vice into a virtue, and we are living with the consequences now, the most selfish of the selfish having wrecked the world economy and got away with it—salaries, stock options, and bonuses restored, like nothing happened—after putting their own empty greed before any other consideration. Quite a legacy.

JR: How great an impact did the 1979 election have on your thoughts about political utopia?

IMB: Almost no impact, at least immediately; my sights were already raised way beyond the impact of such relatively minor events. I was thinking about the Culture, risen from the debris and glories of a dozen civilisations each made up of hundreds of such statistically irrelevant states.

JR: In the past you have said that you are a short-term pessimist and a long-term optimist. Could you expand on this a bit: why are you pessimistic about the short term? What changes do you anticipate taking place between the near and far futures that change your pessimism to optimism?

IMB: On a personal level, it is damage limitation; a sanity-keeping measure. Expect the worst and anything even only half-decent seems like something to celebrate. The pessimism comes from a feeling that as a species we seem unable to pass up any opportunity to behave stupidly, self-harmfully (the Copenhagen climate talks being but the latest example). The long-term optimism comes from the fact that no matter how bad things seem and how idiotically and cruelly we behave . . . well, we've got this far, despite it all, and there are more people on the planet than ever before, and more people living good, productive, relatively happy lives than ever before, and—providing we aren't terminally stupid, or unlucky enough to get clobbered by something we have no control over, like a big meteorite or a gamma ray buster or whatever—we'll solve a lot of problems just by sticking around and doing what we do; developing, progressing, improving, adapting. And possibly by inventing AIs that are smarter and more decent than we are, which will help us get some sort of perspective on ourselves, at the very least. We might just stumble our way blindly, unthinkingly into utopia, in other words, muddling through despite ourselves.

JR: You've talked a bit about the potential for the invention of AI to transform humanity. How much of the scientific debates about AI do you follow? Have you read anything by Hans Moravec?

IMB: I'm not terribly interested in the debates. Maybe I ought to be, but I feel they're like the debates physicists and engineers had about rocketry, decades ago, when they eventually decided that you could never build a rocket able to carry its own weight into orbit—let alone anything else—and that was that. (They just hadn't thought of staged rockets.) I strongly suspect that, barring catastrophes, AI is inevitable, so debates about its possibility are pointless, while any other debates—regarding its nature or characteristics, say—are jumping the gun. Probably still worth having I guess, to prepare ourselves apart from anything else, but essentially premature and of limited use due to their overly speculative nature.

I read Moravec's book *Mind Children* a year or two after it was published and was quite impressed by it. I don't recall that it changed my mind about anything or gave me any fresh ideas (always the secret hope with books like this), but it was interesting.

JR: Ken MacLeod has said that you are optimistic about technology because "the ability of ordinary blokes and folks to work out, using a pocket calculator, when they were being cheated on their pay, which he had actually seen, made Iain feel that technology is empowering."—Do you agree? What were the circumstances in which you saw people checking their pay on calculators?

IMB: Up to a point, yes. I think I saw this happen at the building site for the Inverkip power station, back in the seventies. For a few months I was the office clerk, dealing with pay and bonuses for the work force, for the firm responsible for the main pipe work within the power station.

JR: You also said, in the same discussion that you like to be in control of the technology in your life—checking your email when you want to, not when it tells you, etc.—is this element of being able to control the tech in our lives important to the way you think about the Culture?

IMB: Definitely, yes. A lot of that is to do with the Culture not being Capitalist, so that nobody has to work. People do things for fun, for the challenge, for a hobby, not because if they don't, they'll starve. So the tech is absolutely at the command of the humans (and drones, and AIs/Minds, in the sense that the unthinking—or at least, unfeeling, non-suffering—tech is separate from them), rather than people having the sensation that they are controlled by the technology around them. Also, it's not a coincidence that the presentation of the Culture's relative Utopia—the way that people live on a day-to-day basis—is generally rural, with lots of pleasant green spaces around, but with fast transport links to concentrated urban spaces, where people go to mingle and have fun.

JR: In a panel about utopias at Odyssey Convention you made the distinction between practical utopia and idealistic utopia. What makes a practical utopia?

IMB: In a sense a practical utopia is just doing the best you can with what you have to hand. In other words, a practical utopia is a society which is run for the general benefit of all, rather than for the particular benefit of a few, no matter what level of technological progress you have attained, minimising suffering and maximising well-being. So this can apply to a hunter-gatherer society as well as one based in sophisticated space colonies. In other words, it's a political argument.

An idealistic utopia is one which exists in a post-scarcity environment and can pretty much do whatever it pleases. The slightly depressing realisation—which leads to the short-term pessimism mentioned above—is that we never really do this; we almost never make any serious attempt to minimise suffering and maximise well-being (though, in a sense, we keep on trying to; people establish communes and little sort of mini-attempts-at-utopias all the time, but they never lead to very much). We keep on behaving tribally, xenophobically, selfishly. This is why I'd contend that we are, as things stand, essentially incapable of achieving any practical utopia. We probably need to change ourselves at the genetic level to have any chance of doing so. I'd love to be proved wrong on this, but even so, if I were a betting man, I'd be wagering on the side of the cynics.

JR: You've suggested that we might need to change our genetics or remove the gene for xenophobia as a potential prerequisite for achieving a Culture-like utopia. How much of what it is to be human do you think is in our genes?

IMB: Well, all of it, in a sense. We ain't nothing without our genes. But genes themselves don't create any culture directly, obviously, so the question is about the balance; how much of what we count as creativity—for example—is essentially determined genetically (how much of it could you predict running a really good sim, say, of a statistically relevantly-sized human society) and how much is due to chance and the individual workings of thought, reason and emotion within individual human brains? I think we are, as a species, overly predisposed to irrationality and xenophobia, too quick to turn to violence, and have an insufficiently critical and flexible approach to authority and to institutions that we believe can relieve us of our individual moral responsibilities, and that there may be gene sequences that code for these attributes. Just glad I won't have to sit on the ethics committee that decides whether to do the experiments to find out . . .

JR: The example you gave of utopian fiction (the Hampstead or Campus novel) are both based on a utopia for some that comes at the cost of those who are not shown in the novel. What stops the Culture from being this kind of utopia?

IMB: Well, the fact that you can't tramp off, find somebody who is in any meaningful sense economically supporting—or oppressed by—this society, grab them by the collar and shout "Here's your downtrodden masses!" Hampstead exists, and university campuses exist, within a certain exploitative economic system, obviously. The Culture by its very nature does not. Materially it is entirely self-sufficient and the entities doing what might be described as the dirty work are little more than computers, usually controlling mindless robots; they are not capable of suffering, or experiencing boredom or frustration or dissatisfaction. The entities supervising them might be humans or drones but they exist at a level that lets their work resemble play; a game. It's rewarding, just the way any well-designed game or satisfying job is, and for its own sake.

I only wanted to use Hampstead and Campus novels as examples of kinds of relatively utopian novels; ones in which the protagonists don't have to worry about mundane stuff like working on a farm or in a factory or office to keep a roof over their heads. I was trying to suggest that these were our equivalents of utopias, limited and conditional though they might be; places where people were able to live lives free, to a significant degree, from the exigencies of toil, economic exploitation, and the threat of penury. In the "Reasons: the Culture" section of the appendices in *Consider Phlebas* there's the line, "The only desire the Culture could not fulfil from within itself . . . was the urge not to feel useless." In that need alone it is not self-sufficient, and so it has to go out into the rest of the galaxy to prove to itself, and to others, that its own high opinion of itself is somehow justified. At its worst, it is the equivalent of the lady of the manor going out amongst the peasants of the local village with her bounteous basket of breads and sweetmeats, but it's still better than nothing. And while the lady might—through her husband and the economic control he exerts over his estate and therefore the village—be partly responsible for the destitution she seeks, piecemeal, to alleviate, the Culture isn't. It's just trying terribly hard to be helpful and nice, in situations it did nothing to bring into being.

JR: When you talk about the lady of the manor trying to alleviate the economic conditions her husband brought about, the gender feels significant. To what extent would you consider the Culture to be a feminised society?

IMB: I've always thought of the Culture as being more feminine than male, at least as far as how we as a species would react to it if we were ever exposed to it. To the Culture, of course, such gender-based evaluations are puzzling, not very helpful and profoundly missing the point; in a society with relatively easy sex-change and perfectly asexual Minds running the really complicated stuff, gender is pretty much irrelevant.

I think there's an argument that you need the male predisposition to aggression while you're "growing up" as a species, but that gradually (though absolutely—and preferably immediately—as soon as you invent weapons of mass destruction) you need a different approach; time to pass on the baton, chaps. If we accept that women are, compared to men, generally more caring, less aggressive, and more open to using discussion as a way of resolving disputes, then the less your society and civilisation is concerned with the day-to-day stuff of securing borders, procreating like crazy to keep the numbers up in the face of high rates of infant mortality, and managing and distributing scarce resources and so on, the less you need men calling all the shots.

JR: Almost all your stories involve some kind of game. What is it that interests you about games and game playing?

IMB: I think both stories and games are, at least potentially, kind of rehearsals for life; basically pedagogy, wrapped up in a sweet coating to make the learning fun. And they're both linear, have themes, characters, and so on. So the same things interest me about both games and stories; principally the potential for serious play.

JR: You've used the word "play" to describe your use of form and narrative structure. As I'm sure you know, in recent years the term "play" has been used to describe a certain kind of postmodern engagement with the world. To what extent do you consider your work to be postmodern?

IMB: I confess I don't think about it at all. I've never been good on literary or societal theory. I've long since decided people like me just write what we do and let other people worry about the analytical side.

JR: Farah Mendlesohn, talking about *Excession*, has said that space opera celebrates the human. Do you consider the Culture novels to be a celebration of the human?

IMB: I think space opera in general celebrates a certain manic wildness and vivacity of vision, a refusal to be constrained. I think the Culture celebrates something slightly different from—or at least on the outskirts of—the above, by being about what we call human values but which, I'd argue, are more like sentient values; values to do with intelligence, empathy, altruism, and the promotion of (comfort, contentment, satisfaction, pleasure, joy, bliss, and ecstasy) along with the alleviation of suffering.

JR: Apart from a few bits of poetry and Ziller in *Look to Windward* you haven't written much about artists/writers in the Culture. How important is creativity in the Culture?

IMB: Very, but only at an amateur level, as we would understand it, and not just because there is no need—or way—to be a true professional in any field in a society without money. In the Culture you express yourself creatively because you enjoy it and feel it to be personally fulfilling; you don't do it to prove how completely brilliant you are to peers, potential sexual partners and the world in general because at the back of your mind you know almost any Mind could do it better.

JR: There are very few animals shown in the Culture novels. Are there many animals in the Culture? Also, you use birds a lot in your writing. Do they represent anything in particular for you?

IMB: You're right. Actually, there are not enough animals in the Culture. When I think about it, I always mean to include more, but then I keep forgetting to. Not the thought that counts, sadly, in this case. Birds . . . I don't know. Symbol of freedom, perhaps?

JR: You have written about several characters whose lives involve or have involved an intensely traumatic experience. I'm thinking of Andy in *Complicity* and Zakalwe in *Use of Weapons* in particular here, but there are many others. What is it that interests you so much about trauma and its effects?

IMB: To be frank, it's the excuse it gives me to make my characters do extreme things, or at least put themselves into extreme situations. I'm very conscious that I've lived a pretty easy and non-traumatic life, and I can't imagine me doing the stuff necessary to create the stories I'm interested in (I've too much to lose, I've nothing to prove to somebody who denied me love . . . whatever), so I need to imagine what it would take to make somebody (and specifically somebody I can identify with sufficiently to write convincingly about) behave in such a brave/foolhardy/dangerous manner.

JR: You often write about the perpetrators of violence, far more often than you write about the victims of violence. What is it that interests you about perpetrators?

IMB: They're the instigators, they're the ones who've made a choice to behave badly; that sets them apart, makes them worthy of study (condemnation, too, of course, but that's not the immediate point if you're merely imagining them to write about them). Random killers might happen to kill interesting people, but as a rule we are all just average people, with—mercifully, maybe—nothing much to distinguish us. We live, procreate, die, and that's the way it should be; we've done our bit. In a sense there is no particular further urgency to the understanding of ordinary people, rewarding though that might be in its own way, whereas it is important to understand those who choose to inflict violence on others because they're the ones we need to deal with, and ultimately the ones whose behaviour we need, as a society, to alter or pre-empt.

JR: You have written quite a few novels that use Freudian imagery and tropes—*The Wasp Factory*, *Use of Weapons*, *The Bridge*, *Walking on Glass*—what do you think of Freudian psychoanalysis?

IMB: Never been entirely sold in it. I suspect Freud's theories tell you a great deal about Freud, quite a lot about the monied middle-class in Vienna a hundred-plus years ago, and only a little about people in general. Like Marx, he was too keen to insist that his area of study was genuinely a science. Also like Marx, though, he provides a genuinely useful and insightful (if, especially in Freud's case, limited) way of looking at people and their hidden lives (well, more implied lives with Marx, relating to their economic function within a society).

Anyway, I can honestly say that I've never deliberately included any Freudian imagery in my stories, so what's there must be the result of my subconscious. Uh-oh . . .

## FICTION

*The Wasp Factory*. 1984. London: Macmillan.
*Walking on Glass*. 1985. London: Macmillan.
*The Bridge*. 1986. London: Macmillan.
*Consider Phlebas* (as by Iain M. Banks). 1987. London: Macmillan.
*Espedair Street*. 1987. London: Macmillan.
*The Player of Games* (as by Iain M. Banks). 1988. London: Macmillan.
*Canal Dreams*. 1989. London: Macmillan.
*The State of the Art* (novella, as by Iain M. Banks). 1989. Willimantic, Conn.: Ziesing.
*Use of Weapons* (as by Iain M. Banks). 1990. London: Orbit.
*The Crow Road*. 1991. London: Scribners.
*The State of the Art* (collection, as by Iain M. Banks). 1991. London: Orbit.
*Against a Dark Background* (as by Iain M. Banks). 1993. London: Orbit.
*Complicity*. 1993. London: Little Brown.
*Feersum Endjinn* (as by Iain M. Banks). 1994. London: Orbit.
"Against a Dark Background: Epilogue" (as by Iain M. Banks). 1994. Culture Data Repository, http://www.culturelist.org/cdr/article.cfm?id=142&highlight=against%20a%20dark%20background (accessed August 3, 2015).
*Whit*. 1995. London: Little Brown.
*Excession* (as by Iain M. Banks). 1996. London: Orbit.
*A Song of Stone*. 1997. London: Abacus.
*Inversions* (as by Iain M. Banks). 1998. London: Orbit.
*The Business*. 1999. London: Little Brown.
*Look to Windward* (as by Iain M. Banks). 2000. London: Orbit.
*Dead Air*. 2002. London: Little Brown.
*The Algebraist* (as by Iain M. Banks). 2004. London: Orbit.
*The Steep Approach to Garbadale*. 2007. London: Little Brown.
*Matter* (as by Iain M. Banks). 2008. London: Orbit.
*Transition*. 2009. London: Little Brown.
*Surface Detail* (as by Iain M. Banks). 2010. London: Orbit.
*Stonemouth*. 2012. London: Little Brown.
*The Hydrogen Sonata* (as by Iain M. Banks). 2012. London: Orbit.
*The Quarry*. 2013. London: Little Brown.

NONFICTION

"Iain Banks' Guest of Honour Speech, Eastcon '90." 1990. Matrix 88, 5–6.

"A Few Notes on the Culture" (as by Iain M. Banks). 1994. Available at http://www
.vavatch.co.uk/books/banks/cultnote.htm (accessed December 16, 2014).

*Raw Spirit: in Search of the Perfect Dram.* 2003. London: Century.

"A Personal Statement from Iain Banks." 2013. Available at http://www.iain-banks.net/
2013/04/03/a-personal-statement-from-iain-banks/ (accessed October 6, 2014).

"20 May, Update from Iain." 2013. Available at http://friends.banksophilia.com/74
(accessed October 10, 2014).

"Preface." *The Wasp Factory.* 2013. London: Abacus, ix–xi.

Iain Banks and Ken MacLeod. *Poems.* 2015. London: Little Brown.

## CHAPTER 1. CROSSING THE BRIDGE

1. Alan Brittenham, writing on February 2, 2014, http://friends.banksophilia.com/guestbook, accessed October 10, 2014.

2. March, *Rewriting Scotland*, 83.

3. Quoted on several dustjackets—see, for example, *The Crow Road*, 1991. See also http://www.thetimes.co.uk/tto/life/courtsocial/article3689779.ece.

4. Cobley, "Eye to Eye," 31.

5. Harrison, "Literature of Comfort," 84.

6. Clute, *Strokes*, 82.

7. Brown, *Arts and Parts*.

8. MacLeod, "Continuing Conversations."

9. Smith, "Synopsis of the Culture."

10. MacLeod, "Continuing Conversations."

11. Sawyer, "Iain Banks," 7.

12. Nicholls, *Wordsmiths of Wonder*, 139.

13. Sawyer, "Iain Banks," 5.

14. Nicholls, *Wordsmiths of Wonder*, 138.

15. Garnett, "Iain M. Banks," 69.

16. See Hughes, "Doing the Business," 7.

17. Hastings, "Flying Leap," 7.

18. MacDonald, "Still Magic in the World," 100.

19. Speller, "No Man Is an Island," 28.

20. Ibid., 29.

21. See Jude Roberts interview, herewith.

22. Newman, "Iain Banks," 41.

23. Ibid., 42.

24. Middleton, "Works," 7.

25. See, in particular, Miller, *Alasdair Gray*, chap. 2.

26. Laing, *Divided Self*, 42–43.

27. Craig, *Iain Banks's Complicity*, 54.

28. Cobley, "Eye to Eye," 26.

29. See Kincaid, "Far Too Strange."

30. Butler, "Strange Case of Mr. Banks," 25.

31. McVeigh, "Weaponry of Deceit," 3.

32. This and the following quotations are taken from the original paperback edition of *The Wasp Factory* (1985).

33. Hastings, "Flying Leap," 7.

34. Cobley, "Eye to Eye," 26.

35. See Leishman, "Coalescence."

36. Todd, *Consuming Fictions*, 136.

37. Pattie, "Lessons of *Lanark*," 11.

38. Ibid., 14.

39. Wilson, "Lightly Seared," 59.

40. Ibid., 62–63.

41. Cobley, "Eye to Eye," 31.

42. Martingale, *Gothic Dimensions*, 82.

43. Citations taken from the 1991 U.K. collection rather than the 1989 U.S. novella.

44. Caroti, *Culture Series*, 66.

## CHAPTER 2. BACKING INTO THE CULTURE

1. MacLeod, "Continuing Conversations."

2. Newman, "Iain Banks," 41.

3. Miller, "Walking on Glass," 15.

4. Kincaid, "Walking on Glass," 12.

5. Kincaid, "Bridge," 13.

6. Dickinson, "Bridge," 14.

7. Clute, *Look at the Evidence*, 28.

8. Greenland, "Consider Phlebas," 93.

9. Miller, "Consider Phlebas," 13.

10. Langford, *Complete Critical Assembly*, 170.

11. See Andrew M. Butler, "Thirteen Ways."

12. Palmer, "Galactic Empires," 73.

13. Duggan, "Iain M. Banks," 561.

14. See Caroti, *Culture Series*, 82–83, for an account of the intersecting timelines of these two works.

15. Palmer, "Galactic Empires," 86.

16. Stan Nicholls, "Man of the Culture," *Starlog*, December 1994; quoted in March, *Rewriting Scotland*, 83.

17. Duggan, "Iain M. Banks," 559.

18. Person, "Culture-D Space Opera," 34.

19. Porter, "Player of Games," 13.

20. Miller, "Player of Games," 17.

21. Slocombe, "Games Playing Roles," 136.

22. Craig, *Iain Banks's Complicity*, 12.

23. Sage, "Politics of Petrifaction," 22.

24. Wilson, "Lightly Seared," 59.

25. See, for instance, Hodson, "State of the Art," 16.

26. Person, "Culture-D Space Opera," 35.

27. Wilson, "Lightly Seared," 57.

28. MacLeod, "Phlebas Reconsidered," 2.

29. Gevers, "Cultured Futurist."

30. Goonan, "Use of Weapons," 7.

31. Greenland, "Use of Weapons," 92.

32. Interview with Tim Metcalfe, *GM*, 1989, quoted in Martingale, *Gothic Dimensions*, 441.

33. Greenland, "Use of Weapons," 90.

34. Mendlesohn, "Dialectic of Decadence," 116.

35. Kerslake, *Science Fiction and Empire*, 180.

36. Ibid., 180.

37. Hardesty, "Mercenaries and Special Circumstances," 40.

38. Ibid., 40.

39. Ibid., 43.

40. Wilson, "Lightly Seared," 55.

41. Kerslake, *Science Fiction and Empire*, 187.

42. Hardesty, "Mercenaries and Special Circumstances," 39.

43. MacLeod, "Phlebas Reconsidered," 1.

44. Quantick, "Prose Encounters," 24.

45. Palmer, "Galactic Empires," 79.

46. Spufford, "Iain M. Banks' Universe."

## CHAPTER 3. OUTSIDE CONTEXT PROBLEMS

1. Hartley, "Letter from Adele."

2. Hughes, "Doing the Business," 6.

3. McVeigh, "Canal Dreams," 18.

4. MacGillivray, *Iain Banks*, 8.

5. Branscombe, "Iain M. Banks."

6. Martingale, *Gothic Dimensions*, 300.

7. March, *Rewriting Scotland*, 91.

8. Wilson, "Lightly Seared," 57.

9. Stan Nicholls, "Man of the Culture," *Starlog*, December 1994; quoted in March, *Rewriting Scotland*, 91.

10. Spufford, "Iain M. Banks' Universe."

11. Clute, *Scores*, 28.

12. Gilmore, "Against a Dark Background," 95.

13. Corbett, "Past and Future Language," quoted 126.

14. March, *Rewriting Scotland*, 86.

15. Corbett, "Past and Future Language," 123.

16. Branscombe, "Iain M. Banks."

17. Sage, "Politics of Petrifaction," 23.

18. Interview with *The Scottish Book Collector*, quoted in MacGillivray, *Iain Banks*, 56.

19. Pisarska, *Mediating the World*, 253.

20. Ibid., 253.

21. Clute, *Scores*, 207.

22. Kate Kelman, "A Collision of Selves: Kate Kelman interviews Iain Banks," *Cencrastus* 60, 1998, quoted in Pisarska, *Mediating the World*, 259n5.

23. Rambrout, "Interview."

24. MacGillivray, *Iain Banks*, 7.

25. Pisarska, *Mediating the World*, 255.

26. Taylor, "Crow Road," 30.

27. Latham, "Violent Insertion," 13.

28. Mendlesohn, "Iain M. Banks: *Excession*," 557–58, emphasis in the original.

29. Ibid., 559.

30. Lem, "On Stapledon's *Star Maker*," 345.

31. Duggan, "Inside the Whale," 7.

32. Gevers, "Cultured Futurist."

33. See Jude Roberts interview, herewith.

34. James, *Science Fiction in the 20th Century*, 104–5.

35. Ibid., 106.

36. Ibid., 7.

37. Clarke, "Sublime," 9.

38. March, *Rewriting Scotland*, 87.

39. Oliver Morton, "Iain Banks spoke with Oliver Morton," *Wired*, June 1996, quoted in March, *Rewriting Scotland*, 88.

40. Branscombe, "Iain M. Banks."

41. Ibid.

42. Gilmore, "Excession," 117.

43. Nicholas, "Excession," 12.

44. Duggan, "Inside the Whale," 18–19.

45. Ibid., 19.

46. Wilson, "Lightly Seared on the Reality Grill," 57.

47. Morrow, "Inversions," 16.

48. Dalkin, "Inversions," 25.

49. Langford, *Up Through an Empty House of Stars*, 214–15.

50. Ibid., 215.

51. Dalkin, "Inversions," 26.

52. Caroti, *The Culture Series*, 142.

53. Gevers, "Cultured Futurist."

54. Ibid.

55. See Jude Roberts interview, herewith.

56. Pisarska, *Mediating the World*, 242.

57. Ibid., 246.

58. Eliot, "Waste Land," lines 319–21.

59. Danczak, "Look to Wasteland," 23.

60. Ibid., 27.

61. Eliot, "Waste Land," line 312.

62. Kincaid, "Look to Windward," 18.

63. VanderMeer, "Look to Windward," 15.

## CHAPTER 4. APPROACHING THE WORLDGOD

1. Jonas, "Science Fiction."
2. Poole, "Dead Air."
3. Hughes, "Doing the Business," 6.
4. Parsons, "Interview."
5. Robson, "Algebraist."
6. Willetts, "Iain Banks Speaks," 62.
7. Young, "Algebraist," 25.
8. See Jude Roberts interview, herewith.
9. Wilson, "Lightly Seared," 53.
10. Haigh, "Iain Banks—Transition."
11. Cox, "Textual Crossings," 92.
12. Pisarska, *Mediating the World*, 91.
13. See Jude Roberts interview, herewith, for a discussion of the related issue of Culture Minds within the bodies of the ships.
14. Pisarska, *Mediating the World*, 141.
15. Haigh, "Iain Banks—Transition."
16. Interview with Anthony Brown quoted in Caroti, *Culture Series*, 182.
17. Wilson, "Lightly Seared," 53.
18. Kelly, "Bad Cosmic Ray," 2.
19. See Caroti, *Culture Series*, 185.
20. Ibid., chapter 8.
21. Jones, "Matter."
22. Caroti, *Culture Series*, 199.
23. Parsons, "Interview."
24. Caroti, *Culture Series*, 207.
25. Clute, *Stay*, 164.
26. Ibid., 164.

## CHAPTER 5. AFTERMATH

1. Kelly, "Bad Cosmic Ray," 2.
2. Ibid.
3. Pisarska, *Mediating the World*, 303.
4. Kelly, "Bad Cosmic Ray," 2.
5. Roberts, *Science Fiction*, 155.
6. Norman, "Books of Truth," 37.
7. Spufford, "Iain M. Banks' Universe."
8. Ibid.
9. Norman, "Books of Truth," 41.
10. Parsons, "Interview."
11. Mitchell, "Iain Banks."
12. Quoted in Norman, "Books of Truth," 39–40.
13. Ibid., 46.
14. Norman, "Books of Truth," 46.

15. Stafford, "Iain M. Banks."

16. Winter, "Moments in the Fall," 324.

17. Ibid., 327.

18. Greenaway, "Ordinary People."

19. Winter, "Moments in the Fall," 326.

20. Norman, "Books of Truth," 41.

21. Mitchell, "Iain Banks."

22. Suderman, "Endless Lives."

23. Norman, "Books of Truth," 44.

24. Parsons, "Interview."

25. Mitchell, "Iain Banks."

26. Haigh, "Iain Banks—Transition."

27. Mitchell, "Iain Banks."

28. Ibid.

29. Ibid.

30. Suderman, "Endless Lives."

31. Kelly, "Bad Cosmic Ray," 3.

32. Hughes, "Doing the Business," 7.

33. Pritchard, "Wasp Factory."

34. Hughes, "Doing the Business," 7.

35. Quantick, "Prose Encounters," 24.

36. See Butler, "Thirteen Ways."

37. Hodgson, "Iain Banks Remembered."

38. MacLeod, "Continuing Conversations."

39. Parsons, "Interview."

# BIBLIOGRAPHY OF SECONDARY SOURCES

Iain Banks was very generous with his time and gave innumerable interviews. There are also vast numbers of essays about him and his work. Rather than try to list everything, I have therefore restricted this bibliography to the pieces I found most useful in researching this book.

Armitt, Lucy. *Theorising the Fantastic.* London: Arnold, 1996.

Branscombe, Mary. "Iain M Banks' Latest Culture Novel Is a Tale of Conspiracy, Deception and Eccentricity. So, Iain, We Asked, What's It All About?" *SFX Magazine,* 1996. Available at http://web.archive.org/web/20080206132746/http://www.sandm.co.uk/mary/sfjournm/Excession/excession.html (accessed August 11, 2015).

Brown, Carolyn. "Utopias and Heterotopias: The 'Culture' of Iain M. Banks." In *Impossibility Fiction: Alternativity—Extrapolation—Speculation,* edited by Derek Littlewood and Peter Stockwell, 57–74. Amsterdam: Rodopi, 1996.

Brown, James. "Not Losing the Plot: Politics, Guilt and Storytelling in Banks and MacLeod." In *The True Knowledge of Ken MacLeod,* edited by Andrew M. Butler and Farah Mendlesohn, 55–75. Foundation Studies in Science Fiction 3. Reading, U.K.: Science Fiction Foundation, 2003.

Brown, John. *Arts and Parts.* Broadcast on Scottish TV June 1, 1997. Bundled with the DVD of *The Crow Road.*

Butler, Andrew M. "Strange Case of Mr. Banks: Doubles and *The Wasp Factory.*" *Foundation* 76 (1999): 17–26.

———. "Thirteen Ways of Looking at the British Boom." *Science Fiction Studies* 91 (2003): 374–93.

Caroti, Simone. *The Culture Series of Iain M. Banks: A Critical Introduction.* Jefferson, N.C.: McFarland, 2015.

Clarke, Jim. "The Sublime in Iain M. Banks's 'Culture' Novels." *Vector* 281 (2015): 7–11.

Clute, John. 1988. *Look at the Evidence: Essays and Reviews.* Liverpool: Liverpool University Press, 1995.

———. *Scores: Reviews 1993–2003.* Harold Wood, U.K.: Beccon, 2003.

———. *Stay.* Harold Wood: Beccon, 2014.

———. *Strokes: Essays and Reviews 1966–1986.* Seattle, Wash.: Serconia, 1988.

Cobley, Michael. "Eye to Eye: An Interview with Iain Banks." *Science Fiction Eye* 6 (1990): 22–32.

Colebrook, Martyn, and Katharine Cox, eds. *The Transgressive Iain Banks*. Jefferson, N.C.: McFarland, 2013.

Corbett, John. "Past and Future Language: Matthew Fitt and Iain M. Banks." In *Scotland as Science Fiction*, edited by Caroline McCracken-Flesher, 117–32. Lewisburg, Pa.: Bucknell University Press, 2012.

Cox, Katharine. "Textual Crossings: Transgressive Devices in Banks' Fiction." In Colebrook and Cox, *Transgressive Iain Banks*, 87–99.

Craig, Cairns. *Iain Banks's Complicity*. New York: Continuum, 2002.

Dalkin, Gary. "Inversions." *Vector* 202 (1998): 25–26.

Danczak, Felix. "Look to Wasteland." *Vector* 264 (2010): 23–28.

Dickinson, Mike. "The Bridge." *Vector* 134 (1986): 14.

Duggan, Robert. "Iain M. Banks, Postmodernism and the Gulf War." *Extrapolation* 48, no. 3 (2007): 558–77.

———. "Inside the Whale and Outside Context Problems." *Foundation* 116 (2013): 6–22.

Eliot, T. S. "The Waste Land." 1922. In *Selected Poems*, London: Faber, 1969.

Garnett, David S. "Iain M. Banks." *Journal Wired* (Winter 1989): 51–69.

Garrison, John. "Speculative Nationality: 'Stands Scotland Where It Did?' in the Culture of Iain M. Banks." In *Scotland as Science Fiction*, edited by Caroline McCracken-Flesher, 55–66. Lewisburg, Pa.: Bucknell University Press, 2012.

Gevers, Nick. "Cultured Futurist Iain M. Banks Creates an Ornate Utopia." *Science Fiction Weekly* (2002). Available at http://web.archive.org/web/20080605201003/http://www.scifi.com/sfw/issue274/interview.html (accessed August 11, 2015).

Gilmore, Chris. "Against a Dark Background." *Foundation* 61 (1994): 94–96.

———. "Excession." *Foundation* 70 (1997): 116–18.

Goonan, Kathleen Ann. "Use of Weapons." *New York Review of Science Fiction* 50 (1992): 6–7.

Gray, Alasdair. *Lanark*. London: Granada, 1982.

Greenaway, Jon. "They Are What Is Called Ordinary People—*Engleby, The Wasp Factory* and the Structures of Violence in the British Gothic." *Dark Arts Journal* 1, no. 1 (2015): 34–44. Available at https://thedarkartsjournal.files.wordpress.com/2015/06/the-dark-arts-journal-1-1.pdf (accessed September 20, 2016).

Greenland, Colin. "Consider Phlebas." *Foundation* 40 (1987): 92–95.

———. "Use of Weapons." *Foundation* 50 (1990): 90–94.

Guerrier, Simon. 1999. "Culture Theory: Iain M. Banks's 'Culture' as Utopia." *Foundation* 76 (1999): 28–38.

Haigh, Tim. "Iain Banks—Transition." *Books Podcasts*, September 23, 2009. Available at http://timhaighreadsbooks.com/?p=17#.VmfvB_mLTGg (accessed December 8, 2015).

Hardesty, William H. "Mercenaries and Special Circumstances: Iain M. Banks's Counter-Narrative of Utopia, *Use of Weapons*." *Foundation* 76 (1999): 39–47.

Harrison, M. John. "A Literature of Comfort." 1971. In *Parietal Games: Critical Writings by and on M. John Harrison*, edited by Mark Bould and Michelle Reid. Foundation Studies in Science Fiction 5: 84–88. London: Science Fiction Foundation, 2005.

Hartley, Adele. "A Letter from Adele." *Banksophilia*, June 14, 2013. Available at http://friends.banksophilia.com/a-letter-from-adele-15-june (accessed July 31, 2015).

Hastings, Max. "A Flying Leap from the Junk Pile." *Evening Standard*, December 30, 1983, 7.

Hodgson, Michelle. "Iain Banks Remembered." *Guardian*, December 16, 2013. Available at http://www.theguardian.com/books/2013/dec/16/iain-banks-obituary-michelle-hodgson (accessed December 22, 2015).

Hodson, Dave. "The State of the Art." *Vector* 154 (1990): 15–16.

Horwich, David. "Culture Clash: Ambivalent Heroes and the Ambiguous Utopia in the Work of Iain M. Bank." *Strange Horizons*, January 21, 2002. Available at http://www.strangehorizons.com/2002/20020121/culture_clash.shtml (accessed December 13, 2015).

Hughes, Colin. "Doing the Business." *Guardian*, August 6, 1999.

James, Edward. *Science Fiction in the 20th Century*. Oxford: Oxford University Press, 1994.

Jonas, Gerald. "Science Fiction." *New York Times*, October 7, 2001. Available at http://www.nytimes.com/2001/10/07/books/science-fiction.html (accessed November 19, 2015).

Jones, Gwyneth. "Matter." *Strange Horizons*, April 14, 2008. Available at http://www.strangehorizons.com/reviews/2008/04/matter_by_iain_.shtml (accessed December 13, 2015).

Kelly, Stuart. "A Bad Cosmic Ray with My Name on It." *Guardian Review*, June 15, 2013, 2–4.

Kemp, Stuart. 2009. "Murphy to Film Banks' 'Gift from the Culture.'" *Hollywood Reporter*, October 10, 2009. Available at http://www.hollywoodreporter.com/news/murphy-film-banks-gift-culture-90266 (accessed December 21, 2015).

Kerslake, Patricia. 2010. *Science Fiction and Empire*. Liverpool: Liverpool University Press, 2010.

Kincaid, Paul. "The Bridge." *Vector* 134 (1986): 13–14.

———. "Far Too Strange: The Early Fiction of Iain Banks." *Foundation* 116 (2013): 23–36.

———. "Look to Windward." *Vector* 213 (2000): 18–19.

———. "Walking on Glass." *Paperback Inferno* 62 (1986): 12.

Kneale, James. "'I Have Never Been to Nasqueron': A Geographer Reads Banks." In Colebrook and Cox, *Transgressive Iain Banks*, 45–62.

Laing, R. D. *The Divided Self*. 1960. Harmondsworth: Pelican, 1970.

Langford, David. *The Complete Critical Assembly*. Holicong, Pa.: Cosmos, 2002.

———. *Up through an Empty House of Stars: Reviews and Essays 1980–2002*. Holicong, Pa.: Cosmos, 2003.

Latham, Rob. "Violent Insertion and Destructive Penetration." *New York Review of Science Fiction* 70 (1994): 11–15.

Leishman, David. "Coalescence and the Fiction of Iain Banks." In *Études Écossaises*, December 2009, 215–30. Available at http://etudesecossaises.revues.org/208 (accessed December 4, 2015).

Lem, Stanislaw. "On Stapledon's *Star Maker*." 1987. In *Vintage Visions: Essays on Early Science Fiction*, edited by Arthur B. Evans, 342–51. Middletown, Conn.: Wesleyan University Press, 2014.

MacDonald, Kirsty A. "'Still Magic in the World': Banks and the Psychosomatic Supernatural." In Colebrook and Cox, *Transgressive Iain Banks*, 100–111.

MacGillivray, Alan. *Iain Banks'* The Wasp Factory, The Crow Road *and* Whit. Glasgow: Association for Scottish Literary Studies, 2001.

MacLeod, Ken. "The Culture: Continuing Conversations." Paper presented at The State of the Culture: A One-Day Symposium on Iain Banks's Utopia, Brunel University, Uxbridge, 2013.

————. "Phlebas Reconsidered." In *The True Knowledge of Ken MacLeod*, edited by Andrew M. Butler and Farah Mendlesohn. Foundation Studies in Science Fiction 3: 1–3. Reading, Pa.: Science Fiction Foundation, 2003.

March, Christie L. *Rewriting Scotland: Welsh, McLean, Warner, Banks, Galloway and Kennedy*. Manchester: Manchester University Press, 2002.

Martingale, Moira. *Gothic Dimensions*. Marston Gate, U.K.: Quetzalcoatal, 2013.

McVeigh, Kev. "Canal Dreams" in *Vector* 155 (1990): 18.

————. "The Weaponry of Deceit: Speculations on Reality in *The Wasp Factory*." *Vector* 191 (1997): 3–4.

Mendlesohn, Farah. "Religion and Science Fiction." In *The Cambridge Companion to Science Fiction*, edited by Edward James and Farah Mendlesohn, 264–75. Cambridge: Cambridge University Press, 2003.

————. "The Dialectic of Decadence and Utopia in Iain M. Banks's Culture Novels." *Foundation* 93 (2005): 116–24.

————. "Iain M. Banks: *Excession*." In *A Companion to Science Fiction*, edited by David Seed, 556–66. Oxford: Blackwell, 2005.

Middleton, Tim. "Landscape and the Imagination: Banks' Representation of Argyll in *The Crow Road*." In Colebrook and Cox, *Transgressive Iain Banks*, 63–75.

————. "The Works of Iain M. Banks: A Critical Introduction." *Foundation* 76 (1999): 5–16.

Miller, Faren. "The Bridge." *Locus* 311 (1986): 40.

————. "Consider Phlebas." *Locus* 316 (1987): 13–15.

————. "The Player of Games." *Locus* 335 (1988): 17.

————. "Walking on Glass." *Locus* 303 (1986): 15.

Miller, Gavin. *Alasdair Gray: The Fiction of Communion*. Amsterdam: Rodopi, 2005.

————. "Scottish Science Fiction: Writing Scottish Literature Back into History." *Études Écossaises*, December 2009, 121–33. Available at http://etudesecossaises.revues.org/197 (accessed December 4, 2015).

Mitchell, Chris. "Iain Banks: Whit and Excession; Getting Used to Being God." *Spike*, September 3, 1996. Available at http://www.spikemagazine.com/0996bank.php (accessed December 19, 2015).

Morrow, Kathryn S. "Inversions." *New York Review of Science Fiction* 145 (2000): 16.

Nairn, Thom. "Iain Banks and the Fiction Factory." In *The Scottish Novel since the Seventies*, edited by Gavin Wallace and Randall Stevenson, 127–35. Edinburgh: Edinburgh University Press, 1994.

Newman, Kim. "Iain Banks." *Interzone* 16 (1986): 41–42.

Nicholas, Joseph. "Excession." *Vector* 190 (1996): 12.

Nicholls, Stan. *Wordsmiths of Wonder: Fifty Interviews with Writers of the Fantastic*. London: Orbit, 1993.

Norman, Joe. "'Books of Truth': Iain M. Banks—Atheist, Secularist, Humanist." *Foundation* 116 (2013): 37–50.

Nussbaum, Abigail. "Surface Detail." *Strange Horizons*, June 13, 2011. Available at http://www.strangehorizons.com/reviews/2011/06/surface_detail_.shtml (accessed December 13, 2015).

Palmer, Christopher. "Galactic Empires and the Contemporary Extravaganza: Dan Simmons and Iain M. Banks." *Science Fiction Studies* 77 (1999): 73–90.

Parsons, Michael. "Interview: Iain M. Banks Talks 'Surface Detail' with Wired." *Wired*, October 14, 2010. Available at http://www.wired.co.uk/news/archive/2010–10/14/iain -m-banks-interview (accessed December 19, 2015).

Pattie, David. "The Lessons of *Lanark*: Iain Banks, Alasdair Gray and the Scottish Political Novel." In Colebrook and Cox, *Transgressive Iain Banks*, 9–27.

Person, Lawrence. "The Culture-D Space Opera of Iain M. Banks." *Science Fiction Eye 6* (1990): 33–36.

Pisarska, Katarzyna. *Mediating the World in the Novels of Iain Banks: The Paradigms of Fiction*. Frankfurt: Peter Lang, 2013.

Poole, Stephen. "Dead Air." *Guardian*, September 14, 2002. Available at http://www .theguardian.com/books/2002/sep/14/shopping.fiction (accessed November 19, 2015).

Porter, Maureen. "The Player of Games." *Vector* 147 (1989): 13.

Pritchard, Stephen. "The Wasp Factory—Review." *Observer*, October 6, 2013. Available at http://www.theguardian.com/music/2013/oct/06/wasp-factory-opera-house-review (accessed December 21, 2015).

Quantick, David. "Prose Encounters." *New Musical Express*, June 19, 1993, 24.

Rambrout, Dag. "Interview with Iain M. Banks." *SFFworld*, January 1997. Available at http://www.sffworld.com/1997/01/interview-with-iain-m-banks/ (accessed October 13, 2015).

Roberts, Adam. *Science Fiction*. London: Routledge, 2000.

Robson, Justina. "The Algebraist." *Guardian*, October 23, 2004. Available at http://www .theguardian.com/books/2004/oct/23/sciencefictionfantasyandhorror.iainbanks (accessed November 19, 2015).

Sage, Victor. "The Politics of Petrifaction: Culture, Religion, History in the Fiction of Iain Banks and John Banville." In *Modern Gothic: A Reader*, edited by Victor Sage and Allan Lloyd Smith, 20–37. Manchester: Manchester University Press, 1996.

Sawyer, Andy. "Iain Banks." *Vector* 158 (1991): 5–7.

Slocombe, Will. "Games Playing Roles in Banks' Fiction." In Colebrook and Cox, *Transgressive Iain Banks*, 136–49.

Smith, David. "A Synopsis of the Culture: An Interview with Iain M. Banks." Recorded October 19, 2010.

Speller, Maureen Kincaid. "No Man Is an Island: The Enigma of *The Wasp Factory*." *Steam Engine Time* 1 (2000): 28–29.

Spufford, Francis. "Iain M. Banks' Universe." *New Humanist*, June 10, 2013. Available at https://newhumanist.org.uk/articles/4182/iain-m-banks-universe (accessed January 11, 2015).

Stafford, Robert. "Iain M Banks and the Culture." *Socialist Standard* 1307 (July 2013). Available at http://www.worldsocialism.org/spgb/socialist-standard/2010s/2013/no -1307-july-2013/iain-m-banks-and-culture (accessed December 20, 2015).

Stephenson, William. "'Hippies with Mega Nukes': The Culture, Terror and the War Machine in *Consider Phlebas* and *The Player of Games*." In Colebrook and Cox, *Transgressive Iain Banks*, 165–78.

Suderman, Peter. "The Endless Lives of Iain M. Banks." *Reason*, September 15, 2013. Available at https://reason.com/archives/2013/09/15/the-endless-lives-of-iain-m-banks (accessed December 20, 2015).

Taylor, Martyn. "The Crow Road." *Vector* 174 (1993): 30.

Todd, Richard. *Consuming Fictions: The Booker Prize and Fiction in Britain Today*. London: Bloomsbury, 1996.

VanderMeer, Jeff. "Look to Windward." *New York Review of Science Fiction* 149 (2001): 15–16.

Westfahl, Gary. "Space Opera." *Cambridge Companion to Science Fiction*. Edited by Edward James and Farah Mendlesohn, 197–208. Cambridge: Cambridge University Press, 2003.

Wilkinson, Gary. "Poetic Licence: Iain M. Banks's *Consider Phlebas* and T.S. Eliot's *The Waste Land*." *Vector* 203 (1999): 15–18.

Willetts, Paul. "Iain Banks Speaks." *Book and Magazine Collector* 251 (2005): 58–65.

Wilson, Andrew J. "Lightly Seared on the Reality Grill: Conversations with Iain Menzies Banks." *Foundation* 116 (2013): 51–64.

Winter, Jerome. "'Moments in the Fall': Neoliberal Globalism and Utopian Anarcho-Socialist Desire in Ken MacLeod's Fall Revolution Quartet and Iain M. Banks's Culture Series." *Extrapolation* 55, no. 3 (2014): 323–48.

Young, Pete. "The Algebraist." *Vector* 240 (2005): 25–26.

PAUL KINCAID is a Clareson Award-winning critic and the author of *What It Is We Do When We Read Science Fiction.*

## MODERN MASTERS OF SCIENCE FICTION

John Brunner   *Jad Smith*

William Gibson   *Gary Westfahl*

Gregory Benford   *George Slusser*

Greg Egan   *Karen Burnham*

Ray Bradbury   *David Seed*

Lois McMaster Bujold   *Edward James*

Frederik Pohl   *Michael R. Page*

Alfred Bester   *Jad Smith*

Octavia E. Butler   *Gerry Canavan*

Iain M. Banks   *Paul Kincaid*

THE UNIVERSITY OF ILLINOIS PRESS

is a founding member of the

Association of American University Presses.

University of Illinois Press

1325 South Oak Street

Champaign, IL 61820-6903

www.press.uillinois.edu